Great Britain and the Irish Question 1774–1923

PAUL ADELMAN AND MIKE BYRNE

FOURTH EDITION

HODDER
EDUCATION
AN HACHETTE UK COMPANY

The Publishers would like to thank the following for permission to reproduce copyright material:

Photo credits: p36 Archive.org (from *Portrait gallery of eminent men and women of Europe and America : embracing history, statesmanship, naval and military life, philosophy, the drama, science, literature and art, with biographies* by Duyckinck, Evert A., 1816–1878); **p52** World History Archive/TopFoto; **pp57, 67** The Granger Collection/TopFoto; **p89** Liszt Collection/TopFoto; **p100** https://commons.wikimedia.org/wiki/File:Jan_Vil%C3%ADmek_-_Charles_Stewart_Parnell.jpg?uselang=en-gb; **pp108, 122** TopFoto/HIP; **p148t** Library of Congress, LC-USZ62-135374; **p148b** Baker Street Scans/Alamy; **p166** PA Photos/TopFoto; **p173** Library of Congress, LC-USZ62-67820.

Acknowledgements: An Post, Irish Proclamation of Independence (www.anpost.ie/AnPost/History+and+Heritage/History/1916+Rising/The+Proclamation/), 1916. Andrew Elliot, *Speeches on the Irish Question in 1886* by W.E. Gladstone, 1886. Biteback Publishing, *Peace, Reform and Liberalism: A History of Liberal Politics in Britain 1679–2011* by Robert Ingham and Duncan Brack, editors, 2011. Blackwell, *Protestant Nation to Catholic Nation 1690–1828* by D. George Boyce, 1992. Bloomsbury, *Democracy and Empire: Britain 1865–1914* by E.J. Feuchtwanger, 1985. Colourpoint, *Ireland, 1905–1925: Documents and Analysis*, volume 2 by Russell Rees and Anthony C. Hepburn, 1998. Eyre & Spottiswoode, *Bonar Law – The Unknown Prime Minister* by R. Blake, 1955. George Harrap, *The Life of John Redmond* by Denis Gwyn, 1932. Government of Ireland, Constitution of the Irish Free State (Saorstát Éireann) Act, 1922, Articles of Agreement for a Treaty between Great Britain and Ireland, *Irish Statue Book*, 1922. Harper & Brothers, *The Fall of Feudalism in Ireland* by Michael Davitt, 1904; *The Life of Charles Stewart Parnell* by R. Barry O'Brien, 1898. Harvard University Press, *Aristocracy and People 1815–65* by Norman Gash, 1985. HMSO, *Correspondence Relating to Measures for Relief of Distress in Ireland (Commissariat Series), July 1846–January 1847*, 1847; *Hansard*, HC Deb 11 May 1916, vol 82, cc935–70, 1916. Irish Freedom Press, *How Does She Stand?* by Pádraic H. Pearse, 1915. J. Millikan, *The Speech of the Right Honourable John, Earl of Clare, Lord High Chancellor of Ireland, in the House of Lords of Ireland, on a motion made by him on Monday February 10, 1800*, 1800. James Haly, *Speech of the Right Honorable John Foster, Speaker of the House of Commons of Ireland, Delivered in Committee, on Monday the 17th Day of February, 1800*, 1800. Liberal Publication Department, *The Liberal Magazine*, 1913. Longman, *The Age of Improvement* by Asa Briggs, 1974. Longman & Co., *The Parliamentary History of England, From the Earliest Period to the Year 1803*, 1819. Manchester University Press, *Irish Home Rule, 1867–1921* by Alan O'Day, 1998. Methuen, *Irish Historical Documents* by E. Curtis and R.B. McDowell, 1942. Oxford University Press, *The Age of Reform* by E. Llewellyn Woodward, 1962. Queen's University, Belfast, Act of Union Virtual Library website (www.actofunion.ac.uk/actofunion.htm), 2005. Routledge, *The Irish Revolution, 1916–1923* by Marie Coleman, 2014. Simpkin, Marshall & Co., *Speeches of the Right Hon. W.E. Gladstone, M.P., delivered at Warrington, Ormskirk, Liverpool, Southport, Newton, Leigh and Wigan, in October 1868* by W.E. Gladstone, 1868. Thomas Richardson & Son, *The Dublin Review*, volume XL, 1856. W. Johnston, *The Memoirs, Private and Political, of Daniel O'Connell, Esq.* by Daniel O'Connell, 1836.

Although every effort has been made to ensure that website addresses are correct at time of going to press, Hodder Education cannot be held responsible for the content of any website mentioned in this book. It is sometimes possible to find a relocated web page by typing in the address of the home page for a website in the URL window of your browser.

Hachette UK's policy is to use papers that are natural, renewable and recyclable products and made from wood grown in sustainable forests. The logging and manufacturing processes are expected to conform to the environmental regulations of the country of origin.

Orders: please contact Bookpoint Ltd, 130 Milton Park, Abingdon, Oxon OX14 4SB. Telephone: +44 (0)1235 827720. Fax: +44 (0)1235 400454. Lines are open 9.00a.m.–5.00p.m., Monday to Saturday, with a 24-hour message answering service. Visit our website at www.hoddereducation.co.uk

First published in 1996 by
Hodder Education
An Hachette UK Company
Carmelite House, 50 Victoria Embankment
London EC4Y 0DZ

Impression number	10	9	8	7	6	5	4	3	2	1
Year	2020	2019	2018	2017	2016					

Cover photo by © Mary Evans Picture Library
Produced, illustrated and typeset in Palatino LT Std by Gray Publishing, Tunbridge Wells
Printed and bound by CPI Group (UK) Ltd, Croydon CR0 4YY

A catalogue record for this title is available from the British Library

ISBN 978 1471838620

Contents

Dedication

Keith Randell (1943–2002)

The *Access to History* series was conceived and developed by Keith, who created a series to 'cater for students as they are, not as we might wish them to be'. He leaves a living legacy of a series that for over 20 years has provided a trusted, stimulating and well-loved accompaniment to post-16 study. Our aim with these new editions is to continue to offer students the best possible support for their studies.

CHAPTER 1

Introduction: Anglo-Irish rel 1170–1922

The 'Irish question' was a key, but seemingly insoluble, issue in British politics from the first quarter of the nineteenth century. This chapter introduces you to the nature of the problems posed by Britain's dominance in Ireland and gives an overview of the main pattern of Anglo-Irish affairs. This will allow you to see how detailed analyses of specific events in later chapters fit into a wider context.

It does this through looking at:

★ The background of the relationship between Britain and Ireland before 1800 when Ireland formally became part of a single country – the United Kingdom – with England, Wales and Scotland

★ The nature and implications of what came to be known as the 'Irish question'

★ Different interpretations of the Irish question

Key dates

1541	Henry VIII declared himself King of Ireland by a Royal Proclamation enacted in the following year	**1886**	Gladstone's First Home Rule Bill: rejected by Commons
1610	'Plantation of Ulster'	**1893**	Second Home Rule Bill: rejected by Lords
1641	Ulster Rebellion		
1690	Battle of the Boyne	**1912–14**	A third attempt at Home Rule provoked a crisis as Ulster resisted the move
1782	Irish parliament achieved legislative independence	**1914**	First World War (ended 1918)
1791	Society of United Irishmen founded	**1916**	The 'Easter Rebellion' leaders declared an independent Irish Republic. The attempt failed and the leaders were executed
1800	The Act of Union replaced the constitutional settlement enacted by Henry VIII		
1829	Roman Catholic Emancipation Act	**1921–2**	End of the Act of Union: Northern Ireland remained part of the UK; the rest of Ireland became a New 'Dominion' of the British Empire – the 'Irish Free State'
1845–9	The Great 'Potato Famine' resulted in around a million deaths; perhaps as many as two million people emigrated from Ireland		

England and Ireland 1170–1798

 ▶ *How and why did England come to dominate Ireland?*

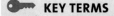

KEY TERMS

Leinster One of the counties of Ireland in 1170 (see Figure 1.1).

Ulster A province of Ireland; the larger part of this is today's Northern Ireland and still within the United Kingdom.

The English connection with Ireland began in 1170 when the King of **Leinster**, wanting military support against the High King of Ireland, who had deprived him of his kingdom, enlisted the aid of a group of English knights under the leadership of Richard de Clare, Earl of Pembroke – popularly known, due to his exceptional skill with a longbow, as 'Strongbow'. In the following year, King Henry II came over to Ireland with a powerful army and pushed forward the conquest of the country. Strongbow, many Irish Gaelic lords and also Church leaders swore allegiance to him.

During the thirteenth century, many of the features of Anglo-Norman feudalism, deriving from the Norman Conquest of England in 1066, were introduced into Ireland. For example, towns and castles were built, the Norman judicial system was introduced, the Irish were reduced to the position of serfs on land that had been seized and a parliament on the English model was established in 1264. The parliament primarily represented the power of the new Anglo-Norman ruling class, whose leaders were rewarded with titles.

The Tudors

The Tudors, with their commitment to a strong, centralising monarchy, were determined to reimpose their rule on Ireland. In 1541, Henry VIII assumed the title 'King of Ireland' and formalised this by a Royal Proclamation in 1542; he then arranged for the Irish parliament to accept his new position. Henry followed this up by imposing a new system of land ownership on the English model. This meant that the estates were now held by virtue of the king's law, not by ancient tradition, and that their holders could be dispossessed if they were guilty of disloyalty. In return for submission, prominent Irish lords were rewarded with English titles; the greatest of them, Con O'Neill of **Ulster**, now became the Earl of Tyrone.

The English Reformation and the break with Rome in 1533 never really obtained a foothold in Ireland and it raised the possibility of foreign intervention in Ireland on behalf of the Pope. Henry VIII had demanded that the Pope annul his marriage so that he could remarry and secure a male heir. When this was refused, Henry was declared by Act of Parliament to be head of the English Church and the break with the Pope and the Roman Catholic Church was made. There was much resentment towards Henry VIII in Ireland because of his anti-papal policy. The prospect of Ireland being used as a backdoor against England was to haunt English rulers and statesmen for centuries to come.

It was Henry's daughter, Queen Elizabeth I, who really carried through the effective conquest of Ireland.

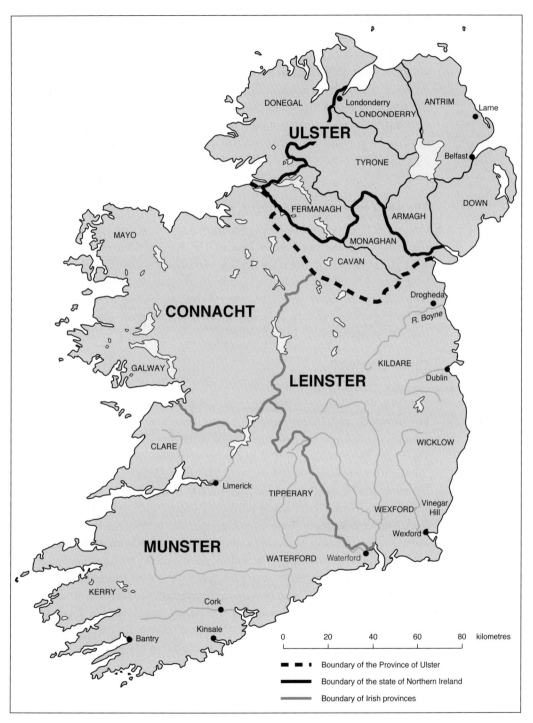

Figure 1.1 The counties of Ireland.

To do this, she relied primarily on English commanders and officials. For the queen and many Elizabethans, the English were engaged in a civilising mission in Ireland. Elizabeth's view of the Irish as 'a rude and barbarous nation' became an assumption of the English governing class for long afterwards. The queen, however, was cautious in her dealings with Irish Roman Catholicism. Although the major statutes of the Elizabethan Church Settlement applied to Ireland, no real attempt was made to impose Protestantism on the Irish people. At her death in 1603, Elizabeth could properly claim to have conquered most of Ireland, although English government still hardly affected the lives of the mass of Irish people.

The early seventeenth century

One of the most significant developments in Anglo-Irish history took place in the reign of Elizabeth's successor, James I. This was the 'Plantation of Ulster' in 1610. The settlement involved the eviction of most of the existing Irish landowners, who were reduced to the status of tenants or labourers for the new landlords, who were mainly Scots. By 1700, Ulster had become mainly a Presbyterian and Anglican province, and the old Catholic ruling class had been displaced. New industry and new towns, including Belfast, began to develop in Ulster.

Oliver Cromwell

The execution of King Charles I in 1649 after his defeat by Parliament in the Civil War left Oliver Cromwell the most powerful man in the country. For both religious and military reasons Cromwell was now determined to conquer Ireland, where Catholics had largely sided with King Charles in the Civil War. He landed there with a powerful army and, as a contemporary chronicler wrote, 'like lightning passed through the land'. He captured the city of Drogheda in September 1649, and the Catholic garrison was slaughtered in cold blood by the troops of the **New Model Army**, partly as an act of revenge for the murder of the Ulster Protestants in 1641. A similar policy was applied after the capture of Wexford. For Catholics, Cromwell's ruthlessness has made his name the most hated in modern Irish history. He abolished the separate Irish parliament, and the Westminster parliament now represented all three kingdoms of England and Wales, Ireland, and Scotland. He also confiscated about 11 million acres of land, mainly in central Ireland, from those who had supported the king. It was given to his soldiers and supporters. At the time of the Cromwell's death in 1658, only about one-fifth of all Irish land remained in the hands of Catholics.

The late seventeenth century

In 1660, King Charles II was restored. Roman Catholics were given religious toleration but Charles II, unwilling to risk his throne by antagonising the Protestant ruling class in England and Ireland, refused to upset the Cromwellian land settlement. The Irish Catholics were, therefore, forced to accept the loss of their lands as permanent. Furthermore, although the separate Irish parliament

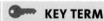 **KEY TERM**

New Model Army
The parliamentary army as remodelled by Cromwell in 1645.

was restored, Catholics were excluded from membership. Charles died in 1685 with no legitimate children.

King Charles II was succeeded by his younger brother James II, an avowed Roman Catholic. For a short time Irish Catholics must have hoped for better things. But James's pro-Catholic policies soon antagonised the dominant Protestant political classes in England. The birth of his son, Prince Charles Edward Stuart, raised the possibility of a succession of Roman Catholic monarchs, and, as a result, leading politicians invited **William of Orange** to invade England and defend the Protestant faith. Thus began the 'Glorious Revolution' of 1688. James fled to France and William and Mary were crowned King and Queen of England as joint rulers. Soon, the exiled James went to Ireland, but his effort to regain the throne ended in failure and he was defeated at the Battle of the Boyne in 1690. Queen Mary died in 1694 and William continued to rule until his death in 1702. The couple had no children, so Queen's Mary's younger sister Anne – also a Protestant – became queen. Despite no fewer than 17 pregnancies, Anne had no surviving children. Therefore, under the terms of what was known as the Act of Settlement of 1701, Anne was to be succeeded by her second cousin – Prince George of the House of Hanover – who was a descendant of the Stuarts through his grandmother, a daughter of King James I. On Queen Anne's death in 1714, he became King George I and so the Protestant succession to the throne was secured permanently.

The Protestant Ascendancy

The downfall of the Catholic cause in Ireland was followed in the eighteenth century by the establishment of the 'Protestant Ascendancy'. This was based on the **Anglican Church of Ireland** members' land ownership and political and religious domination, which lasted until well into the nineteenth century. The Catholic majority became second-class citizens. Ireland was governed indirectly from England, and the powers of the Irish parliament were severely limited.

Nevertheless, even the Anglican ruling classes in Ireland chafed at the restrictions imposed on them and were not immune from feelings of Irish nationalism. The reformers among them, especially 'the Patriots' in the 1750s, demanded more constitutional freedom for the Irish parliament. As a result of that pressure and the impact of the American War of Independence (1775–83), the government eventually yielded, and by the 'constitution of 1782' the Irish parliament achieved legislative independence. During the same period, many of the old restrictions on the Catholics in Ireland were also lifted.

The Society of United Irishmen

As so often in history, however, the beginnings of reform whetted the appetite and encouraged the rise of more extreme political movements. In 1791, the Society of United Irishmen was founded by Wolfe Tone (see page 20) to bring about Irish independence. This could be achieved, Tone believed, by allying with

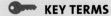

KEY TERMS

William of Orange
A Dutch Protestant Prince married to James II's Protestant daughter, Mary.

Anglican Church of Ireland Established as the State Church in Ireland by Henry VIII.

revolutionary France – at war with England after 1793 – and planning a rebellion in Ireland supported by a French invasion. The rebellion took place in the spring of 1798, but it lacked both leadership and organisation and was quickly defeated by the British army. The surrender of the French invading force in September brought the whole episode to an end. In the eyes of the prime minister, William Pitt, the 1798 rebellion revealed all too clearly the weaknesses of the existing, divided system for the government. Pitt, therefore, put forward a plan for a legislative union between Great Britain and Ireland.

Great Britain and the Irish question

▶ *How did the Irish question emerge?*

▶ *What events led to an Anglo-Irish Treaty?*

The Act of Union of 1800 abolished the status of Ireland as a separate kingdom and joined it with Great Britain to form the United Kingdom of Great Britain and Ireland (see page 23). The separate Irish parliament disappeared, and Ireland was now represented at Westminster. Pitt had intended that union should be accompanied by **Roman Catholic Emancipation**. When this did not take place, the Catholics felt betrayed. In Ireland, a mass movement developed in the 1820s, led by a young lawyer, Daniel O'Connell, to force the British government to grant their claims. This movement represented the first phase of the 'Irish question', and it lasted until the final passing of the Emancipation Act in 1829 (see page 41). The passage of the Roman Catholic Emancipation Act proved to be the most significant achievement of Daniel O'Connell as an Irish Nationalist leader (see pages 34–60). The Act gave Roman Catholics full civil and political rights, with a few minor exceptions; and since they could now become MPs, it was followed by the emergence of a small Irish Party in the House of Commons.

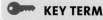

KEY TERM

Roman Catholic Emancipation Prior to this 1829 Act, the Parliamentary Oath of Allegiance required MPs or peers to make statements disavowing fundamental Roman Catholic beliefs in order to sit in the Commons or the Lords.

What, then, was meant by the 'Irish question'? At its heart, according to English politicians, was the unreasonable refusal of the Irish majority to acknowledge the obvious benefits that the Union was bringing. After all, the Roman Catholics from 1829 onwards:

- were in possession of full civil and political rights: they could become MPs, hold public office and participate fully in British political life
- had security against invasion as a result of British power
- benefited economically by being associated with British capital, commerce and industry
- were part of a more advanced, progressive civilisation, which was also the centre of a worldwide empire.

Such arguments cut little ice with the Irish Catholics. They did not regard the increasingly materialistic civilisation of contemporary England as something to be admired. They sensed the contempt for Roman Catholicism and Irish culture which lay behind English views. Moreover, as rapid population growth pressed ever harder on Irish resources, the supposed economic benefits of the Union seemed more and more illusory. In any case, as **Nationalist** leaders argued, the Act of Union had been imposed on them and produced subordination, not equality, for Ireland. The Union, in the words of one Irish Nationalist, was 'a nullity, a usurpation and a fraud'.

The Repeal campaign

The conclusion drawn from all this by O'Connell was his declaration in 1842: 'I want every Irishman to be convinced of this truth, that there is nothing worth looking for, save the power of governing ourselves'. After 1840, he organised a new campaign – modelled on the successful movement for Roman Catholic emancipation – which aimed at the repeal of the Union. The Repeal campaign of the early 1840s formed the second major phase in O'Connell's career as an Irish Nationalist leader. Movements such as this forced the British government to accept the reality of Irish opposition to the Union, although admittedly this was often attributed to the irrationality of the Irish character or the intimidation of the Irish masses by a minority of extremists. In a rather perplexed way, it was gradually accepted that Ireland was a special area within the United Kingdom and demanded special treatment. Nevertheless, every major British politician was convinced that for the good of all, including the Irish people, the Union must be maintained.

After 1830, the most difficult aspect of the Irish question that emerged was: how was loyalty to the Union to be maintained in the teeth of Irish opposition? The answer given by all parties was that the Irish majority must be won over by policies which improved and modernised Irish society and provided the framework for future peace and prosperity. At the same time, special 'coercion' measures could be imposed to stamp out violent opposition. This dual programme (reform and coercion) was pursued by all British governments until the Act of Union was ended in 1921–2.

The first period of Irish reform came from the **Whigs** in the 1830s and Sir Robert Peel and the Conservatives in the 1840s (see Chapter 3). These were mainly administrative measures dealing with education, the Poor Law and local government. Nothing was done yet to tackle the major grievances of the Irish over religion, land and government. The future conservative prime minister Benjamin Disraeli's classic description of the problem in 1844 therefore still applied: 'Thus you have a starving population, an absentee aristocracy, and an alien Church, and in addition the weakest executive in the world. That is the Irish question.'

At the same time as Peel strove to placate the Irish through a programme of reform, he also curbed the Repeal campaign itself in 1843–4, and the movement declined and eventually collapsed after O'Connell's death in 1847.

KEY TERMS

Nationalist A person who seeks to promote the interests of a particular nation.

Whigs A political party that had always been more sympathetic to reform and tolerance in Ireland but which had been largely excluded from government before 1830.

The Great Famine

One reason for the difficulties faced by O'Connell in the later 1840s was the onset of the Great Famine, which, as a result of the failure of the potato crop, led to starvation, disease and death on a large scale in Ireland. It forms a major landmark in the history of modern Ireland. Peel and his successor as prime minister, Lord John Russell, carried through a variety of relief measures (see pages 70–4) to 1849. The consequences of the famine were of enormous importance for Ireland and, indirectly, for the history of the Irish question in Great Britain.

Gladstone and Ireland

Comparative political tranquillity descended on Ireland in the wake of the Great Famine, and the Irish question receded into the background of British politics in the mid-nineteenth century. It re-emerged, however, when the Liberal Party leader, W.E. Gladstone, outlined a new programme of Irish reform after his victory in the 1868 general election. Gladstone dominated the history of the Irish question from 1868 until the failure of his Second Home Rule Bill in 1893 (see Chapter 6).

Whatever Gladstone's motives for taking up the Irish question, his major aim was exactly the same as that of his Whig and **Tory** predecessors: to build up support for the Union in Ireland by remedying outstanding Irish grievances. Indeed, the historian John Vincent, in the 1970s, controversially described Gladstone as 'the most masterly upholder of Unionism since Pitt'.

The two problems Gladstone was particularly concerned with were:

- religion, notably the position of the minority Anglican Church as the Established Church of Ireland
- land, more especially landlord–tenant relations.

The emergence of these two issues had important consequences for the development of the Irish question in British politics. For, whereas earlier Irish reforms were on the whole acceptable to members of all parties, this was not true of Gladstone's. The Conservative Party – traditionally the party of the Church of England – believed that the idea of **disestablishing** the Church of Ireland would (in the contemporary phrase) 'cross the water' and lead to demands for the disestablishment of the Church of England. Similarly, interference with the property rights of landlords in Ireland might encourage attacks on landlords' rights in England. The Irish question after 1868 thus became an important issue dividing the Liberals and Conservatives.

The Irish Church Act of 1869 disestablished and **disendowed** the Anglican Church in Ireland, thus destroying its privileged status and taking over its property. As a result, the religious problem in Ireland was more or less solved. Yet Gladstone's two Irish Land Acts of 1870 and 1881, which limited landlords'

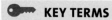

KEY TERMS

Tory A member of the Conservative Party.

Disestablish To deprive a Church of established status and official government support.

Disendow To take away the endowments (funds and property) of an Established Church.

rights over their tenants, did little to resolve the fundamental problems of the Irish rural economy. Nor did Gladstone's legislation as a whole achieve the major political result – namely, Irish support for the Union – for which he had hoped. This was partly because of the emergence of the Irish Land League and the rise of Charles Stewart Parnell as the leader of the Irish Home Rule Party (see Chapter 5).

By the end of 1885, Gladstone was convinced that his programme of reform had failed. Only Home Rule – that is, a measure of self-government for Ireland – would, he believed, now suffice. He was convinced of this by the growing support for the Home Rule Party in Ireland, as shown by the general election in November of that year. Yet both of his Home Rule Bills failed. In 1886, the First Home Rule Bill was rejected by the House of Commons, mainly because of a revolt by an important section of the Liberal Party. In 1893, the Second Home Rule Bill was passed by the Commons but rejected by a massive majority in the House of Lords.

Gladstone retired as Liberal leader in 1894, and, in the general election the following year, his party suffered an overwhelming defeat. The Liberals remained out of power until 1905. They won a landslide victory in 1906, but it was not until 1911 that they took up for a third time the idea of Irish Home Rule.

The Ulster problem

A major factor in Gladstone's failure to achieve Home Rule for Ireland was the opposition he encountered from Ulster. Ulster was different from the rest of Ireland in many ways:

- There was a majority Protestant population overall, although the size of the majority varied in different counties and in some Catholics actually predominated.
- The city of Belfast was the centre of a thriving industry of global importance – shipbuilding – whereas the rest of Ireland was overwhelmingly agricultural.
- In both 1886 and again in 1893, Ulster had mobilised in conjunction with unionist support in Britain to oppose and defeat Home Rule. In both instances, Liberal governments had soon been replaced by the Conservatives and in 1886 the Liberals had split permanently over the issue.

Despite this, the Liberal government headed by H.H. Asquith, which took office at the end of 1905, was eventually forced to take up again the thorny problem of Home Rule that had twice defeated Gladstone. This was because a great constitutional crisis between the House of Commons and the House of Lords resulted in:

- two general elections in 1910, which left the government dependent on Irish MPs for their majority and
- a Parliament Act in 1911, which changed the constitution.

The 1911 Act meant that a bill passed by the Commons could only be held up by the Lords for a maximum of two years, and therefore for the first time a Home Rule Bill could eventually become law even if rejected by the Upper House. In this new context, the Irish question came to dominate British politics in the years before the outbreak of the First World War.

Asquith's Home Rule Bill, presented to the Commons in April 1912, was a moderate measure, similar in most respects to Gladstone's 1893 bill. In particular, like that measure, it provided for Home Rule for all Ireland. But, in the intervening period, the divisions between Catholics and Protestants in Ireland had hardened, and the Liberals now found themselves faced by the united, stubborn resistance of the Ulster **Unionists** (see Chapter 7). In opposing the Liberals' policy over Ireland, the Ulstermen were backed up by the Conservative Party in England, which was prepared to use Ulster extremism to destroy the new Home Rule Bill, and, they hoped, the Liberal government. The crisis mounted.

Although compromise solutions were suggested – based on the possibility of 'excluding' the distinctly Protestant counties of Ulster from the operation of Home Rule – no agreement had been reached by the time Great Britain entered the First World War on 4 August 1914. The Home Rule Bill was passed but suspended for the duration of the war and never actually enforced.

The making of the Anglo-Irish settlement

The war had a profound effect on the development of the Irish question. In Ireland it led to the Irish Nationalist Party being superseded by the more militant organisation of Sinn Féin, which was committed to complete independence and the establishment of an Irish Republic. The war also helped to give the Irish question an international dimension: the influence of the United States (with its large Irish–American community) was boosted, while Allied statesmen at the Paris Peace Conference in 1919 voiced a commitment to national self-determination.

Even while the war was still on, attempts were made by the **coalition government** to obtain agreement between the Irish nationalists and unionists on an immediate political settlement based on the principle of **Home Rule plus 'exclusion'**. All failed. In 1916, an abortive attempt at rebellion by nationalist extremists initially led to widespread hostility against the rebels from the Irish population. However, when the leaders of the rebellion were executed the mood changed. This was revealed dramatically in the general election of 1918 that followed the end of the war in November 1918. Sinn Féin won almost every seat in southern Ireland (see Chapter 8).

Sinn Féin leaders, now claiming to be the rightful representatives of the Irish people, demanded an English withdrawal. Sinn Féin set up its own parliament in Dublin and proclaimed the establishment of the Irish Republic. Since the British government had no intention of abandoning its sovereignty over Ireland, these demands led to the outbreak of a vicious war between the two sides.

In 1920, the British government made one more attempt to produce an acceptable political settlement. The Government of Ireland Act of that year was based on the principle of Home Rule for both parts of Ireland: local parliaments and representative governments were to be set up for both Northern Ireland (consisting of the six most Protestant counties) and Southern Ireland (26 counties). In the north, an Ulster Unionist government soon came into power; but in the south the Act was completely ignored by Sinn Féin, whose leaders insisted on nothing less than full independence for the whole of Ireland. Once again, British views on Ireland were far behind the tempo of events. The Anglo-Irish War therefore continued.

By the spring of 1921, however, both the British government and the Irish republican leadership were war-weary. A truce was agreed to in July. It was followed by long, drawn-out negotiations between an Irish delegation and a small ministerial team headed by Lloyd George, which led eventually to the signing of an Anglo-Irish Treaty in December 1921. It was ratified in the following year. This brought an end to the war. Politically, it led to the establishment of a virtually independent Irish Free State of 26 counties, although the existence of the state of Northern Ireland as a *fait accompli* was also recognised (see Figure 1.1 on page 3).

 # The key debate

> ▶ *What has influenced historians' interpretations of the Irish question?*

To some extent, historians' outlooks on the Irish question have been determined by their nationality. So, when studying the relationship between England and Ireland it is important to consider the following.

English historians

England's dominance over Ireland meant that, inevitably, Ireland had little direct impact on the development of its more powerful neighbour. For English historians, therefore, the Anglo-Irish relationship has formed only a minor part of modern English history. Even when the Irish question has impinged more directly on England, as during the Home Rule crises and the Anglo-Irish War, the attitude of English historians has on the whole been Anglo-centric: Irish affairs are looked at through English eyes and with English concerns in mind.

Patricia Jalland, writing in 1980, and A.B. Cooke and John Vincent in 1974 are outstanding examples of this approach. This, of course, does not mean that all English historians have been unsympathetic in terms of recognising the problems of Ireland and the desire for reform or even Irish independence.

Irish nationalist historians

For Irish nationalist historians – the dominant group in Irish historical writing up to about the 1960s – the very shape and substance of modern Irish history has been determined by the forced connection with England. For these historians, Irish history since the later eighteenth century is the story of a united people – conscious of their separate national identity and inspired by a long line of outstanding nationalist leaders – joining together to oppose the tyranny of England and, in the end, compelling it to retreat and abandon most of Ireland. The fulfilment of that story, with a united Ireland, must eventually come. Thus, as P.S. O'Hegarty wrote in 1952, Irish history is 'the story of a people coming out of captivity … finding every artery of national life occupied by the enemy, recovering them one by one, and coming out at last into the full blaze of the sun'.

For nationalist historians then, Irish history since 1800 has a pattern and a purpose: historical development proceeds along a fixed line to a predetermined end. Yet, such nationalist history is too simple:

- It highlights the role of nationalist heroes and martyrs, often inspired by the Catholic faith, as the embodiment of the will of the Irish people.
- It provides a 'mythical' interpretation of key events, based on their emotional appeal – the 1798 rebellion and the Easter Rebellion of 1916, for example – to sustain that nationalist fervour.

This sort of history reads the past through the eyes of the present, and its purpose is to raise Irish nationalist consciousness and justify the revolutionary tradition.

KEY TERM

Revisionist A historian who has significantly 'revised' or challenged the previously accepted view of a particular historical question.

Revisionists

Since the 1960s, so-called **'revisionists'** have come to the fore, in deliberate opposition to the nationalist tradition. They have a far less committed view of Irish history and the Anglo-Irish relationship. The revisionists see no special pattern or purpose in Irish history, nor do they regard the English connection as the only factor that explains Irish development. As historians, they serve no particular cause and have no public mission other than the desire to use the established techniques of the professional historian to achieve the 'truth' about the past.

They have, therefore, tried to penetrate behind the myths and simplifications of the nationalist historians to the detailed, often complicated, context in which historical events actually occur. This has often led them to see disunity and conflict in many aspects of Irish history, where the nationalists see only unity and continuity. In particular – to the fury of many – they have sounded a more sceptical note in discussing the ideals and methods of modern Irish nationalism, and have insisted on giving full weight to the reality of Ulster unionism. They have also laid a new stress on the importance of social and economic history. Much of the recent work on land ownership in Ireland, for example – which has exploded many myths about the conditions of landlords and tenants and the results of land reform – has been due to their inspiration.

One result of this detailed work has been to cast doubt on the traditional view that all Ireland's economic ills can be blamed on England. Indeed, revisionist history has shown that during particular periods, economic prosperity was a reality for some groups in Irish Catholic society. All these issues are discussed at length in Roy Foster's outstanding revisionist history, *Modern Ireland 1600–1972* (1988).

Modern historians

The revisionists have, in turn, been fiercely attacked by a number of younger Irish historians sympathetic to nationalist aspirations. It has been argued that revisionist history lacks 'empathy and imagination'; it plays down what has been called (by Dr Brendan Bradshaw, its major critic) 'the catastrophic dimension' in Irish history, especially in relation to the Great Famine. Revisionist history is thus out of touch, it is suggested, with the deepest feelings of the Irish majority. Bradshaw is critical of the false 'objectivity' of the revisionists. Yet, Bradshaw has, in turn, been criticised by one senior historian for abandoning 'the status of history as a detached scholarly activity'. The history of Ireland and its relationship with Britain is likely always to be one of historical debate and controversy.

CHAPTER 2

The making of the Act of Union 1800

The focus of this chapter is the Act of Union, which its supporters hoped would improve Anglo-Irish relations but in fact it did the opposite. Yet the Act, although important for what followed, was itself part of a broad historical process. Therefore, in order to identify the fundamental issues, it is important to have an understanding of the period before 1800, as well as the Act of Union itself. For this reason, this chapter explores the significance of the Act of Union through the following key themes:

★ The Protestant Ascendancy in eighteenth-century Ireland

★ The age of revolution

★ The Act of Union 1800

Key dates

1750s	The Patriots formed	1791		Society of United Irishmen formed
1760	The Catholic Committee formed	1795		Orange Order in Ulster
1779–80	Free trade for Ireland	1798	**May–Dec.**	Irish Rebellion
1782	Constitutional reform in Ireland	1800		The Act of Union passed

KEY TERMS

Jacobite rebellions
A series of military campaigns attempting to restore the Stuart kings to the throne. A Jacobite was a supporter of James II of England or of the Stuart pretenders after 1688.

Penal laws The body of discriminatory and oppressive legislation directed against Roman Catholics and Protestant nonconformists.

1 The Protestant Ascendancy in eighteenth-century Ireland

▶ *In what ways was Ireland subordinate to England before 1800?*

The 'Protestant Ascendancy' over Ireland is a term used to express the dominance of a minority of landowners, Anglican clergy and members of the professions over all aspects of life in Ireland: social, economic and political. Their control over Ireland effectively ensured England's supremacy. The defeat of James II at the Battle of the Boyne in 1690 meant the triumph of Protestantism and the defeat of Catholicism in England and Ireland, a supremacy confirmed by the accession of the Protestant King George I in 1714, and the subsequent defeat of the **Jacobite rebellions** of 1715 and 1745. **Penal laws** were passed against Catholics after 1689 aimed at ensuring that they could never again threaten English supremacy:

- Catholics could not vote, sit in parliament or hold any public office.
- In addition – in an age when land and political power went hand in hand – Irish Catholics were limited in their right to purchase or inherit land.
- Catholics were forbidden to bear arms or enlist in the armed forces.
- Marriage between Catholics and Protestants was banned.
- Catholics could not leave their land to their eldest son. On death, a Catholic's estate was required to be divided between his surviving sons, unless the eldest son converted to Protestantism. Catholics could not avoid this by converting temporarily and then going back to Catholicism because there were also laws to invalidate their earlier conversion if they did so. The effect of this law was to reduce the size of the estates and political influence of Catholic landowners.

These are only some of the better known examples of a multitude of restrictions and prohibitions. Catholics did, in practice, possess religious toleration, but the penal code impeded their right to a Catholic education and forced a number of their clergy to emigrate. However, over the course of the eighteenth century almost all the penal laws were gradually repealed at different times; for example, the ban on intermarriage was repealed in 1778. By the time of the Act of Union of 1800, only the wording of the Parliamentary Oath of Allegiance remained as a general barrier to Roman Catholic political rights, although the position of lord-lieutenant of Ireland (see below) remained limited to Anglicans until 1920.

Some of these penal laws applied also to the **Irish Dissenters**, including the powerful Presbyterian community of Ulster. Although they possessed freedom of religion and could generally vote, as non-Anglicans they were denied the right to hold public office. This was the result of the so-called Test and Corporations Acts, initiated in 1662, which excluded non-Anglicans from public offices. In England and Wales, the Acts were widely ignored by the nineteenth century, but not so in Ireland. The 'Test Acts' were formally repealed in 1828. Indeed, the property qualifications for voting meant that even most Anglicans were excluded from the ranks of the Ascendancy; although they could, of course, regard it as operating on their behalf.

 **KEY TERM**

Irish Dissenters Protestants who disagreed with the teachings of the Church of Ireland.

Land

All this paved the way for the emergence of the 'Ascendancy' in eighteenth-century Ireland, with the Anglican social elite dominating Irish politics, society and the economy. This elite's power stemmed from ownership of the bulk of the land. By the mid-eighteenth century, Catholics owned only about five per cent of the land, at a time when they formed about 75 per cent of the population. A small class of Catholic gentry did survive, mainly in the west, but the majority of Catholics now existed as small tenant farmers, renting land from their Protestant landlords, or as landless labourers living in conditions of appalling squalor and poverty.

KEY TERMS

Established Church
A Church that is constitutionally and legally recognised as the official Church of the nation.

Tithe All landholders, irrespective of their religion, had to pay an annual tithe (or religious tax) to the Church of Ireland of ten per cent of the value of the agricultural produce of their land.

Legislature The body which has the power to pass laws. In a democracy this is an elected parliament.

Executive The top-level part of a government which makes the key decisions on policy; in the UK this is the Cabinet, which comprises the prime minister and other leading government ministers.

Religion

The other pillar of the Ascendancy was the Anglican Church of Ireland. Since by law it was the **Established Church** – even though it represented only about fifteen per cent of the people of Ireland – it possessed wealth, privileges and influence. It had, for example, representatives sitting in the Irish House of Lords, and possessed the right to collect **tithes** from the whole population; something which aroused bitter resentment among Catholics and Presbyterians alike. Not surprisingly, the Church of Ireland was regarded as a major instrument in the English control of Ireland.

Government

Unlike its Scottish neighbour, which by the Act of Union of 1707 had joined with England to form the Kingdom of Great Britain, Ireland remained a separate and dependent kingdom, as it had been since the reign of Henry VIII. In a number of ways Ireland's status was akin to that of a colony:

- Administration was headed by the lord-lieutenant (or viceroy), the British government's representative in Ireland, who was generally an English aristocrat and sometimes a member of the Cabinet. The lord-lieutenant was effectively the monarch's direct representative and so increasingly a constitutional figurehead rather than the political leader of Ireland.
- Below the lord-lieutenant were the various ministers and officials, many of them Englishmen, who were responsible for the day-to-day running of the Irish government and were known collectively as 'the Castle', since Dublin Castle was the viceroy's official residence.
- The chief secretary for Ireland was responsible for getting the government's legislation through the Irish parliament. This was a major task which could only be accomplished successfully by building up support through the lavish distribution of titles and lucrative offices controlled by the government. The chief secretary increasingly became, in effect, the prime minister of Ireland.

Parliament

Although the Irish parliament had existed since the thirteenth century and was modelled on that of England, its powers were severely limited. By Poyning's Law of 1494 and the later Declaratory Act of 1719, Ireland was subject to the laws of the Westminster parliament. Its own parliament could only pass laws ultimately approved by the British government. Thus, the Irish parliament lacked any real legislative initiative, and, since the lord-lieutenant was the nominee of the British government, the Irish **legislature** had no control over its own **executive**. Moreover, the Irish parliament met only when summoned by the Crown. The Septennial Act of 1715, which provided for general elections at least every seven years, did not apply to Ireland.

Nevertheless, despite its weaknesses, the Irish parliament did not always respond to government direction. This was particularly so when questions involving finance or Irish economic interests were involved and the parliament could rely on the backing of public opinion. In 1725, for example, the government was forced to withdraw a new Irish coinage manufactured in England.

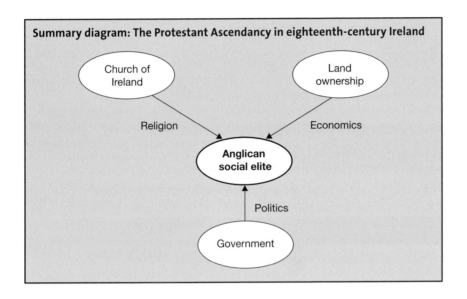

Summary diagram: The Protestant Ascendancy in eighteenth-century Ireland

2 The age of revolution

▶ *What factors produced moves for reform in Ireland?*

In the later eighteenth century, Protestant nationalism steadily advanced in Ireland. There was a growing feeling in the Protestant communities that, although they were divided by race and religion from the majority of Irish people, they were Irish by nationality and should put the interests of Ireland first. This conviction led in the 1750s to the emergence in the Irish House of Commons of the minority group of MPs known as the 'Patriots', whose most notable leader was Henry Grattan. His personality, his powers of oratory and his devotion to the cause made him a natural leader.

The Patriots denounced the subordination of Ireland to Great Britain. They demanded commercial equality for Ireland and legislative independence for the Irish parliament, to be accompanied by regular elections and an attack on the corruption of the Castle's rule. Nor were the Catholics unaffected by these developments. The formation of the Catholic Committee in 1760 as a moderate organisation for the redress of Catholic grievances is a reflection of this. As Grattan said: 'the Irish Protestant can never be free, till the Irish Catholic has ceased to be a slave'. Something of an unofficial alliance was built up during this period between the moderate reformers in both communities.

In the 1760s, the British government was prepared to make some concessions. For instance, it was conceded that the lord-lieutenant should be permanently resident in Ireland, and the process of reforming the **patronage system** was begun. In addition, an Octennial Act was passed in 1768, so that general elections had to be held at least every eight years. However, it was the outbreaks of the American War of Independence in 1775 and the French Revolution in 1789 that did most to encourage the process of reform, and which profoundly affected the relationship between Great Britain and Ireland.

The American War of Independence

Whereas the Catholics in Ireland remained loyal to the Crown during the American War of Independence (1775–83), and thereby won some minor improvements in the penal code, the Protestants were more sympathetic to the Americans. They too saw themselves as suffering from subordination to the parliament in Westminster. The **Ulster Presbyterians**, in particular, had strong links with America through emigration, and the political ideas of the American rebels, exemplified by their slogan 'No Taxation without Representation', appealed to their own radical outlook. 'We are all Americans here', wrote one Patriot, 'except such as are attached to the Castle or are papists [Catholics]'.

The influence of Grattan and the Patriots was boosted by the support of the Volunteer movement, which sprang up spontaneously in 1778 and numbered 30,000–40,000 members two years later. The Volunteers pledged to repel any foreign invader, but they undoubtedly represented the military arm of Protestant nationalism. Their strong support for the political programme of the Patriots is shown by one of their marching songs:

> 'No laws shall ever bind but those we frame ourselves.
> The Britons now shall find us as free as they're themselves.
> Hibernia's Volunteers, boys, have worked the glorious cause
> And will with mighty heart and head abolish Poyning's Laws.'

The British prime minister, Lord North, recognised the power wielded by the Volunteer and Patriot alliance in favour of reform. His government yielded to the economic demands of the Irish opposition, so that in 1779–80 most of the restrictions on Irish commerce were abolished and 'free trade for Ireland' was introduced. Greater change occurred, however, when North resigned after the British surrender to the American rebels at Yorktown, Virginia, in 1782. He was replaced by Lord Rockingham and the Whigs, who for years had been strong supporters of the Patriots' cause.

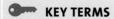 **KEY TERMS**

Patronage system
The award and distribution of favours.

Ulster Presbyterians
The largest Protestant group in Ireland; of Scots–Irish descent.

Grattan's parliament

By the 'constitution of 1782', which the Whigs now introduced, Poyning's Law and the Declaratory Act of 1719 were repealed, and the Irish parliament for the first time in its history achieved legislative independence. This meant that although the Crown retained a final veto over legislation, the initiative belonged to the Irish House of Commons, which could pass its own laws without the consent of the government in Great Britain. In this way, 'Grattan's parliament', as it is always known – in tribute to its greatest member – began its short life. 'Ireland is now a nation', he proclaimed. 'In that new character I hail her'.

Despite Grattan's euphoria, the changes were more apparent than real. Ireland's parliament still had no control over the Executive, and the lord-lieutenants could still contrive, although with greater difficulty than previously, to control the Commons' proceedings through the time-honoured methods of influence, patronage and electoral corruption. All this meant that the major demand of the reformers (as with their fellow radicals in England) now became parliamentary reform, aimed at making the Irish parliament truly representative of the people. For Patriots, like Grattan, this implied political rights for Catholics too, something which the Catholic Committee itself had been vigorously demanding. Yet, this was an issue over which the Ascendancy itself was divided, and in the later 1780s parliament rejected any attempt to reform the 'constitution of 1782'. Nor could the reformers now expect much sympathy at Westminster. The accession of the Younger Pitt to office as prime minister in 1783 began a long period of strong and stable government in defence of the political and social *status quo*.

There were also growing economic and social problems in Ireland. Although these years saw a considerable increase in the prosperity of the Irish middle classes, especially in Ulster, owing to the expansion of trade, the rapid increase in the Irish population throughout the eighteenth century increased the competition for land, which helped to cause sporadic outbreaks of violence. All these problems were to come to a head during the period of the French Revolution.

The French Revolution

The outbreak of the French Revolution stimulated the demand for further reform throughout Britain and Ireland, especially in Ulster where the Volunteer movement, although in decline elsewhere, remained powerful. Even the Catholic Committee became more radical. It was the need to pacify the Catholics, especially after the outbreak of war with France in 1793, and fears of a Catholic–Presbyterian anti-government alliance, that led Pitt to force further reforms on a reluctant viceroy and parliament. In 1793, Catholics were granted the right to vote, and most civil and military posts in Ireland were thrown open to them. In this way, a young Catholic lawyer, Daniel O'Connell – the future 'Liberator' (see Chapter 3) – became a member of the Irish Bar.

These concessions did little to improve the status of the Irish Catholics since they were still denied the right to sit in parliament or to hold public office, and the old pattern of Anglican-dominated politics remained. Hence, the era of the French Revolution placed the demand for Roman Catholic emancipation firmly on the political agenda of the opposition both in Ireland and in England, and this question was inextricably linked with the wider aim of parliamentary reform. The government's obstinate refusal to shift its position on either the 'emancipation' or the 'parliamentary reform' question during this period not only helped to push Catholic and Protestant radicals closer together, but also inevitably encouraged the growth of more extreme reform movements. The 1790s therefore saw the emergence of a new, and ultimately more **militant**, organisation, the Society of United Irishmen, led by a young Protestant lawyer, Wolfe Tone.

The Society of United Irishmen

The Society of United Irishmen was originally formed in 1791 as an organisation of radical clubs in Ulster. Its aim was to influence Irish opinion in favour of:

- Catholic emancipation
- parliamentary reform.

In the years that followed, the society transformed itself into a more secretive, extremist and quasi-military organisation. This was particularly a result of the increasingly **reactionary** attitudes of the Irish government and parliament, and the developing revolutionary fervour of Wolfe Tone. It now appealed deliberately to all Irishmen and aimed at the establishment of an independent Irish republic. By 1797, the Society was believed to possess more than 100,000 active supporters. Wolfe Tone became more intensely anti-British and pro-French, and since Britain and France were now at war, the idea of military help from France as the only means of salvation for Ireland became more and more appealing. 'To subvert the tyranny of our execrable government', he wrote, 'to break the connection with England, the never-failing source of all our political evils, and to assert the independence of my country – these are my objects'.

The notion of liberation from British rule was bound to have an appeal, not just to middle-class radicals, but also to the Catholic peasantry, who had their own economic grievances against Protestant landlords and the Anglican Church. This led to fierce outbreaks of **sectarian** strife in the north. In response, a number of Ulster Protestants combined together in 1795 to form the **loyalist** Orange Order, based largely on the former Volunteers, to defend Protestantism and the British Crown. Some Catholics therefore turned to the Society of United Irishmen to defend them against this Protestant backlash.

By this time, the British government, alarmed at the growth of subversive ideas in the middle of a major war, was preparing to move against the Irish radicals. Wolfe Tone fled to America in 1795 and from there he made his way to Paris,

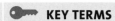

KEY TERMS

Militant Engaged in violence as part of a struggle for the achievement of a political goal.

Reactionary Resistant to any form of progressive change.

Sectarian Part of an extreme religious movement.

Loyalist Supporter of the British government.

where he began plotting with the French authorities for an invasion of Ireland. A fleet did set sail at the end of 1796 and reached Bantry Bay, but owing to a storm it was forced to withdraw.

Action had already been taken by the British to stamp out the radical opposition. Earlier in 1796, magistrates in Ireland had been given wider powers to seize arms and arrest suspects. Even more provocatively, a force of loyalist Protestant **yeomanry** had been set up to act on behalf of the government. Now, in 1797, a mainly yeomanry force under the command of General Lake moved against the United Irishmen in Belfast, determined to destroy their leadership and their support. 'Our aim', said one officer, 'was to excite terror and by that means obtain our end speedily'. To a large extent their brutal campaign of repression succeeded; and in the following year the yeomanry moved against the United Irishmen in the south, especially in Dublin. **Martial law** was proclaimed. It was in these circumstances that the United Irishmen, now largely leaderless and with their organisation in disarray, decided that their only hope now was through rebellion coupled with a French invasion.

The rebellion of 1798

The disintegration of the Society of United Irishmen meant that it was unable to impose its grip on the long-awaited rebellion which broke out in Ireland on 23 May 1798. The rebellion therefore consisted of a series of separate uprisings, based primarily on local grievances rather than any overriding set of ideas or a concerted plan. At the time, some members of the Ascendancy saw it as basically a Catholic rebellion against Protestantism. But Lord Cornwallis, the viceroy, denounced 'the folly of substituting Catholic instead of Jacobin [French revolutionary] as the foundation of the present rebellion', and a fellow member of the government similarly argued that it was due to 'French policies and French success … [and] the jargon of equality'.

In fact, it was only among a minority in Ulster that French revolutionary ideas were important, and the rebellion there, as in the west of Ireland, was a limited affair. The main area where the outbreak was bitter and protracted was in the south-east, especially in Wexford, and there it did take the form of a bloody religious war. Groups of Protestants were massacred by Catholic insurgents, and the yeomanry responded in kind, sometimes resorting to a **'scorched earth' policy** against Catholic property. Given the strength and determination of the government forces, the rebellion had no real chance of success, and after General Lake's victory at Vinegar Hill on 21 June, it rapidly petered out. The captured rebel leaders were executed or suffered transportation, but the rank-and-file were allowed to return to their homes. Although the rebellion lasted barely a month, it has been estimated that by the end of that summer the death toll on both sides amounted to about 30,000. It has been suggested that 'The 1798 rising was probably the most concentrated episode of violence in Irish history'.

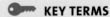

KEY TERMS

Yeomanry Volunteer regiments.

Martial law Rule by military authorities, imposed on a civilian population especially in time of war or when civil authority has broken down.

'Scorched earth' policy Burning any land, crops or trees so as to leave nothing salvageable to the enemy.

French invasion

The fact that it was only in August, after the rebellion was more or less over, that the French made their invasion attempt ensured that it was virtually a doomed enterprise from the start. The French landed in County Mayo in the west with barely 1000 men and were forced to surrender early in September. By that time, another French expedition, including Wolfe Tone, had set sail for Ireland, but it was scattered by a British naval force and most of the French ships were captured. Tone was one of the prisoners taken. He was condemned to death as a rebel but cheated the hangman's noose by killing himself. He was only 35.

The hoped-for 'Year of Liberation' ended with the apparent triumph of the forces of reaction. But things were never to be the same again. In the long run, the life and death of Wolfe Tone and the history of the Society of United Irishmen became part of the mythology of **Irish republican nationalism**, which adopted the society's colour – green – as its symbol. More immediately, the demand for fundamental constitutional change was gaining ground. Even before the rebellion there were fears by members of the governing class in both Britain and Ireland that, as a result of the disagreements arising out of the constitution of 1782, the two countries would drift farther and farther apart. This was bound to risk the security of both. The fears and doubts inspired by the events of 1798 meant, therefore, that the arguments in favour of a union of the two kingdoms became more powerful and imperative to the British government and its supporters on both sides of the Irish Sea.

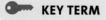 **KEY TERM**

Irish republican nationalism The desire for the establishment of an Irish Republic.

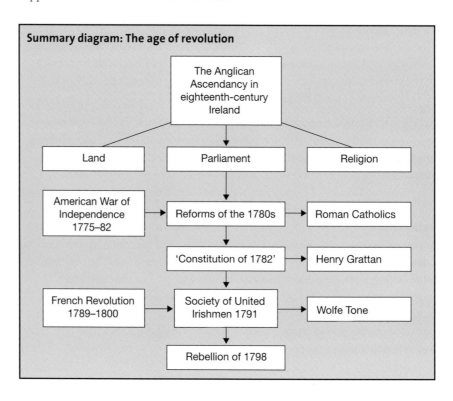

Summary diagram: The age of revolution

The Act of Union 1800

> ▶ *Why did William Pitt the Younger decide to bring forward an Act of Union between Great Britain and Ireland in 1800?*

Even before the end of the Irish Rebellion, William Pitt had begun to consider the possibility of a union between the two kingdoms of Great Britain and Ireland, coupled with Catholic emancipation. The Irish parliament considered the issue of union at the end of January 1799 in a series of highly charged debates held amid intense public interest and excitement in Dublin. In the end, the government proposal was narrowly defeated. But Pitt remained determined to get an Act of Union passed. He paved the way for legislation by dismissing ministers and officials opposed to union, and he then gave Viscount Castlereagh, the chief secretary, the task of winning over Irish public opinion. In the course of the next year both unionist and anti-unionist forces attempted to build up support for their respective causes. Most Irishmen, inevitably worried about the hardships of their daily lives, were probably unconcerned, and the politically motivated minority were profoundly divided. Some groups found it difficult to decide and just awaited events. What, then, were the arguments in favour of and against union?

Arguments for the union

Pro-unionists stressed the hard facts of geography and military power. Ireland was the weak link in the system of imperial defence; union, however, would enable the British government to assume direct responsibility for the defence of Ireland against rebellion and foreign invasion. Furthermore, the present system of government divided between London and Dublin, together with a separate and now independent Irish parliament, only encouraged divisions, acrimony and inefficiency – weaknesses which could be fatal in the middle of a great war. Besides, the fate of the Ascendancy itself was at stake. Its very existence had always rested ultimately on the military power of Great Britain; union would finally confirm this simple but inescapable fact.

As Lord Clare, the lord chancellor, argued to his fellow members of the Irish parliament with brutal clarity:

SOURCE A

From ***The Speech of the Right Honourable John, Earl of Clare, Lord High Chancellor of Ireland, in the House of Lords of Ireland, on a motion made by him on Monday February 10, 1800***, J. Millikan, 1800.

From their first settlement they [the English settlers] have been hemmed in on every side by the old inhabitants of this island, brooding over their discontents in sullen indignation. What was the security of the English settlers for their physical existence? And what is the security of their descendants at this day? The powerful and commanding position of Great Britain. If, by any fatality it fails, you are at the mercy of the old inhabitants of this island.

According to Source A, what did English settlers have to fear?

KEY TERM

Scottish Union Scotland had been united with England in 1707.

William Pitt preferred to stress the more positive benefits of union, especially in the economic field. Union would enable Ireland to become part of the wider British economy, and, as the **Scottish Union** had shown, this would produce clear advantages for the Irish people, especially by encouraging economic growth and prosperity. Moreover, the fact that the Roman Catholics would be a minority within a United Kingdom (whereas they were the overwhelming majority in Ireland itself) would remove the traditional fears of Protestants, and would make them more prepared to grant equal rights to their Catholic fellow-citizens. As Castlereagh said, 'strength and confidence will encourage liberality'. In a wider sense too, the hatreds of Irish life would be tempered by 'a moral assimilation' (in the phrase of an Anglican cleric) into British society, and this would undermine the age-old differences between the Irish Celt and the Anglo-Saxon, and thus sustain the union.

As Pitt explained to the British House of Commons in January 1799 in supporting the idea of union:

SOURCE B

From *The Parliamentary History of England, From the Earliest Period to the Year 1803*, Longman & Co., 1819, p. 273.

What are the positive advantages that Ireland is to derive from it? … the protection which she will secure to herself in the hour of danger, the most effectual means of increasing her commerce and improving her agriculture, the command of English capital, the infusion of English manners and English industry, necessarily tending to ameliorate her condition … and to terminate those feuds and dissensions which now distract the country, and which she does not possess, within herself, the power either to control or extinguish … But … the question is not only what Ireland is to gain, but what she is to preserve … In this view, what she gains is the preservation of all those blessings arising from the British constitution, and which are inseparable from her connection with Great Britain.

? According to Pitt in Source B, what was to be the key factor in securing the future for Ireland?

Arguments against the union

The arguments of the opponents of union were more emotional, and were based primarily on a vague feeling of Irish nationality. Opponents insisted that Ireland was a separate society with its own distinctive institutions and interests, and should therefore possess its own independent parliament, even though it bore allegiance to the British Crown. The record of that parliament, based on the constitution of 1782, had clearly justified its existence. Ireland was now a more prosperous and cultivated society, the arts flourished, and Dublin was a major European city. 'God and nature', affirmed one anti-unionist MP, 'never intended Ireland to be a province, and by God she never shall'.

It was, argued the opponents of union, the Ascendancy that had helped Ireland to make so much progress in the eighteenth century, and it was the Ascendancy which had crushed the rebellion of 1798. 'How was the rebellion put down?' asked another like-minded MP. 'By the zeal and loyalty of the gentlemen of Ireland rallying round the laws, the constitution and the independence of their country.' Destroy that independence, and Ireland would once again be under the heel of Great Britain and decline into a provincial backwater.

As Sir John Foster, the attorney-general, one of the major parliamentary opponents of union, argued:

SOURCE C

From *Speech of the Right Honorable John Foster, Speaker of the House of Commons of Ireland, Delivered in Committee, on Monday the 17th Day of February, 1800*, James Haly, 1800, p. 3.

Can those who hear me, deny, that since the period of 1782, this country has risen in civilization, wealth and manufactures, until interrupted by the present war, … much more than it ever did itself in a like period before? And what has this improvement been owing to, but the spirit, the content and enterprise which a free constitution inspired? … I admit that this kingdom is dependent on the crown of Britain … but it is dependent only on the crown … whereas if we adopt the proposed Union … we shall be brought back to the miserable state in which we were, when governed by the laws of another parliament, sitting in another land, ruled by their will, not by our own.

According to Source C what was the key factor in improving the state of Ireland since 1782?

The arguments put forward by the opponents of the union possessed one fatal flaw: the 'nation' they claimed to speak for – like the Irish parliament itself – represented only a tiny minority of the Irish people. The Catholics still remained outside the political nation. By and large the Ascendancy had continued to set its face against both Catholic emancipation and parliamentary reform. After the events of 1798 all it wished to do was to return to the *status quo* – back to the very situation which had brought it to the verge of disaster. 'The noble lord calls upon us for an alternative', said one leading anti-unionist MP, addressing Lord Castlereagh, 'we want no alternative – we call for a sacred adherence to the constitution of 1782'. Admittedly, some anti-unionists, like Henry Grattan, did support both Catholic Emancipation and parliamentary reform, but that stance merely revealed the divisions within the anti-unionist camp. All this made it difficult for them to make an effective stand against the attacks of their opponents.

The passage of the Act

During the months that followed Pitt's initial failure, events appeared to move in favour of the government. Since, as we have seen, the anti-unionists seemed to have nothing positive to offer, leading members of the Roman Catholic clergy and **laity** came out in support of union, encouraged by the belief that Catholic emancipation would follow. Fears of French invasion resurfaced in 1799–1800, and this once again produced fear and alarm and helped to shake

KEY TERM

Laity The main body of Church members who do not belong to the clergy.

the anti-unionist resolve of some members of the Ascendancy. What also helped was the dominant position of William Pitt as prime minister. There was no chance now of an anti-unionist administration coming to power in Britain, and so Pitt controlled patronage.

The last point is particularly important. In the end, everything would turn on the vote in the Irish House of Commons, and Castlereagh was determined to ensure that it went the government's way. He prepared the ground by employing influence, pressure and bribery on a massive scale to ensure that MPs voted in favour of union. As a result, some anti-unionist MPs were induced to change their minds or to give up their seats; and a flood of new MPs – around one-fifth of the total – entered the Irish House of Commons between January 1799 and January 1800. Hence, when the Irish parliament met again in early 1800 to reconsider the government's motion in favour of union, it consented by a vote of 158 to 115. In the spring, both houses of the Irish parliament accepted the detailed plans for the Act of Union, and, after a few minor amendments, so too did the Westminster parliament. The Act of Union received Royal Assent in August 1800.

Why, then, did the Irish parliament agree in this way to its own extinction? For some observers at the time, this was entirely due to Castlereagh's flagrant use of corruption. As one opposition ballad put it:

> How did they pass the Union?
> By perjury and fraud;
> By slaves who sold their land for gold
> As Judas sold his God …
> And thus was passed the Union
> By Pitt and Castlereagh;
> Could Satan send for such an end
> More worthy tools than they?

Yet, most historians have concluded that this is too simple a view. There was nothing exceptional about the methods employed by Castlereagh in 1799–1800, only about their scale. The anti-unionists won the first round against the government in 1799 because they were united in resistance to the principle of union; they then failed because they had no agreed alternative once it became apparent that the government was determined to push ahead with its plan. Their failure seems more important than corruption in the government victory.

Crucially, Pitt was forced in the end to abandon his plan for combining union with Catholic Emancipation owing to the opposition of King George III. He refused to accept Catholic Emancipation, arguing that to do so would violate his coronation oath to protect the Church of England and the Protestant Succession. The king threatened to use his right of royal veto over legislation if Pitt did not give in. No monarch had actually used the power of veto for nearly a century and Pitt was not willing to force the king into such an extreme position. On the other hand, he was personally committed to Catholic Emancipation as part of the Act of Union. As a result, in March 1801, Pitt resigned as prime minister. He was replaced by Henry Addington, who later became better known as Viscount Sidmouth. Addington was the speaker of the House of Commons at the time. He was personally against Catholic Emancipation and was prepared to head a government that would agree to the king's demand. Pitt's resignation avoided the danger of a clash between parliament and the king but at the cost of great bitterness in Ireland.

The terms of the union

By the Act of Union, the 'United Kingdom of Great Britain and Ireland' was established on 1 January 1801 on the following basis:

- The separate Irish parliament disappeared, and Ireland was incorporated into the British parliamentary system.
- To the House of Lords were added four Irish **spiritual lords** and 28 **temporal lords** elected for life by the whole body of Irish peers.
- Ireland elected 100 MPs to the House of Commons: two for each county, two each for the cities of Dublin and Cork, one each for 31 other cities and boroughs, and one for the University of Dublin.
- In spiritual matters, the Churches of Ireland and England were united as the Established Church of England and Ireland.
- Free trade was established between the two countries, and (with a few minor exceptions) there were to be equal commercial privileges.
- The financial systems of the two countries were to remain separate for the time being. Ireland was to contribute two-seventeenths to the expenditure of the United Kingdom and Great Britain was to contribute fifteen-seventeenths.
- The legal systems and laws of the two countries remained as they were.

The impact of the union

The high hopes of the supporters of the Union went largely unfulfilled. There were two basic reasons for this: the political incorporation of Ireland into the United Kingdom was a half-hearted affair, and the economic advantages for Ireland envisaged by Pitt were not realised.

In many ways, Ireland was still treated as a separate country – as 'a half-alien dependency', in one historian's phrase:

- The lord-lieutenant remained as the Crown's representative or viceroy; increasingly, the figurehead of the government of Ireland still based at Dublin Castle. The lord-lieutenant was permanently located in Ireland. Occasionally, lord-lieutenants were given a Cabinet place but this became increasingly unusual after the Act of Union.

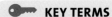 **KEY TERMS**

Spiritual lords High-ranking churchmen such as bishops.

Temporal lords Peers of the Realm with the right to sit in the House of Lords. In descending order of seniority, these are dukes, marquises, earls, viscounts and barons.

- The chief secretary for Ireland continued to deal with the administration of Irish affairs on behalf of the British government – effectively the prime minister of Ireland. The chief secretary was mainly based in Ireland but was expected to travel to London to brief the Cabinet on Irish affairs when required. Chief secretaries for Ireland sometimes were accorded Cabinet rank but this was not the usual practice.
- The Protestant Ascendancy continued to control Ireland and run its local politics as they had done before 1801.

All this meant that Irish Protestantism – especially the Ulster Presbyterians, who now built up strong economic and religious links with England – came to be identified with loyalty to the Union. By contrast, the Catholics soon became increasingly anti-unionist and began to develop a strong sense of their own separate Irish religious and national identity. They felt betrayed when union was not followed by Catholic emancipation.

Additionally, it soon became apparent, in the age of the British industrial revolution, that Irish industries (with the exception of Ulster linen) had no chance of competing effectively with those of Great Britain. Nor was Ireland regarded as a sound and safe field for investment by British bankers and businessmen. Far from economic resources flowing from England to Ireland (as Pitt had prophesied), the traffic proved to be all the other way, as rapid population growth led to large-scale emigration from Ireland to England and Scotland.

Emmet's Rebellion 1803

The Union was still in its infancy when a new rebellion occurred. The extent to which it was directly provoked by the Union is debatable since the organiser, Robert Emmet, was an associate of Wolfe Tone, who was a close friend of his older brother Thomas Emmet. Like Tone and many other nationalist leaders, the Emmets were Protestants. As a result of his relationship with Tone, Robert Emmet had been deeply involved in the failed rebellion of 1798. Following that – with an arrest warrant issued for him – he fled to the Continent, where he attempted to persuade the French to support a new rebellion. However, the French government was by now under the control of the emerging military dictator Napoleon Bonaparte, whose policy from 1799 was to secure a peace agreement with Britain. After long negotiations this was eventually agreed in March 1802 in the 'Peace of Amiens', so-called after the French city where it was signed. The peace lasted only until May 1803 but for the time being Emmet had no hope of securing French support and he returned to Ireland secretly in October 1802 to carry through the rebellion without French aid.

Emmet was not able to secure complete support in Ireland for his plans, and although they remained unknown to the authorities, an accidental explosion at one of his secret arms depots forced him to bring forward his revolt earlier than he had planned. In addition, there was great confusion over when exactly the rebellion would be staged and over the supply of arms for potential rebels approaching Dublin. In the end, Emmet went ahead with his plan on 23 July 1803, issuing a 'Proclamation of Irish Independence' as the rallying call. The plan involved seizing control of several key places in Dublin then waiting in the hope that this would provoke a general rising. The main target was Dublin Castle, the centre of British authority. However, the action was largely limited to Thomas Street in Dublin, where clashes with British forces provoked a general riot rather than a popular rebellion. During the riot, a British soldier was attacked and murdered by the mob – an event witnessed personally by Emmet. Sickened by what he saw, Emmet attempted to call the whole thing off. However, only a small group of those involved regarded themselves as under Emmet's command, so the rioting continued and in the evening the mob hacked to death the Lord Chief Justice of Ireland, Lord Kilwarden, who was attempting to reach Dublin Castle from his residence on the outskirts of the city. By the time the clashes had ended, 50 rebels were dead along with twenty from the authorities.

The end of Emmet

Emmet initially escaped but was eventually was arrested in late August 1803. Within a month he had been tried for treason and executed. He was hanged in Thomas Street – the scene of the riot – and his body then decapitated. Sixteen other people involved in the rebellion were also executed. Compared to the 1798 rising it had been insignificant in scale. Its main interest for historians is as evidence of the growing distance between Irish nationalism and revolutionary France. Emmet, like many veterans of 1798, was bitter about the feebleness of the French effort. Nevertheless, he initially persisted with the idea that French assistance was vital to success in liberating Ireland from British rule. In the end, however, he was forced to abandon this approach. The Irish historian Thomas Bartlett has pointed to the increasing sense of 'Britishness' which developed in Ireland after the 1798 rebellion and resulted in the distancing of Irish nationalists from France. Emmet came to typify this. In effect, Emmet ended up arguing for an Irish nationalism that relied on its own internal dynamic. He did this most famously in his 1803 Proclamation, which many Irish historians see as highly significant: it was later used as a model for the Irish Declaration of Independence made by the rebels of 1916.

Patrick Pearse, one of the 1916 rebels who would himself be executed in the wake of another failed rising, summed up Emmet and his rebellion as follows:

SOURCE D

According to Source D, what was Emmet's great achievement?

From Pádraic H. Pearse, *How Does She Stand?* Irish Freedom Press, 1915, pp. 69–70.

*No failure, judged as the world judges these things, was ever more complete, more pathetic than Emmet's. And yet he has left us a prouder memory than the memory of Brian victorious at **Clontarf** or of Owen Roe victorious at **Benburb**. It is the memory of a sacrifice Christ-like in its perfection. … And his death was august. In the great space of Thomas Street an immense silent crowd; in front of Saint Catherine's Church a gallows upon a platform; a young man climbs to it, quiet, serene, almost smiling, they say – ah, he was very brave; there is no cheer from the crowd, no groan; this man is to die for them, but no man dares to say aloud 'God bless you, Robert Emmet'. Dublin must one day wash out in blood the shameful memory of that quiescence … when the hangman kicked aside the plank and his body was launched into the air.*

KEY TERMS

Clontarf A battle won by Brian Boru, High King of Ireland in 1014, against a joint force of Vikings and Irish rebels.

Benburb A battle won by Owen Roe O'Neill, commanding forces of the Irish Confederacy, which supported Charles I in the Civil War. He defeated forces from Scotland that invaded Ulster with the intention of purging Roman Catholicism and imposing Presbyterianism on Ireland in 1646.

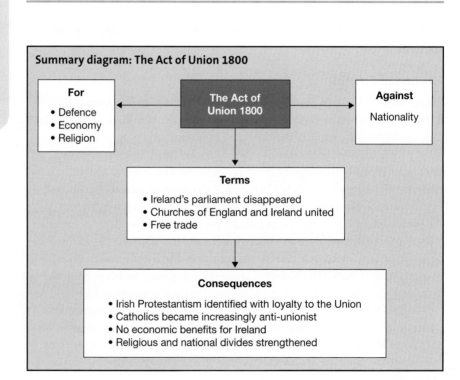

Summary diagram: The Act of Union 1800

Chapter summary

The Act of Union was intended to finally define the relationship between Great Britain and Ireland as one country. It came at the end of a drawn-out process of Britain bringing most of the penal laws against Catholics to an end and allowing a new constitutional settlement in the form of the 1782 'Grattan' parliament. Pitt, in particular, had been committed to reform across a broad front prior to the onset of the French Revolution. This had included moderate parliamentary reform, financial and economic reforms and reform for Ireland. Pitt's reforming instincts, however, were seriously affected by the revolution in France. Initially, Pitt welcomed this, thinking it would lead France to a parliamentary system like that of Britain. However, when the truly revolutionary nature of events in France became apparent, and war with France ensued, he changed position and adopted a repressive attitude aimed at preventing Britain from taking the same path as France. The impact of the French Revolution in Ireland poisoned the progress that had been made. The 1798 rebellion gave the Act of Union a context of repression that Pitt, who had considered the move for several years, had never intended. The failure to grant Catholic Emancipation as part of the settlement simply sealed the fate of the Union as a cause of tension for the future.

Refresher questions

Use these questions to remind yourself of the key material covered in this chapter.

1 In what ways did the penal laws discriminate against Catholics?

2 How successful were the 'Patriots' in achieving their aims?

3 What was the impact of the French Revolution?

4 What impact did the American War of Independence have on Anglo-Irish relations?

5 To what extent was Grattan's parliament a positive step forward for Ireland?

6 What were the aims of the 'United Irishmen'?

7 Why was there a rebellion in Ireland in 1798?

8 What were the arguments for and against the Act of Union?

9 To what extent was Pitt able to achieve his aims in passing the Act of Union?

10 Why did those opposed to the Act of Union fail to prevent it?

 Question practice

ESSAY QUESTIONS

1 How far do you agree with the view that 'Grattan's parliament' (1782–1800) was a complete failure?

2 How significant were the penal laws in shaping events in Ireland between 1774 and 1800?

SOURCE ANALYSIS QUESTION

1 Evaluate the interpretations in both of the passages below and explain which you think is the more convincing explanation of the significance of the Act of Union 1800.

PASSAGE A

From D. George Boyce, 'Ireland 1828–1923: from ascendancy to democracy', in *Protestant Nation to Catholic Nation 1690–1828*, Blackwell, 1992, pp. 8–10.

The events of May to September 1798 only emphasized and deepened the differences between Catholics, Protestants and Dissenters. In 1800 a peace was imposed on Ireland … That peace was followed by an Act of Union … secured by Pitt after two years of intensive political pressure on the Irish parliament. Most Roman Catholics supported the idea of Union, or were at least neutral towards it for the British Government had advanced their cause steadily before the debacle of the Fitzwilliam episode in 1795. There was considerable Protestant opposition to the Union. An Irish parliament dominated by Protestants was, up to a point, master of its own fate. Protestant resentment did not disappear overnight … Protestant acceptance was as a final settlement of Anglo-Irish affairs and a guarantee of their political survival in Ireland. The Churches of England and Ireland were united … as an essential part of the making of the United Kingdom. The Protestant establishment was thus formally incorporated into the Union … to attack that establishment was to attack the very basis of the Union, or so Protestants maintained. This placed Roman Catholics at a disadvantage. Not only must they convince British public opinion of the justice of their claims for full civil rights, but they must also persuade British opinion that Catholic rights were compatible with the continuation of the United Kingdom. Roman Catholics had hoped the Union would be accompanied by Catholic emancipation … Pitt was strongly in favour. Because England was such an overwhelmingly Protestant country she found it hard to accept Roman Catholics in her Parliament: Roman Catholics who for centuries had been regarded as disloyal and even treasonable people.

PASSAGE B

Adapted from Asa Briggs, *The Age of Improvement*, Longman, 1974, pp. 195–7.

During the 1780s … Pitt tried in vain to improve economic relations between the two countries … during the 1790s in the French Revolution, he attempted to quieten growing political, economic and religious turmoil in Ireland by conciliating Irish Catholics. The climax of his policy was the preparation of an Act of Union between the two countries. In 1795, when for a few months the liberal-minded Earl Fitzwilliam was in power in Dublin, George III with his usual stubbornness showed beyond all doubt that he would never countenance full Catholic emancipation. Fitzwilliam was abruptly recalled. The rebellion of 1798 and its aftermath compelled Pitt to take a different line from the King. In 1800 he bribed the Irish Parliament into supporting an Act of Union – it had resisted the measure a year earlier – and tried to follow it up, as many of his supporters had promised, by introducing a Catholic emancipation. Catholics should be admitted to Parliament on taking an amended oath of allegiance. Such a measure, Pitt told the King, 'would be attended by no danger to the Established Church or to the Protestant interest in Great Britain or Ireland – now the Union has taken place'. Pitt's logic did not satisfy George III's scruples and … with the King on the verge of yet another mental breakdown, Pitt did not wish to coerce him. He resigned on 14th March 1801 … Pitt promised not to revive the question of Catholic emancipation during the King's lifetime and to resist any attempts on the part of other statesmen to reopen the subject … both Pitt and his contemporaries knew that even to try to discuss Catholic emancipation with the King after 1801 would be likely to lead to a further bout of insanity.

CHAPTER 3

Daniel O'Connell, 'the Liberator'

This chapter covers important events in Anglo-Irish history, including the mobilisation of mass support in the Catholic Association and the passing of the Emancipation Act and other reforms. But it is important to focus not just on what happened but also on why events happened and their consequences. Pay particular attention to the role of Daniel O'Connell and to the alternative strategy of Sir Robert Peel. You also need to grapple with the contentious issue of how we should evaluate O'Connell's historical stature. The chapter considers these issues through the following themes:

★ The campaign for Catholic Emancipation

★ O'Connell and the Whigs 1830–40

★ The repeal campaign 1840–4

★ Peel and Irish reform

★ O'Connell: the final years

Key dates

1823	May	Formation of the Catholic Association
1828	July	O'Connell elected MP for County Clare
1829	April	Roman Catholic Emancipation Act
1833		Coercion Act
1835	Feb.	Lichfield House Compact: an alliance of Whigs and Irish lasting until 1840

1840		Repeal Association founded by O'Connell
1843	Oct.	Repeal meeting at Clontarf banned
1846		Young Ireland leaders left the Catholic Association
1847		Death of O'Connell

1 The campaign for Catholic Emancipation

▶ *What were the main causes of the Emancipation Crisis?*

🔑 **KEY TERM**

Agrarian Rural (usually but not always) and agricultural.

The religious and national divide in Ireland, contrary to the hopes of men like William Pitt, was strengthened rather than weakened as a result of the Act of Union. An upsurge of **agrarian** outrage and crime prompted Sir Arthur Wellesley (later to become the Duke of Wellington), the chief secretary in 1807, to insist that Ireland 'must be considered to be the enemy's country' – a reference to the ongoing war with France in which Ireland was still considered suspect as to loyalty. It was in these circumstances that a new, outstanding leader of Catholic Ireland at last emerged in the 1820s in the person of Daniel O'Connell, who was prepared to use popular power to challenge the will of the British state.

The early years of the nineteenth century were a depressing time for the supporters of Catholic Emancipation. In England there was still much popular prejudice against Roman Catholics, for political as well as religious reasons. Although the old idea that Catholics were actively plotting to overthrow the **Hanoverian dynasty** had faded, most members of the political classes believed that it would be unwise to give full political rights to Roman Catholics. It was argued that their loyalties were divided between allegiance to the Crown and support for the Pope in Rome. In 1811, George III was finally declared insane after many years of erratic mental health. The Prince of Wales took over his royal powers, taking the title 'Prince Regent'. Like his father, he maintained an obstinate opposition to Catholic Emancipation during the years of his Regency, 1811–20. When George III died in 1820, the Prince Regent became George IV, reigning from 1820 until his death in 1830. As regent and as king he insisted that the government must not even discuss Catholic Emancipation. In order to ensure this would be the case, he followed the principle that the prime minister must be personally committed against Catholic Emancipation and prepared to ensure that all Cabinet ministers, whatever their personal view, for or against, would accept the embargo on raising the issue.

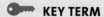

KEY TERM

Hanoverian dynasty
The English royal house that reigned from 1714 to 1901 (from George I to Victoria).

Catholics in Ireland

In Ireland, the Catholic cause made little headway. The leaders of the Emancipation campaign, who were mainly members of the Roman Catholic upper class, were unwilling to seek active popular support and were cautious and conciliatory in their dealings with the authorities. They were even unwilling to support a compromise Emancipation Bill which, while granting political and civil rights to Catholics, included what became known as the 'veto'. This would allow the British government the right to vet ecclesiastical appointments to the Roman Catholic Church in the United Kingdom in order to ensure that only 'loyal' clerics were appointed. This timid attitude was vigorously denounced by Daniel O'Connell. He rejected the veto, believing that it was vital to maintain the freedom of the Catholic Church from interference by a British government. To do otherwise would be a retrograde step, back to the days of the penal code.

Despite the attitude of the king, a majority of MPs were actually in favour of Catholic Emancipation. In 1821 and 1826, Catholic Emancipation Bills obtained a majority in the House of Commons, but were rejected by the Lords. In many ways the 1821 failure was a turning point for O'Connell and the cause he represented. 'Twenty years … have passed away', he said, 'and we are still slaves.' Faced with the permanent hostility of the Crown and the House of

Daniel O'Connell

1775	Born in Kerry
1794–6	Studied law in London
1798	Called to the Irish Bar
1811	Set up the Catholic Board
1815	Killed an opponent in a duel
1823	Founded the Catholic Association
1828	Won the County Clare election
1830	Entered the Commons as the first Catholic MP in modern history
1841–2	Lord Mayor of Dublin
1844	Imprisoned for incitement to violence
1847	Died

Early life

Daniel O'Connell was born on 6 August 1775 in Kerry in the west of Ireland. He was Roman Catholic and Irish was his first language, although he was fully bilingual in Irish and English. He was educated in France and then studied law at Lincoln's Inn in London between 1794 and 1796 to qualify as a barrister. In London, he was influenced by the ideas of the English radicals on political and religious liberty, principles which remained with him throughout his life.

Legal career

After London he continued his law studies in Dublin and was eventually called to the Irish Bar in 1798. He built up a large and profitable practice as a barrister travelling around the Irish legal circuit and coming into touch with the people and problems of Catholic Ireland, where he became known as 'the Counsellor'. All this helped to prepare him for his future political career.

Political career

O'Connell first came into prominence in Irish politics by helping to frame a petition in 1805 for the removal of Catholic disabilities, an appeal rejected by the British government. Then he became the leader of the radical wing of the 'Catholic Board', which he set up in 1811 to campaign for Catholic Emancipation. In 1815, he made a speech condemning the Dublin Corporation. However, the insulting tone of his comments led one member of the Corporation to challenge him to a duel with pistols. O'Connell's shot killed his opponent, leaving him conscience-stricken and determined never to fight a duel again. In the meantime, the campaign for Catholic Emancipation was stalling. The Catholic Board was composed essentially of the middle-class elite of Irish society and made little popular progress – even the annual subscription for membership was far beyond the means of ordinary Irishmen. In 1823, O'Connell founded the Catholic Association, which under his leadership became the driving force behind Catholic Emancipation in 1829.

Lords, he believed that the Emancipation movement in Ireland must now reconsider its aims and methods if the deadlock was to be broken. That was now to be accomplished with the formation of the Catholic Association in 1823–4.

The Catholic Association

The Catholic Association was formed by O'Connell and his supporters in 1823 as a constitutional organisation for the achievement of Catholic civil and political rights. However, it did not become a genuine mass movement until 1824 when, in a masterstroke of policy, O'Connell introduced the famous 'Catholic Rent' of one penny a month for supporters, instead of the high subscription originally proposed. This enabled the Association to become a truly national organisation with strong roots among the peasantry, and turned the old ineffective pressure group into what has been called 'the crusade of an irresistible mass movement'.

The aims and strategies of the Catholic Association

Aims

The main aim of the Catholic Association, like the Catholic Board, was Catholic Emancipation. However, unlike the Board, it also attempted to embrace a wider range of issues, such as electoral reform, reform of the Church of Ireland, tenants' rights and economic development, in order to advance the interests of the whole Catholic community. Initially, the Association was elitist like the Catholic Board, for example, the annual subscription of one guinea (£1.1s.0d. or £1.05 in modern currency) per year was the equivalent of six months' rent for the average farmer. However, in 1824 O'Connell decided on a new category of 'associate membership' which was established with a cheap subscription rate of one penny (1d.; about 0.4p) per month – which became known as the 'Catholic Rent'. This opened up membership to Catholics from poorer backgrounds and the narrow class base barrier of the Catholic Board was removed. Although membership of the Association was not confined to Catholics, O'Connell did aim at making the Irish Roman Catholic Church an integral part of the whole movement, since, as he rightly realised, the role of the parish priests was of crucial importance in spreading the message and helping to collect the Catholic Rent. Indeed, the Catholic Rent was to become the mainstay of the work of the Association as a whole. Its collection was enormously successful: £20,000 was raised in the first nine months alone in 1824–5, and £35,000 was collected between 1826 and 1829. Some of this vast sum – primarily as a gesture towards the Church – was used for educational and other communal purposes; but the bulk of the money was used to finance the Association's work as a national organisation of protest and agitation.

Strategies

The Association was run from Dublin by a committee of O'Connell and his friends and supporters, who directed and encouraged activities at regional and local levels. An important and effective part of the Association's work was the organisation of great open-air public meetings which were often addressed by O'Connell himself. He proved to be an outstanding public speaker; his background and his work as a lawyer meant that he knew his audiences, and his magnificent voice and clear, conversational style of oratory enabled him to build up a marvellous rapport with the Catholic masses. For the peasantry in particular, O'Connell seemed the incarnation of their hopes and ambitions, not only in a material but in a religious sense. He became known as 'the Deliverer'. In turn, the peasant traditions of secret societies and local agitation helped to reinforce the work of the Association at grass-roots level.

As a public orator, O'Connell spoke with two voices. On the one hand, in speaking to his fellow countrymen, he demanded justice for Ireland, which meant Emancipation and the redress of Catholic grievances, to be obtained by peaceful means. But at the same time he was addressing the British government.

Brinkmanship The policy of seeking advantage by creating the impression that one is willing and able to push a dangerous situation to the limit rather than to concede.

Demagogue A popular orator who appeals to the passions and prejudices of his audience.

40-shilling freeholders Those who possessed a 'freehold' (a property held for life or in unconditional inheritance) worth at least 40s. a year in rental value, which entitled them to vote.

Here, in a series of veiled threats, he hinted that British failure to yield to the Association's demands could lead to mass disobedience, possible violence and eventual separation. This policy of '**brinkmanship**' was dangerous but, as later events were to show, also successful.

Apart from its innovative ways of raising money, its organisational work and its great public meetings, the Catholic Association also used the press and public posters to build up support. In the words of the great Irish historian Oliver MacDonagh, in his major biography of O'Connell published in 1990, the Association was a sophisticated political organisation: 'a pioneer … of mass constitutional politics and pacific popular democracy'.

Supporters

Geographically, its main area of support proved to be in Munster in south-west Ireland, and later in the south-east; the north, where O'Connell was seen by the powerful Protestant community as a Roman Catholic **demagogue**, proved to be largely barren territory. Three main Catholic groups provided organisational support for the Association:

- the urban middle classes – particularly lawyers – who hoped to gain most, economically and professionally, from Emancipation
- the rural middle classes, whose links with the peasantry and local politics were particularly important
- the parish priests, who became the most important emissaries of the Association at local level.

The British government's response

The rapid progress of the Association and O'Connell's often bellicose language at public meetings alarmed the authorities, and he was arrested in 1824 on a charge of incitement to rebellion, although the prosecution failed. In 1825, the government did suppress the Association, but it was soon reorganised by O'Connell. In 1825, too, another Emancipation Bill passed through the House of Commons, but was again rejected by the House of Lords. The deadlock therefore still remained.

The 1826 election

The following year, however, saw the beginning of a new phase in the history of the Emancipation campaign. 1826 was an election year, and the Association decided to intervene directly and deliberately in the Irish elections. This time, in unprecedented fashion, it called on the voters in selected counties to support only pro-Emancipation candidates, whether they were Whigs or Tories. This meant that the Catholic **40-shilling freeholders** – the mainstay of the county electorate and normally a deferential group – were being urged to defy their Protestant landlords. A number were indeed prepared to do so.

The meticulous organisation of the Catholic voters by the Association, with the cooperation of the local priests, achieved a considerable success: four pro-Emancipation candidates were returned. The most remarkable contest was at Waterford, where the English landowners, the Beresfords, had controlled the seat for generations. On this occasion, Lord George Beresford was defeated by Villiers Stuart, an ally of O'Connell's.

It was the fact that the Catholic voters in these counties had the backing of a powerful national organisation in the form of the Catholic Association that enabled them to defy their landlords with relative impunity. The Association, proclaimed R.L. Shiel, one of O'Connell's lieutenants, was now 'master of the representation of Ireland'.

The lessons of the 1826 general election were not lost on the British government either. As Robert Peel (home secretary) wrote: 'the instrument of deference and supremacy had been converted into a weapon fatal to the authority of the landlord'. O'Connell himself was now the key figure in Irish politics. It was at this point that the Tory prime minister, Lord Liverpool, who had successfully maintained government unity since 1812 under difficult circumstances of war and economic problems as well as the Irish situation, suffered a stroke. He was forced to resign, precipitating a crisis that profoundly affected the situation in Ireland.

The Emancipation Crisis 1828–9

Liverpool's forced departure in February 1827 brought to a head the divisions within the Cabinet over Catholic Emancipation. On one side were its opponents, notably Robert Peel and the Duke of Wellington, who, as supporters of the rights and privileges of the Established Church of England, were opposed to Emancipation on principle. On the other were those members of the Cabinet, led by George Canning, who was a long-time supporter of Emancipation believing, as his early mentor William Pitt had done, that it would help to bind Ireland more securely to the Union, and enable British governments to deal more effectively with Irish problems.

After weeks of discussions with George IV – who disliked him personally as well as opposing his support for Emancipation – Canning finally became prime minister in April. In agreeing to this, George IV was breaking his own policy of always having a prime minister opposed to Emancipation, but Canning's political experience and his popularity with many MPs meant that any government without him would be unlikely to survive and Canning, after years of experience, was not willing to serve under another leader. The king was forced to swallow his pride and appoint Canning, although he insisted on continuing the embargo on discussions about Emancipation in the Cabinet and insisted also on personally approving all Cabinet appointments (which was an unusual demand). However, Canning's position on Emancipation led Peel and

Wellington to refuse to join his ministry. This meant that Canning was forced to take some Whig leaders into his government in order to fill all the posts. In this situation, few politicians believed that the issue of Catholic Emancipation could be ignored for long, whatever the king thought.

However, in September 1827 Canning suddenly fell ill and died. The obvious choice to replace him was Wellington, but the king had wanted Wellington and Peel to enter Canning's government to balance it against Catholic Emancipation, and their refusal to do so angered him. Consequently, to general disbelief, he replaced Canning with a totally ineffectual prime minister, Lord Goderich, who did not want the job, and who only accepted the role in deference to the king, and then took the first opportunity he could to resign. Wellington finally became prime minister in January 1828 and Peel agreed to resume office as home secretary and – as second-in-command in a government led by a peer – leader of the House of Commons. Unfortunately, the elevation of the ultra-conservative Wellington to the premiership soon led to the resignation of Canning's former supporters and the Whig reinforcements he had recruited from the new government.

The Tory Party was now in complete disarray, and in no fit state therefore to deal with a major crisis. The repeal of the **Test and Corporations Acts** in February 1828 at the instigation of a leading Whig MP, Lord John Russell, was bound to make it difficult for the Tory leaders to ignore the issue of Catholic Emancipation. The government was unable to resist the repeal of the Test and Corporations Acts because a majority of the Commons was in favour of it. Wellington could have organised its defeat in the Lords but he was unwilling to provoke an outright confrontation with the Commons over the issue, especially since the Acts were by then largely disregarded for the most part. However, exactly the same situation existed in regard to Catholic Emancipation except, of course, that this barrier was strictly imposed. It was a by-election in a parliamentary constituency in Ireland that now brought matters to a head.

The County Clare election 1828

Early in 1828, an Irish Tory MP, William Vesey Fitzgerald, was appointed **president of the Board of Trade** and, as was customary at that time for any ordinary MP accepting a government position, he had to stand for re-election since he was no longer able to act independently as an MP. In this case, the constituency was County Clare in the west of Ireland. Fitzgerald was in fact a very popular landlord locally and a well-known supporter of Catholic Emancipation; but, seeing the political opportunity, O'Connell decided to stand as a candidate for the seat himself.

O'Connell's candidature at County Clare presented the government with a serious dilemma. Since O'Connell was a Roman Catholic he would be unable to take his seat in the House of Commons if elected without a change in the parliamentary oath – in effect, Catholic Emancipation. Yet, to oppose his right

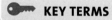

KEY TERMS

Test and Corporations Acts Acts of 1661 and 1673 excluding Roman Catholics, Protestant Dissenters, and followers of Judaism and other faiths from public office.

President of the Board of Trade The title of a position in the government that was sometimes given Cabinet status and sometimes not. It is now a secondary title of the Secretary of State for Trade and Industry.

to enter the Commons would run the risk of widespread public disorder and violence in Ireland, with the unenviable prospect of further Catholic candidacies at elections in the future. The situation was all the more difficult because the House of Commons had a majority in favour of Emancipation and would hardly be prepared to support measures to hold down Irish opinion by force.

In the event, things worked out exactly as O'Connell had anticipated. With the backing of the Catholic Association and the local priests, the Catholic voters were prepared once again to defy their landlords, and O'Connell won an easy victory in July (with 2057 votes to Fitzgerald's 982). The latter wrote to Peel that O'Connell's organisation was 'so complete and so formidable that no man can contemplate without alarm what is to follow in this wretched country'.

'This business', wrote one English MP of the Clare election, 'must bring the Catholic question to a crisis and conclusion'. So it turned out. The Duke of Wellington, as a soldier and ex-Irish secretary, took the threat of violence seriously, and concluded that, on purely practical grounds, Emancipation must be conceded, even if this meant bullying the king, browbeating the House of Lords and facing the prospect of a Tory revolt in the House of Commons, and, of course, compromising his own firmly held beliefs. Peel, after some hesitation, accepted the logic of the duke's case, and agreed to shoulder the burden of getting the proposed bill through the House of Commons. This decision was critical because as home secretary and leader of the Commons, Peel was the only government minister with the status and ability to take on the job.

The crisis provoked opposition to Emancipation in Ulster. The introduction of proposals to bring about Catholic Emancipation in September 1828 saw the setting up of so-called 'Brunswick Clubs'. The title derived from George I, the first Hanoverian king, whose succession had secured the Protestant monarchy in 1714. Although the family name of Hanover was the most familiar one, George also held the title Duke of Brunswick. It was this connection to a key point in the preservation of the Protestant supremacy that gave the clubs their name. The clubs hoped to force the British government to abort the constitutional change to the parliamentary oath, but they had virtually no impact on Wellington and Peel. Once the legislation passed in March 1829 they were effectively dead. It was, however, an indication of the dimension of Ulster resistance for the future.

The Roman Catholic Emancipation Act 1829

The Catholic Emancipation Bill passed through the House of Commons early in 1829 as a result of the support of the Whigs and pro-emancipationist Tories (142 Tory MPs voted against). The demoralised Lords, not daring to defy the duke, subsequently passed it by a two-to-one majority – many abstained from the vote. King George IV angrily accepted the inevitable, and the bill became law in April 1829. The influence of the Protestant supporters of Emancipation in the House of Commons was essential to the passing of the Act, and they were helped by the disunity of the Tory Party. The lion's share of credit for the victory was, understandably, claimed by O'Connell, who now acquired the title – in Ireland – of 'the Liberator'.

The Roman Catholic Emancipation Act of 1829 was a simple one. The existing parliamentary oath of allegiance required the person swearing the oath to deny the doctrines of **transubstantiation** and the **invocation of saints**, both key aspects of Roman Catholic belief. The Act – which was formally known as 'An Act for the Relief of His Majesty's Roman Catholic Subjects' – repealed this requirement and instituted a new oath which Roman Catholics were able to swear without renouncing their religion. It was, in effect, the final concession giving virtually full civil and political rights to Roman Catholics, with very few exceptions, such as the office of lord chancellor – the highest legal officer in the judiciary and a member of the Cabinet.

On the other hand, to reduce the political impact of the concession, the franchise qualification in Ireland was raised from a 40-shilling (£2) freehold to a **£10 household suffrage**, and this cut the Irish electorate from around 216,000 to around 37,000. Despite this, O'Connell welcomed the bill with enthusiasm. 'Peel's bill for Emancipation', he wrote to his wife in March 1829, 'is good – very good; frank, direct, complete; no veto, no control'. He was not over-worried by the electoral restrictions, since, although he had mobilised them, he believed that the 40-shilling freeholders were still too much under the control of the landlords.

Much more important were the opportunities opened up by the Emancipation Act for Catholic advancement in politics, the professions and government service, and O'Connell believed that this was bound to lead to the eventual destruction of the Protestant Ascendancy in Ireland. In that sense, the Act was, as the Liberator claimed, 'one of the greatest triumphs recorded in history – a bloodless revolution'. Nevertheless, fundamental change in Ireland after 1829 was slow. Since the Emancipation Act was regarded by Irish Protestants as primarily a Catholic victory, sectarianism increased. This meant that in practice, despite O'Connell's protestations to the contrary, the achievement of the 1829 Act marked another stage in the identification of Irish nationalism with Catholicism. 'Our politics', as an Irish land agent wrote only a few years later, 'have little or nothing to do with any general principle or feeling save that of Catholic versus Protestant.'

In Great Britain, however, the Emancipation Act was followed by swift and dramatic changes in politics. It helped to precipitate:

- the break-up of the old Tory Party and the rise of a new Conservative Party
- the triumph of the Whigs and their allies at the general election of 1830; and, subsequently, the passage of important political and social reforms in the 1830s.

These years also saw the emergence of a small but significant Irish Party in the House of Commons, led by O'Connell. He was able to use his position to play off

KEY TERMS

Transubstantiation
The belief that during the Roman Catholic Mass the bread and wine of the sacrament are literally transformed into the body and blood of Christ, rather than the Anglican belief that this is a symbolic transformation.

Invocation of saints
The belief that saints can be prayed to in order that they may intercede with God on behalf of the person praying. The Anglican Church does not agree with the Roman Catholic view of this and some other Protestant Churches completely reject this idea.

£10 household suffrage
The vote to the male head of every household possessing £10 a year or more.

Conservatives and thus extract reforms for Ireland. But O'Connell more than just a parliamentary politician. The County Clare own what could be achieved by the power of mass opinion in ed by political activists and under clerical influence. 'The policy ...manship', as one historian puts it, 'received the seal of success'. What had been achieved once, as both O'Connell and his enemies perceived, could perhaps be achieved again. This meant that the 'Irish question', as the years after 1829 were to show, could never be reduced to a purely parliamentary dimension. Nevertheless, the importance of O'Connell's position should not be overstated. It should be remembered that the Whigs had a long record of sympathy for Irish grievances, and as such – although not all Whigs were in agreement on all issues – there was a real sense among many Whig leaders that they had a duty to resolve at least some of the problems that had prevented both Irish acceptance of the Union and tranquillity in Ireland.

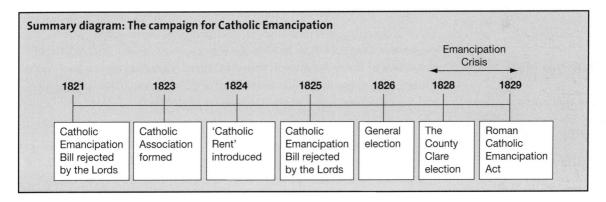

Summary diagram: The campaign for Catholic Emancipation

Emancipation Crisis

1821	1823	1824	1825	1826	1828	1829
Catholic Emancipation Bill rejected by the Lords	Catholic Association formed	'Catholic Rent' introduced	Catholic Emancipation Bill rejected by the Lords	General election	The County Clare election	Roman Catholic Emancipation Act

② O'Connell and the Whigs 1830–40

▶ *How fruitful was the alliance forged between O'Connell and the Whig government in the 1830s?*

After the success of the Emancipation campaign, O'Connell was able to give up practising law and devote his whole time to politics. He received a gift of £20,000 from Irish Catholics in recognition of his great services, and further regular payments thereafter, known as the 'O'Connell Tribute'. He now possessed a dual position as both an Irish national leader and a British parliamentary politician. His immediate task was to decide what role to adopt:

- should he concentrate on a policy of repeal of the Act of Union and rely on another campaign in Ireland to ensure its success?
- or should he use his new position in the House of Commons to press for immediate reforms for Ireland?

O'Connell's long-term aim was clearly repeal. 'I have an ultimate object', he had proclaimed in 1813, 'it is the Repeal of the Union and the restoration to Old Ireland of her independence.' But the Liberator was primarily an opportunist in politics. He was never prepared to come down firmly on the side of either repeal or reform; and in practice he veered from one to the other as and when circumstances dictated, and often spoke with the voice of repeal in Ireland and of reform in England.

The case for reform

However, it soon became clear, in the years immediately following emancipation, that it would be difficult to mount a new mass campaign in Ireland in favour of repeal, although some sporadic agitation was organised.

In the first place, many members of the Catholic middle classes wanted to see some of the fruits of Emancipation in terms of jobs and opportunities as soon as possible, and this implied reform. A number of leading Catholic bishops also supported a policy of 'reform first'. Furthermore, the actions of the Catholic peasantry – many of whom had lost the vote and most of whom felt frustrated by the lack of any real change in their conditions – demanded immediate action. Their refusal to pay their tithes to the Anglican Church led to the outbreak of a vicious '**tithe war**' in the 1830s. It was accompanied by:

- forcible and generally unsuccessful attempts by the authorities to collect the tithe with the use of police and soldiers
- the virtual breakdown of law and order in many parts of Ireland; in 1832, for example, there were 242 murders, 300 attempted murders and 560 cases of arson throughout Ireland.

For the new Whig government after 1830, the immediate priority in Ireland was the restoration of law and order, a policy which, implicitly, many leaders of the Roman Catholic laity and clergy were prepared to accept despite their opposition to tithes.

The Great Reform Act 1832

From O'Connell's point of view, the situation in parliament seemed more promising, even though he was treated with open contempt as an outsider by many MPs. In the general election of 1830, 30 Irish (O'Connellite) MPs were returned to the House of Commons, and emerged as an influential third party. They supported the new Whig prime minister, Earl Grey, in getting a Parliamentary Reform Act through Parliament in 1831–2. The Act extended the right to vote to a limited extent and redistributed some seats in favour of the new industrial towns. Constitutionally, three versions of the Reform Act were required: one for England and Wales; one for Scotland and one for Ireland. But the terms of the Irish version were disappointing to the Irish. The vote was not restored to the 40-shilling freeholders, and Ireland obtained only five new MPs,

 **KEY TERM**

Tithe war Violent resistance to paying the tithe that lasted from 1831 to 1838.

bringing the total to 105. Nevertheless, in the first post-reform general election in 1833, the O'Connellites emerged with 39 MPs, and thus became the largest group of Irish MPs in the House of Commons.

The Coercion Act

However, O'Connell was not yet prepared to cooperate fully with the Whigs, an attitude which seemed even more justified when they passed a new Coercion Act for Ireland in 1833, to last for just one year. This was one of the toughest pieces of law-and-order legislation to affect Ireland in the nineteenth century. It gave the authorities wide powers of arbitrary arrest and imprisonment and control of public meetings. The Act did succeed in diminishing the amount of violent crime and stifling repeal agitation, and even received the tacit support of Irish Catholic bishops. O'Connell, however, denounced its authors as 'the base, brutal and bloody Whigs'.

Reform of education

Yet, despite the rhetoric, there were good reasons for the Whigs and O'Connellites to come together, for the Whigs had already begun a programme of Irish reform. In 1832, Lord Edward Stanley, as Irish secretary, introduced a system of 'national schools' which, although it failed to satisfy his aim of overcoming religious sectarianism, did much to attack basic illiteracy.

The Irish Church Act

In the following year, the Irish Church Act was passed. This reformed the unrepresentative Church of Ireland by abolishing ten **sees**, including two archbishoprics; and it was suggested that the confiscated Church funds obtained from this be used for secular purposes. Whatever the defects of this legislation, it soon became apparent to O'Connell that the new reformed parliament was no more in favour of repeal than the old one had been. A resolution in favour of repeal in 1834 was defeated in the Commons by a massive vote of 523 to 38, with only one British MP voting in favour. Even English liberals and radicals, it appeared, were averse to the prospect of a separate, Roman Catholic-dominated Irish parliament. For O'Connell, therefore, if repeal was ruled out, cooperation with the Whigs offered the best prospect of a continuation of Irish reform.

The Whigs became keener on more formal Irish support during 1834 as divisions began to emerge in their ranks. In November of that year, owing to disputes arising principally out of the **sequestration clauses** of the Irish Church Act, which offended many Anglicans, two Cabinet ministers resigned and were supported by some 40 backbenchers. As a result, Earl Grey gave up his post as prime minister and was succeeded by Lord Melbourne. O'Connell had disliked and distrusted Grey; he was much more inclined to establish closer relations with Melbourne.

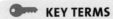

KEY TERMS

See A bishop's official seat or area of authority.

Sequestration clauses Parts of the Irish Church Act that authorised the seizure of Church property.

The Lichfield House Compact

The Whigs' difficulties underlined the increasing centrality of Irish issues in British politics. Melbourne found it difficult to carry on as prime minister, and often clashed with King William IV. Four government ministers, including Lord Edward Stanley, resigned in May 1834 over proposals suggested by Lord John Russell to deal with the tithes issue by a partial reform of the Irish Anglican Church, and the project was shelved. When the leader of the House of Commons, Lord Althorp, was forced to leave his post and go to the House of Lords as Earl Spencer when his father died, matters came to a head. Melbourne argued that the only Whig MP with the ability to replace Althorp was Lord John Russell. William IV detested Russell (whom he felt was far too radical on reforming Ireland) and refused to agree. Melbourne then tried to force the king's acceptance by hinting that if Russell was not appointed he might have to resign. To Melbourne's astonishment the king chose to interpret this as an actual resignation and effectively dismissed Melbourne from the premiership. Sir Robert Peel, now acknowledged as the Conservative leader rather than Wellington, was appointed prime minister, as head of a minority administration.

In the general election that followed in January 1835, the Conservatives gained more than 100 seats, but Peel's party still remained a minority in the House of Commons despite its remarkable recovery. Peel stayed in office really to protect the king from embarrassment. He knew that the Whigs still had a majority in the House of Commons, even without the support of O'Connell's Irish MPs. Any hope that Peel might be able to prolong his government vanished in February in what became known as the 'Lichfield House Compact', negotiated in February and March 1835 in a series of meetings at the home of the prominent Whig Lord Lichfield. The Lichfield Compact was an agreement between the Whig government, O'Connell and a group of 'Radicals' who were nominally Whigs but often acted independently as individuals or loosely in association with each other – to cooperate in the interests of reform.

The significance of the Compact

The significance of the agreement is debatable. The historian Robert Stewart argued in his 1989 book *Party and Politics 1830–1852* that the Compact marked the origin of the Liberal Party and saw it as the key development for party politics in the period. However, it can equally be argued that it merely confirmed what was already the position in reality since neither the Irish nor the Whig/Radicals could work with Peel. In any event, within a few weeks the government was suffering regular defeats in the House of Commons. Peel resigned in April and rejected William IV's plea to hold another general election, telling the king that he must accept Melbourne back as prime minister. Russell duly became leader of the House of Commons. Formally, this Whig–Irish alliance lasted until 1840, when O'Connell, disillusioned by the relative lack of progress on Irish grievances, opted to put forward repeal of the Union as his objective. This was as totally unacceptable to the Whigs as it was to the Conservatives. One undoubted effect of the Compact was to convince some 30 or so of the more conservative-minded Whigs – who had grave fears that reform in Ireland might become too radical – to join Peel and the Conservatives during 1835. Some important figures made the switch, notably Lord Edward Stanley who, as Lord Derby, would later become leader of the Conservative Party.

Further reform

Fears of more unrest in Ireland, together with an acceptance of the legitimacy of many Irish grievances, made the Whigs amenable to the case for further Irish reform. A new spirit of fairness and impartiality was now applied to the administration of Ireland, mainly due to the efforts of Thomas Drummond, the Irish under-secretary:

- Catholics were appointed to high offices in the Irish judiciary and the Castle.
- A new national police force was established, with Catholics encouraged to join.
- The political powers of the Protestant Orange Order were curbed.

Drummond insisted that the police and military were no longer to be used automatically to defend the claims of the landlords or to collect tithes – 'property has its duties as well as its rights', as he said in a famous phrase. In fact, as far as the tithe question was concerned, an Act of 1838 introduced a compromise solution by which the tithe now became a fixed additional rent charge, payable by the landlord.

Lord John Russell, who became home secretary as well as leader of the Commons in 1835, also tried to introduce into Ireland a number of major English reforms. In 1838, a new Irish Poor Law Act system based on the principles of the 1834 Poor Law Amendment Act, which applied to England and Wales, was set up. The 1834 Act had established a central authority for poor relief – the Poor Law Commission – which based its policy on the idea that able-bodied people who applied for poor relief should be compelled to enter a workhouse to receive it. It also provided for the segregation and different treatment of different classes of applicants, such as the old and infirm and children. The Irish version was based largely on this system. The main provisions of the 1838 Act were:

- The extension of the powers of the Poor Law Commission to Ireland, with the appointment of assistant commissioners who were to implement the Act in Ireland.
- The division of the country into Poor Law Unions based on Irish electoral divisions.
- Boards of guardians to be set up to run each Union – most to be elected, but some such as local magistrates to be appointed by virtue of their office.
- The setting up of a workhouse in each Union.
- The collection of a local poor rate to finance the system.
- Financial assistance for emigration. This provision was unique to the Irish Act.

In 1840, the Municipal Corporations (Ireland) Act attempted to apply to Ireland the major features of an 1835 Act that had reformed English and Welsh urban government. This provided for the election of unpaid local councillors every three years as a municipal corporation to represent the local community. However, owing to the opposition of the House of Lords, the Irish Corporations Act was much narrower than its English counterpart because it:

- was based on a £10 household suffrage, rather than as in England and Wales where all ratepayers were eligible to vote
- had more limited powers, so that control of the police, for example, was excluded.

In addition, the 1840 Act abolished 58 Irish corporations. Nevertheless, the new regime in Irish local government did offer opportunities to Catholics. The O'Connellites won control of ten local councils, and in 1841 O'Connell was elected Lord Mayor of Dublin, the first Catholic to hold that position since the reign of James II. Catholics were also appointed as sheriffs and magistrates, and became members of Poor Law boards of guardians.

The end of the Whig–Irish alliance

The year 1840 marked the end of the formal Whig–Irish alliance. Despite O'Connell's initial enthusiasm, the Irish Catholics seemed to gain little of real substance from a decade of Whig reform. Ireland was still treated differently from England, and the power of the Protestant Ascendancy there still remained unbroken; it was the Whigs who appeared to gain most from the alliance. The contemporary description of the O'Connellites as 'the Irish tail' to the Whig parliamentary party was not inappropriate. For while the Whigs obtained the one thing they vitally needed – Irish parliamentary support – O'Connell was forced to compromise time and time again in order to keep the government in power. Moreover, his concentration on parliamentary politics after 1835 to some extent cut him off from his Irish roots. This was reflected in the decline of the 'O'Connell Tribute' and the waning of his own personal influence in Ireland.

O'Connell had always insisted that 'if that experiment failed, I would come back with tenfold force to the repeal'. The signal for the new policy came in 1840 with the formation of the National Repeal Association and his break with the Whigs. A mass agitation in favour of repeal became virtually certain when, as a result of the Conservatives' triumph at the general election of 1841, Sir Robert Peel became prime minister. Apart from other considerations, there was a personal antipathy between O'Connell and Peel which went back to the latter's time as Irish secretary in the years 1812–18. For Peel, O'Connell was still 'the great blackguard', while for the free-and-easy Irish leader the prime minister was a cold and callous Englishman whose 'smile was like the silver plate on a coffin'.

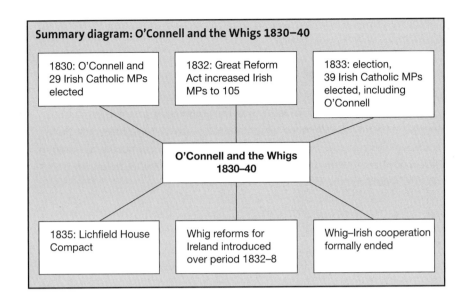

Summary diagram: O'Connell and the Whigs 1830–40

1830: O'Connell and 29 Irish Catholic MPs elected

1832: Great Reform Act increased Irish MPs to 105

1833: election, 39 Irish Catholic MPs elected, including O'Connell

O'Connell and the Whigs 1830–40

1835: Lichfield House Compact

Whig reforms for Ireland introduced over period 1832–8

Whig–Irish cooperation formally ended

3   The repeal campaign 1840–4

▶ *Why did O'Connell's attempts to secure repeal of the Act of Union fail?*

O'Connell's main efforts after 1840 were concentrated on a national repeal campaign in Ireland. 'Repeal', he proclaimed, 'is the sole basis which the people will accept … Repeal alone is and must be the grand basis of all future operations, hit or miss, win or lose.' In many ways it resembled, although on a much larger scale, the campaign in favour of Catholic Emancipation in the 1820s.

Support for repeal

Repeal rested upon the support of two major groups:

- the peasantry, to whom it seemed to offer a reduction of the landlords' power
- the Catholic Church.

As far as the Church was concerned, O'Connell could rely once again on the loyalty of the parish priests; but this time many bishops were prepared to come out openly in support, notably Archbishop MacHale, the most powerful man in the Irish Catholic Church. This did mean, however, that O'Connell was forced to go along with the Church's views on contentious questions such as education, which was bound to antagonise Protestants. One difference, however, between the present campaign and the earlier one was that this time the Catholic middle classes were less committed, since many of them were more concerned with the immediate material concerns rather than the problematic future advantages of repeal. On the other hand, O'Connell did have the support of a small but

KEY TERM

Young Ireland Radical Irish nationalist movement founded by Irish intellectuals in 1841. It promoted the study of Irish history, the Irish language, Irish national ideas and independence. Its belief in violent agitation led it to break away from O'Connell in 1846.

significant group of more extreme nationalists, known as '**Young Ireland**', led by the Protestant Thomas Davis.

What did repeal mean?

On this fundamental point O'Connell was vague and ambiguous. If it meant a return to the *status quo* before 1800, then this implied the re-establishment of the Irish parliament, though on a more representative basis. This would then be followed by measures to improve conditions for the Irish people, although to allay the fears of the propertied classes O'Connell went out of his way to stress that this would not mean any 'social revolution'.

But what exactly would be done about social, economic and religious affairs? And what powers would be enjoyed by the new parliament in a new Anglo-Irish relationship?

A speech by O'Connell to a large audience on 14 May 1843 is a typical example:

? In what ways can the speech reported in Source A be seen as representing a limited aim?

SOURCE A

From *The Nation*, 20 May 1843, quoted in E. Curtis and R.B. McDowell, *Irish Historical Documents*, Methuen, 1942, pp. 269–74.

My first object is to get Ireland for the Irish … Old Ireland and liberty! That is what I am struggling for … What numberless advantages would not the Irish enjoy if they possessed their own country? A domestic parliament would encourage Irish manufactures … Irish commerce and protect Irish agriculture. The labourer, the artisan, and the shopkeeper would all be benefited by the repeal of the union … They say we want separation from England, but what I want is to prevent separation taking place … what motive could we have to separate if we obtain all these blessings? … I want you to do nothing that is not open and legal, but if the people unite with me and follow my advice it is impossible not to get the Repeal … there is no pursuit of Roman Catholic interests as opposed to Protestant … the object in view is the benefit of the whole nation.

Some historians to refuse to take seriously O'Connell's support for repeal as a genuine political aim. They have suggested that the whole repeal campaign was merely an attempt to blackmail the British government into granting further and more fundamental reforms within the framework of the Union. 'He used Repeal', argued Oliver MacDonagh, in his 1990 biography of O'Connell, 'as a popular rallying-cry, a mode of intimidating governments and a hoped-for bargaining counter'.

Organisation and finance of the campaign

The repeal campaign was financed by the 'Repeal Rent', which was similar to the 'Catholic Rent' of the earlier campaign, and brought in ample funds. This enabled an efficient, national movement to be established again. The outstanding characteristic of the new campaign in the early 1840s was the organisation of 'monster meetings', strictly controlled by O'Connell on a peaceful basis. These tactics did lead to a massive mobilisation of the Irish Catholics, especially in the key year 1843; and overall between 3 million and 4 million people may have attended these meetings, representing the pinnacle of his career as a popular leader. Their aim was, he said, 'to convince our enemies … I want to make England feel her weakness if she refuses to give the justice we require'.

Although occasionally O'Connell hinted at the possible use of force, fundamentally the Repeal Association was a vast pressure group which aimed (like the contemporary **Anti-Corn Law League**, with which it was often compared) to arouse and channel opinion through propaganda and large-scale public agitation, and thus force the government to repeal the Act of Union. This was, after all, a tactic which had worked successfully against the British government in 1828–9 in the crisis over Catholic Emancipation.

The failure of the campaign

However, Peel was in a much stronger position now than he and Wellington had been during the Emancipation Crisis. This was because:

- As prime minister in 1841 he headed a government with a large majority in the House of Commons – quite unlike the Tory government's position in 1828–9.
- The Conservative Party was united against repeal as it had not been over Catholic Emancipation. There was no majority in the House of Commons for repeal in the way there had been for Emancipation in 1828–9 and indeed for many years prior to that – in 1841 even the Whig opposition agreed that the Union must be maintained.

In contrast, O'Connell's position was weaker than it had been in 1828–9:

- The Irish electorate was no longer so formidable, owing to the disenfranchisement of the 40-shilling freeholders in 1829.
- O'Connell's support was not as united as it appeared. Middle-class Catholics had serious doubts about repeal and were worried by the implications of a mass agitation and radicalism generally.
- 'Young Ireland' differed sharply with O'Connell over tactics and long-term aims.

In contrast, Protestant opinion in England and Ireland was totally opposed to repeal. Peel was prepared to take a moderate line and tolerate the repeal movement so long as it remained strictly within the law. Initially, he played down the alarmist clamour of the lord-lieutenant and the Irish Protestants for the immediate suppression of the Association. However, in a speech in the Commons in May 1843, Peel spelled out the total commitment of his support for the Union. 'Deprecating as I do all war, but, above all, civil war, yet there

 **KEY TERM**

Anti-Corn Law League
Organisation formed in 1839 to work for the repeal of the English Corn Laws. The Corn Laws, which regulated the grain trade and restricted imports of grain, were repealed in 1846, although in reality this was not solely due to the campaign of the League.

SOURCE B

KING O'CONNELL AT TARA.

This *Punch* cartoon, 'King O'Connell at Tara', published in London in 1843, shows Daniel O'Connell as King of the Irish.

? Why do you think O'Connell might have been represented in this way in Source B?

is no alternative which I do not think preferable to the dismemberment of this empire.' The army was duly strengthened in Ireland. Peel was making it clear that on this occasion the government was determined not to back down, as had happened in 1829.

The repeal campaign came to a head in the autumn of 1843. The momentum of the movement itself pushed O'Connell and other leaders into more threatening postures, with hints of mass unrest and military action. Peel waited for the right tactical moment to arrive, and then acted suddenly and swiftly. The monster meeting, planned by O'Connell to take place at Clontarf on 7 October, was banned by the authorities. The Irish leader accepted the decision peacefully, and his followers acquiesced, although many of them were disappointed and resentful.

'Clontarf' marks the effective end of the repeal campaign. Yet, the Liberator believed that not all was lost. The work of the Repeal Association, he suggested, had at least 'aroused the English nation from slumber. Our grievances are beginning to be admitted by all parties … to be afflicting.' It was followed by a new period of Irish reform, initiated this time by the Irish leader's formidable adversary, Sir Robert Peel.

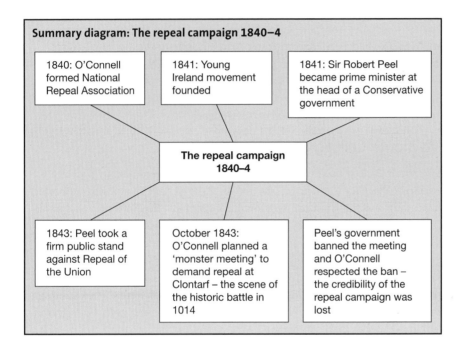

Summary diagram: The repeal campaign 1840–4

1840: O'Connell formed National Repeal Association	**1841:** Young Ireland movement founded	**1841:** Sir Robert Peel became prime minister at the head of a Conservative government

The repeal campaign 1840–4

1843: Peel took a firm public stand against Repeal of the Union	**October 1843:** O'Connell planned a 'monster meeting' to demand repeal at Clontarf – the scene of the historic battle in 1014	Peel's government banned the meeting and O'Connell respected the ban – the credibility of the repeal campaign was lost

④ Peel and Irish reform

▶ *How successful was Peel's strategy of reform in Ireland?*

The lesson that Peel drew from the confrontation with O'Connell was that 'mere force … will do nothing as a permanent remedy for the social ills of Ireland'. What he aimed at was to build up in Catholic Ireland, especially among the middle classes, a feeling of confidence in the effectiveness and impartiality of British government and the law. In this way, the Irish Catholic majority would become reconciled to the benefits of the Union. Peel therefore continued the Whigs' policy of appointing suitable Catholics to official posts in Ireland, particularly in the judiciary.

In 1844, Peel went further, and submitted to the Cabinet a programme of wide-ranging Irish reform covering such controversial topics as the franchise, landlord–tenant relations and, above all, Catholic education. One of Peel's main aims here was the need to break the 'powerful combination' (as he termed it) of

O'Connell and the Catholic clergy – the dynamic behind repeal. It was this aim that was the essential cornerstone of his Irish policy. As part of this strategy the British government even embarked on an attempt – ultimately unsuccessfully – to obtain the Pope's unequivocal condemnation of the political activities of the Irish priesthood.

But (apart from an Act dealing with Catholic charities) the early part of Peel's programme was not very successful. A proposed new Franchise Bill, based on a £5 freeholder franchise, gained little support in the House of Commons and was dropped. A bill for providing compensation to evicted Irish tenants, for improvements made to their holdings, was rejected by the House of Lords. These failures meant that Peel's reform programme came to depend more and more on the improvement of Irish education, and, in particular, on the vexed question of State support for Maynooth College.

Maynooth College

Maynooth College had been established by the Irish parliament in 1795 as a training college for Catholic priests, and after the Act of Union it was supported financially by a small annual parliamentary grant. By the 1840s the college was clearly facing financial difficulties. In 1845, therefore, Peel decided to support a bill increasing the State grant to the college. His attitude, which represented a dramatic change in his views, was purely political: a greater injection of state funds and an improvement in the college's status would surely encourage the rise of a more 'respectable', less politicised, class of parish clergy. The penury and backwardness of the college, he argued, 'all combine to send forth a priesthood embittered rather than conciliated … and connected … with the lower classes of society'.

Peel's Maynooth Bill, however, led to a storm of protest throughout the United Kingdom, since it seemed to provide State encouragement for the Roman Catholic Church. It also split the parliamentary Conservative Party. In the end, it only became law as a result of the firm support of the Irish in the House of Commons, and the Whigs in both houses of parliament.

The Colleges Bill

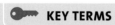

KEY TERMS

Non-denominational
Not aligned to any one denomination of the Christian Church.

Interdenominational With the participation of various religious denominations.

With the Maynooth problem out of the way, Peel was able to pass on to the final phase of his Irish programme – the Colleges Bill. This passed fairly easily through parliament (although O'Connell opposed it) and led to the establishment of **non-denominational** university colleges at Belfast, Cork and Galway, thus providing wider and cheaper opportunities for higher education in Ireland, outside the Anglican foundation of Trinity College, Dublin. But the aim of **interdenominational** teaching was once again, as over the national schools in the 1830s, bedevilled by religious sectarianism, since the Catholic Church was not prepared to support colleges over whose teaching it had no control.

The Devon Commission 1843–5

Peel set up a major inquiry in November 1843 under the Earl of Devon to look into the situation of the tenant farmers in Ireland. It was officially called the Commission on Occupation of Land (Ireland) but is more popularly called the 'Devon Commission'. The Commission reported in 1845, pointing out that the population of Ireland had exploded from 6 million people to close on 8 million people. It also concluded that the land leases were unfair to tenants and were too favourable to the, usually, Anglo-Irish landowners. The Commission showed that the majority of Irish tenants had no form of protection at all. They could be, and often were, summarily evicted from their tenancies. Outside Ulster, they also had no claim to the so-called 'Ulster Custom' of landholding, which granted tenants important rights:

- legally set periods of tenancy duration during which the tenant could not be evicted if the set rent was paid
- the right to sell the tenancy to another person – subject to the landowner's approval
- the right to compensation for any improvements made to the holding by the tenant at the end of the tenancy agreement if it was not renewed.

The Devon Commission recommended that such rights be extended across Ireland. However, its publication in 1845 came at a time of political crisis over the onset of famine in Ireland and the issue of the repeal of the Corn Laws. A bill to give effect to some of its recommendations was introduced in the House of Lords in 1845 but failed to secure enough support to proceed. Nonetheless, its findings did influence the later reforms carried out by Gladstone – a strong supporter of Peel's ideas – in his 1868–74 government.

Limits to Peel's reforms

How important, then, was Peel's work for Ireland? Peel knew the Irish situation well, as he had been a very successful chief secretary for Ireland – effectively the head of government there – from 1812 to 1818. His Irish reforms certainly displayed courage and resolution: as a recent historian of the subject writes, 'considered in the context of the time and the prejudices of his party they were remarkable'. But Peel was not in a position to force through long-term solutions to the problems of Ireland. He was facing a dire financial and economic situation in 1841 and all his energies were spent in dealing with this. Consequently, nothing was done to alter the status of the Church of Ireland, and nothing was done for economic improvement or land reform. Mistrust of the British government and opposition to the Union still remained strong, therefore, among Irish Catholics. Inevitably, these feelings were exacerbated by the horrors and bitterness of the Great Famine of 1846–9 (see Chapter 4).

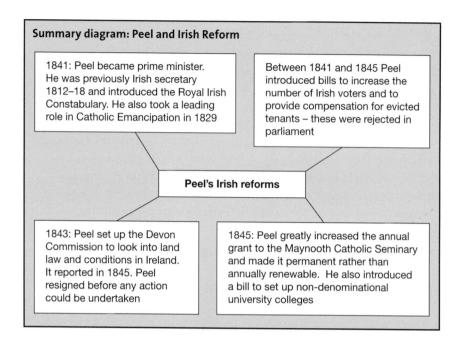

Summary diagram: Peel and Irish Reform

1841: Peel became prime minister. He was previously Irish secretary 1812–18 and introduced the Royal Irish Constabulary. He also took a leading role in Catholic Emancipation in 1829

Between 1841 and 1845 Peel introduced bills to increase the number of Irish voters and to provide compensation for evicted tenants – these were rejected in parliament

Peel's Irish reforms

1843: Peel set up the Devon Commission to look into land law and conditions in Ireland. It reported in 1845. Peel resigned before any action could be undertaken

1845: Peel greatly increased the annual grant to the Maynooth Catholic Seminary and made it permanent rather than annually renewable. He also introduced a bill to set up non-denominational university colleges

 # 5 O'Connell: the final years

▶ *Was O'Connell out of touch in his final years?*

The successful banning of the Clontarf meeting was a turning point in O'Connell's work for Ireland. Already ageing – he was now nearly 70 – the Liberator's career went into permanent decline after the autumn of 1843. In May 1844, he was arrested and imprisoned for incitement to violence, even though the verdict against him was soon quashed by the House of Lords. Physically and mentally these events took their toll. 'O'Connell', wrote Thomas Davis, the leader of Young Ireland, 'will run no more risks … from the day of his release the cause will be going back and going down'.

Split with 'Young Ireland'

The cause of repeal was indeed worsened by O'Connell's personal and ideological disputes with the leaders of Young Ireland. They resented the Liberator's opportunism – his commitment to parliamentary politics and alliances and support for reforms – as well as his authoritarianism. As **doctrinaire** nationalists, Thomas Davis and his colleagues were concerned above all with the raising of Irish national consciousness, as the basis for an eventual independent Irish Republic.

They also differed with O'Connell over religion. Davis, a Protestant, wanted religion kept out of the repeal movement but, out of loyalty to his Church and as

KEY TERM

Doctrinaire Committed to carry principles to their extremes without compromise; in this case the cause for an independent Ireland.

SOURCE C

A contemporary wood engraving of O'Connell's triumphant procession through Dublin following his release from prison in September 1844. O'Connell spent three months in prison accused of attempting to repeal the Act of Union.

a reward for their support in the repeal campaign, O'Connell felt duty bound to support the Catholic bishops in their opposition to the new university colleges proposed by Peel. The final break between the two groups of repealers came over O'Connell's rigid commitment to peaceful agitation. In 1846, the leaders of Young Ireland came out in favour of the possible use of force in support of repeal (see page 56), and over this issue they were either expelled from or left the Association.

By that time, however, Ireland was in the throes of the Great Famine and movements such as the Repeal Association – now divided and weakened anyway – appeared increasingly remote and irrelevant. O'Connell's attempt to revive the alliance with the Whigs after the fall of Peel in June 1846 seemed one last futile gesture, especially as it was the Whig government of Lord John Russell that was blamed for the incompetence of the relief measures in Ireland during the grim winter of 1846–7. 'The Liberator' spoke for the last time in the House of Commons in February 1847, and delivered a moving appeal for parliament

> Study Source C. How useful is this source to an understanding of the strengths and weaknesses of O'Connell's position in 1844?

'to act not only liberally but generously to find out the means of putting a stop to this terrible disaster'. Then, aware of his failing powers, he set off for Italy determined to spend his last days in Rome, but he died in Genoa on 15 May 1847.

How impressive were O'Connell's achievements?

'No other single person', wrote the Irish historian J.C. Beckett (1969), 'has left such an unmistakable mark on the history of Ireland.' How valid is this assessment of O'Connell's achievements?

- His greatest success was undoubtedly the passing of the Roman Catholic Emancipation Act of 1829, which stemmed directly from his strategy of contesting the County Clare by-election in the summer of 1828. The Act not only remedied an old grievance and injustice but, by granting Roman Catholics virtually full civil and political rights, led gradually but inevitably to the destruction of the power of the Protestant Ascendancy in Ireland. More immediately, by granting Roman Catholics the right to become MPs, it led directly to the emergence of an Irish party in the House of Commons. As a result, O'Connell became recognised – even by his opponents – as an outstanding parliamentarian and party leader.
- However, O'Connell's success needs to be seen in the wider context which worked to his advantage. The opportunity was opened for him by Wellington's decision to appoint Vesey Fitzgerald to a government post. Presumably Wellington assumed that since Fitzgerald was pro-emancipation his re-election was a formality; this was a major mistake. Even so, the pressure that then mounted on Wellington and Peel to concede emancipation was arguably as much related to the majority support for it in the House of Commons as to O'Connell's campaign. Had majority opinion in both houses been overwhelmingly against Emancipation in 1828 – as it was against repeal in the 1840s – the outcome might have been different.

O'Connell's significance

O'Connell and his party helped to bring the Irish question to the attention of the British parliament, and Irish conditions and grievances became a permanent – although not always prominent – part of British domestic politics. Moreover, as one historian of the Irish Party writes: 'Whatever the final judgement on O'Connell's party, there can be no doubt that it had some success as a political pressure group.' This success was seen in the Irish reforms passed by the Whig governments of Grey and Melbourne, although (as has been noted previously) they were in any case sympathetic to Irish grievances. Despite his personal hostility to O'Connell, and the fact that he commanded an independent Conservative majority in the House of Commons, Sir Robert Peel, too, was prepared to support a measure of Irish reform. Indeed, Peel's determination to press ahead with reforming the Maynooth Grant in 1845 brought him into direct conflict with his party. The repeal of the Corn Laws in 1846, in which Peel sacrificed his political career and broke the unity of his party, was also related at least in part to the famine conditions in Ireland, although his decision was consistent with the economic policy he had been following since 1842. It is clear therefore that while O'Connell deserves some credit for the reforms of the 1830s – as with Catholic Emancipation – he benefited from favourable circumstances in both contexts. When he tried to promote repeal in the 1840s without a favourable set of circumstances to build on he failed utterly.

O'Connell's legacy

Historians have also emphasised the importance of the methods pursued by O'Connell, via the Catholic Association and, later, the Repeal Association. Both movements appealed consciously to all classes in Ireland; and both aimed deliberately at the peaceful organisation of mass opinion to change the law. 'O'Connell', it has been said, 'chose to use **extra-parliamentary** means to achieve constitutional ends.' By their use of such devices as popular fundraising, large-scale public meetings, national organisation and leadership, and the involvement of local activists, the two associations were the forerunners of modern political pressure groups and parties. As Oliver MacDonagh noted in his 1990 biography of O'Connell: 'he was perhaps the greatest innovator in modern democratic politics as well as the originator of almost all the basic strategies of Anglo-Irish constitutional relations'.

KEY TERM

Extra-parliamentary
Political methods that go outside politics. Direct action and civil disobedience are examples of extra-parliamentary tactics.

One other aspect of his work is of vital importance. O'Connell was undoubtedly a great national leader, and he persistently claimed to speak for all the Irish people. But his origins and background, his rapport with the Irish Catholic masses and their priests, the message and appeal of the great associations he led, and his support for the leaders of the Irish Catholic Church on major issues, as well as the unremitting hostility of Irish Protestantism – all these made him inevitably a great national Catholic leader. To quote MacDonagh again: 'he was in part the faithful reflector and in part the actual shaper of the emergent Irish nationalist Catholic culture'. As a result, O'Connell's career helped unwittingly to divide rather than bring together the two great religious communities of Ireland.

O'Connell's failures

After 1840, O'Connell's record is clearly one of failure. The collapse of the repeal campaign after 1843 and O'Connell's ineffectiveness during the Great Famine were followed by the eclipse of the Irish parliamentary party after his death in 1847. All this led to a certain reaction in Ireland against the Liberator's methods of peaceful agitation coupled with involvement in parliamentary politics. The year 1848, suggests one of his modern biographers, marks the end of 'the O'Connellite tradition in Irish politics … rendered obsolete by changes in the direction, methods and ideas of the Irish nationalist movement'.

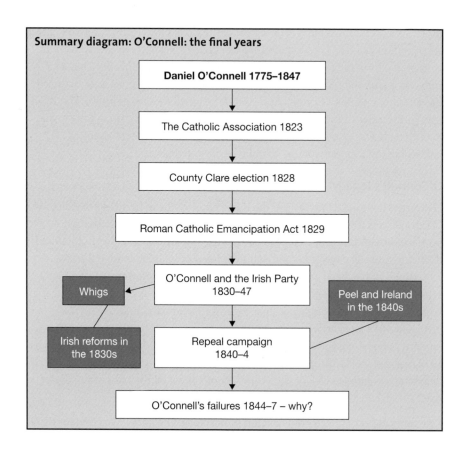

Summary diagram: O'Connell: the final years

Daniel O'Connell 1775–1847
↓
The Catholic Association 1823
↓
County Clare election 1828
↓
Roman Catholic Emancipation Act 1829
↓
O'Connell and the Irish Party 1830–47 → Whigs → Irish reforms in the 1830s
↓
Repeal campaign 1840–4 ← Peel and Ireland in the 1840s
↓
O'Connell's failures 1844–7 – why?

Chapter summary

Daniel O'Connell undoubtedly had a great impact on the course of Irish history. However, his right to the title 'the Liberator' is very questionable. It rests entirely on his role in bringing about Catholic Emancipation in 1829. In reality, Emancipation was 'liberating' only for the minority of Roman Catholic men who could meet the property qualifications for election to parliament and had the leisure and means to support themselves as MPs. Nor was Emancipation his victory alone. O'Connell created a mass movement and then used it to good effect in exploiting the opening that Wellington allowed in 1828 by appointing Vesey Fitzgerald to the government and forcing him to seek re-election for County Clare. He forced the British government to confront an issue that had been divisive for as long as the Union had existed. But O'Connell was essentially an elite politician. He made no effort to resist or revise the significant increase in voting qualifications in Ireland introduced in 1829 and maintained by the 1832 Reform Act. In fairness, he had little real scope to go beyond what he achieved in 1828–9. For much of the 1830s the Whigs enjoyed a comfortable majority in the House of Commons. The 1837 general election reduced their advantage greatly but the alliance with O'Connell was more of a convenience than a necessity. Once Peel came to power, O'Connell's position was even weaker.

Refresher questions

Use these questions to remind yourself of the key material covered in this chapter.

1 Why were Roman Catholics unable to sit in the British parliament?

2 What were Daniel O'Connell's key attributes as a leader?

3 How did O'Connell change his strategy for advancing the cause of Catholic Emancipation in the 1820s?

4 What circumstances allowed O'Connell to force the issue of Emancipation on to the political agenda?

5 How important was the Catholic Association in bringing about Emancipation in 1829?

6 How significant was the coming to power of the Whigs in 1830 for Ireland?

7 What was the purpose of the Lichfield House Compact?

8 How and why did O'Connell's political strategy change in the 1840s?

9 What was Peel's attitude to the situation in Ireland in the 1840s?

10 Why did the campaign for repeal of the Act of Union fail?

11 Does O'Connell deserve to be called 'the Liberator'?

 Question practice

ESSAY QUESTION

1 To what extent was royal opposition the most significant factor affecting the issue of Catholic Emancipation in the years 1800–29?

SOURCE ANALYSIS QUESTION

1 Assess the value of Source 1 (page 62) for revealing tensions in Ireland over Catholic Emancipation and the part played by Daniel O'Connell in exploiting these tensions. Explain your answer, using the source, the information given about its origin and your own knowledge about the historical context.

INTERPRETATION QUESTION

1 Evaluate the interpretations in both Passages A (page 62) and B (page 63) and explain which you think is the more convincing assessment of the ability of O'Connell as a political leader in the 1830s.

SOURCE 1

Adapted from O'Connell's election address to the voters of County Clare in 1828, quoted in Daniel O'Connell, *The Memoirs, Private and Political, of Daniel O'Connell, Esq.*, W. Johnston, 1836, p. 438.

It is true that as a Catholic I cannot, and of course never will, take the oaths at present prescribed to members of Parliament; but the authority which created these oaths can abrogate [end] them, and I entertain a confident hope that, if you elect me, the most bigoted of our enemies will see the necessity of removing from the chosen representative of the people an obstacle which would prevent him from doing his duty to his King and Country.

The oath at present required by law is: 'That the Sacrifice of the Mass and the invocation of the blessed Virgin Mary and other saints as now practised in the Church of Rome are impious and idolatrous'. I will of course never stain my soul with such an oath. I leave that to my opponent, Mr. Vesey Fitzgerald. He has often taken that horrible oath; he is ready to take it again and asks your votes to enable him so to swear. I would rather be torn limb from limb than take it. Electors of the County Clare! Choose between me, who abominates that oath and Mr. Vesey Fitzgerald, who has sworn it full twenty times! Return me to Parliament, and it is probable that such a blasphemous oath will be abolished forever. As your representative, I will try the question with the friends in Parliament of Mr. Vesey Fitzgerald. They may send me to prison. I am ready to go there to promote the cause of the Catholics, and of universal liberty. The discussion which the attempt to exclude your representative from the House of Commons must excite, will create a sensation all over Europe, and produce such a burst of contemptuous indignation against British bigotry in every enlightened country in the world, that the voice of all the great and good in England … being joined to the universal shout of the nations of the Earth, will overpower every opposition, and render it impossible for Peel and Wellington any longer to close the doors of the constitution against the Catholics of Ireland.

PASSAGE A

Adapted from D. George Boyce, 'Ireland 1828–1923: from ascendancy to democracy', in *Protestant Nation to Catholic Nation 1690–1828*, Blackwell, 1992.

O'Connell's victory in County Clare in June 1828 was not the only reason why the British government conceded Catholic emancipation. It was the culmination of a long and arduous campaign, and of the gradual weakening of the Protestant resolve to stand firm. This raised a question of vital importance for the Union between Great Britain and Ireland. Was its purpose to reform Ireland to reconcile the Catholic majority to the Union, or was the Union designed to protect the Protestant interest? O'Connell was uncertain which way to go – his immediate call was for the repeal of the Union and the restoration of the Irish Parliament. But he was a realist, and willing to concentrate on reform within the Union. The next few years revealed only frustration and disappointment. Parts of the Irish countryside were plunged into a state of terror as the tithe war raged. O'Connell fought the 1835 general election on the question of repeal of the Union but he quickly saw the advantages of making some kind of agreement with the Whigs. Ireland needed government and the Whig government introduced important reforms in public health, sanitation and the management of the poor. The Irish Poor Law of 1838 revealed the advantages and disadvantages – addressing the problem of the poor but attempting to apply English remedies to an Irish defect. Influential English opinion tended to lay the blame for Ireland's economic ills, her poverty, her backwardness, at the door of the landlords, yet landlords would – O'Connell himself believed – be ruined by a poor rate they could not afford.

PASSAGE B

Adapted from Norman Gash, *Aristocracy and People 1815–65*, Harvard University Press, 1985.

The Lichfield House compact of February 1835, though at the time no more than a tactical decision by whigs, radicals and O'Connell's Irish to combine for the immediate purpose of evicting Peel, was in fact the point of origin for the Victorian Liberal party – the genuinely independent radicals in the Commons – were reduced by 1841 to a mere handful. The same process of consolidation was at work in O'Connell's Irish party. After 1835 he proved a remarkably loyal ally of the whigs, content to forgo office for himself and suspend his campaign for repeal of the Union until the advent of a conservative ministry. Even if these were no more than clever tactics designed to extract benefit from a friendly government while retaining his long-term objective of repeal as the ultimate strategy, he lost as much as he gained. At the 1832 election his party, fighting as an independent organization, had emerged as the largest in Ireland. The conservatives, who up to 1830 normally won a majority of Irish seats, returned less than a third. In 1835 and 1837, however, when there was close cooperation between Irish nationalists and the whigs, O'Connell's electoral ascendancy perceptibly weakened. It was true that whig losses in England made his support a parliamentary necessity. But in Ireland the Liberal party was now preponderantly whig rather than O'Connellite. Whig association and patronage continued to eat into O'Connell's parliamentary following. The 1841 election left the whigs the largest single Irish party, closely followed by the conservatives with O'Connell's repealers holding only 18 seats.

CHAPTER 4

The Irish famine 1845–9

The famine of 1845–9 is often seen as a great turning point in Irish history. Certainly, its consequences were profound, socially, economically and politically. You have to decide what caused the famine, whether more could have been done to mitigate its consequences and, above all, what effects it had on the Irish question – the relationship between Britain and Ireland. This chapter will look at the famine through the following themes:

★ Background to and causes of the Great Famine
★ The response of the British government
★ The results of the Great Famine

Key dates

1845	Sept.	Beginning of potato blight	1848		Poor Law used as means of relief
1846	July	Repeal of the Corn Laws		July	Young Ireland rebellion failed
		Peel replaced as prime minister by Lord Russell	1849		Better conditions returned
					Encumbered Estates Act, facilitating sale of estates
1847		Soup kitchens provided relief	1850		Irish Tenant League founded

1 Background to and causes of the Great Famine

▶ *What was the 'Great Famine'?*

What became known as the 'Great Famine' in Irish history began quite unexpectedly in the late summer of 1845. That summer had been a fine, warm one, and reports from the west of Ireland spoke of potato crops of 'the most luxuriant character … promising abundant yield'. But once the potatoes began to be harvested, it soon became apparent that they were hopelessly diseased and unfit for consumption by either man or beast. By early 1846, the **blight** had spread to most parts of Ireland and about three-quarters of the country's potato crop was wiped out. The potato blight affected large areas of Europe but only in Ireland would it have such catastrophic consequences, because only in Ireland were so many people totally dependent upon the potato for their survival.

KEY TERM

Blight General term for any sudden and severe crop disease.

Introduction

Since the potato was the staple food of Ireland, millions were now haunted by the prospect of widespread famine. Sir Robert Peel, the Conservative prime minister, took remedial measures to prevent this; but although there were no deaths from starvation during his administration, there was widespread hunger among the peasantry, soon accompanied by the spread of fever, mainly typhus. It seemed apparent that unless there was a better potato harvest in the following year, or alternative supplies of cheap food became available, the Irish people faced massive starvation and death.

Hopes that the next harvest would be unaffected by the potato blight proved unfounded.

A parish priest wrote early in August 1846:

SOURCE A

From Reverend Theobald Mathew writing to Mr Trevelyan, 7 August 1846, quoted in *Correspondence Relating to Measures for Relief of Distress in Ireland (Commissariat Series), July 1846–January 1847*, HMSO, 1847, p. 4.

On the 27th of last month I passed from Cork to Dublin, and this doomed plant bloomed in all the luxuriance of an abundant harvest. Returning on the 3rd [of August], I beheld, with sorrow, one wide waste of putrefying vegetation. In many places the wretched people were seated on the fences of their decaying gardens, wringing their hands, and wailing bitterly the destruction that had left them foodless.

In what way does Source A shed light on the difficulties posed by the potato blight? **?**

The situation was similar throughout the whole of Ireland and, weakened by earlier deprivation and with all their resources used up during the previous year of hunger, the Irish peasantry faced a grim winter in 1846–7. Despite the varied package of relief measures introduced by the new Whig prime minister, Lord John Russell, thousands soon succumbed to starvation and disease. Others determined to leave Ireland at any cost, and the great tide of emigration across the Atlantic became a flood.

The potato harvest in 1847, although free from blight, was small and had little effect on the general situation. In 1848, the blight returned in full force, and that year proved to be one of the worst in terms of death and distress during the whole history of the Great Famine. It was not until the end of 1849 that the disappearance of the potato blight and the total effect of the relief measures brought the Great Famine to an end.

The Great Famine

Ireland had suffered famine earlier, notably in 1817 and 1822. What was remarkable about the Great Famine was its extent and intensity. This time, it affected the whole country for a period of more than four years with profound long-term consequences for the Irish people. The immediate cause of the famine was a fungal disease that attacked the potato crop. The wider origins and character of the Great Famine were directly related to the structure of Irish social and economic life, and especially its land system. As the Devon Royal Commission reported in 1845, shortly before the outbreak of the famine: 'the source of all Ireland's misfortunes and poverty was the fatal system of **land tenure** existing in the country'.

Land tenure

As we saw in Chapter 2 (see page 15), the general character of the Irish land system had been shaped by the confiscations of earlier centuries, which led to the bulk of the cultivated land falling into the hands of a small class of Protestant landowners. Some of the original estates were still held virtually intact by great aristocrats, whose agents ran them on their behalf. But over the years most of these estates had been carved up into smaller units and were leased out to middlemen on long leases at fixed rents. This new class of landowners had in turn divided up their estates into smaller farms, and they often charged high rents and lived as absentees in England.

The process of division and subdivision accelerated even further in the later eighteenth and early nineteenth centuries, until by the eve of the Great Famine:

- 24 per cent of holdings were between one and five acres (rented by the **cottiers**)
- 40 per cent were between five and 15 acres
- only about seven per cent were over 30 acres.

At the very bottom of the rural scale were the million or so 'landless' labourers who worked for the farmers – when they could get work. This was not very easy when many farms were so small and labour was so plentiful, and many labourers were forced to become **migratory workers** to England for part of the year. **Underemployment** was one of the great social evils of rural Ireland. Even the domestic work of spinning and weaving, with which many smallholders and labourers had eked out their livelihood in earlier years, was now drying up as a result of the decline of the Irish woollen and domestic linen industries in the early nineteenth century. Unlike English farm labourers, the Irish labourers were not usually paid wholly in wages but were also rewarded with scraps of land, on which they could just exist by relying on the potato. The labourers were thus virtually indistinguishable from the cottiers. It was the tiny size of peasant holdings that was therefore the characteristic feature of the Irish rural scene. Why was this?

Population increase

One major cause was the dramatic rise in the Irish population, which was roughly 5 million in 1780 and reached about 8 million in 1845, despite the fact that 1.5 million Irishmen emigrated to North America in the generation

KEY TERMS

Land tenure The manner in which land was owned by an individual, who was said to 'hold' the land.

Cottier An Irish tenant holding land.

Migratory workers People who move from one area to another in search of work.

Underemployment The condition of having too large a part of the labour force unemployed due to the demand for labour being less than the supply of labour available for work.

SOURCE B

A contemporary print depicting an Irish family searching for potatoes in 1846–7. Notice how poor the family looks.

Study Source B. How much impact was likely to result from the publication of a source such as this?

following the Act of Union. This population explosion was primarily due to early marriage and a very high birth rate, and probably to the general improvements in health and diet that occurred in the relatively prosperous years of the later eighteenth century. This prosperity was the result of high prices for Irish agricultural produce in England (where the population was also increasing rapidly).

In a country such as Ireland with virtually no industry outside Ulster, and where the overwhelming majority of the people were dependent on agriculture, such an upsurge in population growth was bound to lead to intense competition for land, even at the high rents that then prevailed. Possession of a plot of land became literally the difference between life and death. Fathers who themselves rented smallholdings were prepared to subdivide them further in order to help their families. 'A parent must provide for his children in some way', as one tenant-farmer said, 'and he cannot send them all the way to America.'

Potatoes

What both encouraged subdivision and made it economically workable was the spread of the potato as the staple crop. The potato had enormous advantages for the Irish peasant. It was easy to grow (although impossible to store for long) and could flourish on relatively poor soil. Above all, it was an economical and nutritious crop which produced high yields: one-and-a-half acres of land could provide food for a year for a family of five or six. It could also be used to feed a pig and poultry. Subsistence on the potato also enabled the peasantry, especially in the more prosperous east, to concentrate on **cash crops** – wheat, oats, flax, dairy produce – to pay their rent, while for the larger farmers the provision of a tiny plot for potatoes provided a cheap way of paying their labourers.

Thus, population and the potato advanced together. On the eve of the famine about 2 million acres (one-third of the cultivated land) was used for potatoes and provided food for some 3 million people. It was in the west particularly, where plots were smallest, that there was the greatest dependence on the potato and the grimmest poverty. There, the peasants' normal diet consisted of 12–14 pounds (approximately 5–6 kg) of potatoes daily, together with a little buttermilk and oatmeal. Conditions for these tenants – and even more so for the landless labourers – were particularly wretched.

Basic and monotonous as their normal diet was, conditions were even worse during the notorious 'hungry months' of the summer. These were at the end of the old season of potatoes and before the new had been harvested. Then, many of the peasantry existed in a state of semi-starvation, lacking the money to buy food and being forced to obtain meal on credit. It was this large class of cottiers and labourers, living on the very edge of existence, who were particularly vulnerable to any sudden deterioration in the state of the potato crop.

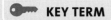

KEY TERM

Cash crop A crop grown for sale rather than for feeding the producer's livestock or family.

Summary diagram: Background to and causes of the Great Famine

Penal laws of eighteenth century caused smaller and smaller holdings for farmers	Small plots led to the cultivation of the potato as the staple diet for the poorer rural classes

Background to and causes of the Great Famine

Potato blight, although widespread in North America and Europe in 1845, was catastrophic for Irish people who depended on potatoes as their main or sole source of food	Irish peasants increasingly cultivated crops other than the potato for rent rather than consumption

2 The response of the British government

▶ *What did the British government do to combat the famine?*

Reports of the partial failure of the potato crop came to the attention of the British government in September 1845. It gave Sir Robert Peel, the prime minister, the opportunity for carrying through the repeal of the Corn Laws which imposed taxes on foreign grain imports and which he had believed for some time were no longer economically defensible. To maintain the Corn Laws while Irish people starved would be unacceptable in principle. But, as the prime minister realised, the repeal of the Corn Laws in itself could have little effect on the situation in Ireland, given the fact that the Irish peasantry could not afford to buy grain at any price and that supplies from Europe were in any case limited. Hence, at the same time he also acted quickly to introduce relief measures to stave off potential famine in Ireland:

- The government began by spending £100,000 on a supply of Indian Corn (maize) from America, which was sold cheaply and so kept down the price of other grains.
- Peel's main effort, however, was devoted to encouraging the Irish landlords to organise local committees to raise money for the relief of the distressed, and to provide more work on their estates. 'Our main reliance', he said, 'must be placed on the co-operation of the landed interest with local aid.'
- In similar fashion, the **Irish Board of Works**, with the aid of Treasury grants, began to employ men to work on such undertakings as road repairs and road building.

KEY TERM

Irish Board of Works
Established in 1831 to carry out public works schemes such as road building.

The impact of Peel's measures

Peel's measures were successful in fulfilling their immediate purpose of preventing exceptional hardship during the months between the autumn of 1845 and the summer of 1846. Even the nationalist newspaper, *The Freeman's Journal*, was prepared to give the prime minister his due. 'The limited distress which Sir Robert Peel was called upon to meet', it wrote, 'he provided for fairly and fully. No man died of famine during his administration.' However, the use of Indian Corn had adverse consequences. To begin with, it was not very nutritious and hardly an adequate substitute for potatoes. It was difficult to cook, especially for those with no previous experience of cooking it. Poorly cooked it led to diarrhoea and it some cases intestinal bleeding. It may well have added to the misery as much as relieving it.

In August 1846, the potato blight struck again on a wider scale and in more virulent fashion, and the peasantry were even less prepared than earlier since their reserves had now been used up. Millions faced starvation. By that time

Peel was out of power. He had successfully pushed through the repeal of the Corn Laws in the face of opposition from the majority of his backbenchers. But he was shortly afterwards defeated over his proposal for a new Irish Coercion Act – which he believed was necessary to deal with potential food riots – by a 'blackguard combination' (as Wellington termed it) of all the opposition groups in the House of Commons together with the anti-repeal Conservatives. As a result, the Whigs came into power. It was Lord John Russell, therefore, who now became prime minister and found himself facing the grim prospect of massive famine and death in Ireland.

Government attitudes

The view of the extreme nationalists, expressed at the time, was that the aim of the British government was to allow the famine to take its course so that the Catholic Irish majority would decrease and the land would be cleared of surplus population. Some even suggested that the potato blight was deliberate. Such ideas found their way into the popular mythology of Irish people well into the twentieth century. These ideas have no basis in reality. Yet the impatience and prejudice of English politicians and their ignorance of Irish conditions did lead some of them to blame the Irish themselves for their troubles. 'The real difficulty', wrote the newly appointed lord-lieutenant, Lord Clarendon, in May 1847, 'lies with the people themselves – they are always in the mud … their idleness and helplessness can hardly be believed.' Nor were many Englishmen prepared to accept the logic of those Irishmen who argued that the existence of the Union meant that the whole of the United Kingdom – and not just Ireland – should accept responsibility for the Great Famine. For most of them, including the prime minister, it was the Irish landlord class who should bear the main burden.

A greater impediment to vigorous action by the British government was its increasing commitment to the economic principle of *laissez-faire*. This idea argued that governments must not interfere with market forces and the **price mechanism**. It stood at the heart of Peel's policy to reduce taxes on imports and exports, which he followed from 1842 and was then accepted by subsequent governments. Thus, in order not to undermine the interests of traders and retailers, food must not be provided freely or below market prices. 'It must be thoroughly understood', announced Russell on assuming office, 'that we cannot feed the people.' This principle need not extend to charitable support, which was seen as quite different from government action.

In the same way, public works had to be of general utility and were not to benefit particular individuals or interests. In this outlook, Russell was strongly supported by his chancellor of the exchequer and even more assiduously and dogmatically by Charles Trevelyan, the Treasury official primarily responsible for the organisation of famine relief. Although an upright and hard-working official, Trevelyan's addiction to red tape and his unswerving commitment to

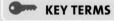 **KEY TERMS**

Laissez-faire An approach where the government avoids intervening in economic and social matters, allowing market forces to operate freely.

Price mechanism
The process of supply and demand by which markets set prices. When supply outstripped demand prices would naturally fall and, in reverse, prices would increase with limited supplies.

'the operation of natural causes' (his own pet phrase) have made him the evil genius of the Great Famine for a number of modern historians.

For all these reasons, although Russell was genuinely moved by Irish suffering, the measures that were introduced in the early autumn of 1846 were haphazard and limited.

Early relief measures

The public works system was extended, and labourers were to be paid less than **subsistence-level wages** to work on unproductive tasks on roads and bridges. By the spring of 1847, about three-quarters of a million men were employed on such schemes. In addition, by a special **Labour Rate Act**, the screw was to be tightened on landlords to provide work or pay a 'labour rate' – a burden which many of them resented and found onerous. The demands by both landlords and nationalists for real productive work to be provided – for instance, land reclamation and railway construction – were brushed aside by Charles Trevelyan in typical fashion: 'For the government to undertake by its own direct agency the detailed drainage and improvements of the whole country, is a task for which the nature and functions of government are totally unsuited.'

The measures taken by the government to avert famine proved to be hopelessly inadequate. It is true that, in response to high prices, grain flooded into the country and offset the food exports that had continued since the early days of the famine. But the wages paid to the labourers under private or public schemes were insufficient to enable them to afford the rocketing prices of the imported wheat and flour.

Starvation

The winter of 1846–7 was grim for the peasantry. The first deaths from starvation were now reported, and in the wake of famine came disease. The limited number of hospitals and **dispensaries** were unable to cope. Fever was spreading throughout Ireland as the stricken peasantry in the west moved into eastern rural areas and then poured into the towns. An eyewitness from Cork described how 'Crowds of starving creatures flock in from the rural districts and take possession of some hall-door or the outside of some public building where they place a little straw and remain until they die. Disease has in consequence spread itself through the town.'

Relief measures 1847–9

By January 1847, even Trevelyan appeared to recognise the extent of the government's failure. 'The tide of distress', he wrote to a colleague, 'has for some time been steadily rising and appears now to have completely overflowed the barriers we endeavoured to oppose to it.' Russell therefore abruptly changed his policy.

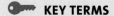

KEY TERMS

Subsistence-level wages The minimum amount needed to provide for the necessities of life in order to survive.

Labour Rate Act Passed in 1846, this Act stated that Irish hunger relief and work creation schemes were to be funded from Irish local taxation.

Dispensary A place where medical care and medicines are available.

In the spring of 1847, the public works projects and the labour rate were abandoned, and the government now pinned its hopes for relief on direct help: free distribution of food via soup kitchens. However, this was to be funded through the local rates, although the government was prepared to advance money to the local authorities, which was to be repaid later. By August, over 3 million people were being fed in this way, although, of course, the scheme came too late to help the many who had already died of hunger or disease.

Food was also provided by private charity and voluntary organisations, especially by the Quakers, who did magnificent work in the stricken west of Ireland. But since the government had always insisted that the free distribution of food was a temporary measure, and the harvest of late summer and autumn in 1847 was a good one, the soup-kitchen system was brought to an end, with little warning, in September of that year.

The Irish Poor Law Extension Act 1847

The government now decided to provide relief entirely through the Poor Law system that had been set up in 1838. As a result, about 200,000 of the ill, hungry and destitute were accepted into the workhouses, although those who possessed more than a quarter of an acre of land were refused entry. Since the workhouses had been designed to cope with only about half that number, the conditions in them were appalling and disease spread rapidly. In 1847, there were 130 deaths in the Limerick workhouse alone.

The Irish Poor Law Extension Act of 1847 actually consisted of several separate measures, two of which were particularly important:

- The first, in June 1847, was 'An Act to Make Further Provision for the Relief of the Destitute Poor in Ireland'. This officially allowed – for the first time – the option of giving relief to the old, the infirm, the sick, and to poor widows with dependent children in their homes rather than workhouses. If a union's workhouse was full, or harbouring an infectious disease, out-relief could also be offered to other classes of destitute persons for up to two months. In the case of able-bodied claimants, however, out-relief was to be provided only in the form of food. The Act also gave the Poor Law commissioners further powers to dissolve or alter unions, to dissolve a board of guardians, and to purchase additional land for use as a cemetery or the erection of fever wards.
- The following month, 'An Act to Provide for the Execution of the Laws of the Relief of the Poor in Ireland' set up an Irish Poor Law Commission as an independent body, and no longer under the control of the commissioners for England and Wales.

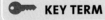

KEY TERM

Poor Law Unions After 1838, workhouses in Ireland were administered locally by groups or unions of electoral divisions.

Since famine relief was to be financed out of the Irish Poor Law rates, many **Poor Law Unions** soon became bankrupt. As the *Cork Examiner* had written prophetically in 1846: 'We should not wonder if these workhouses became the charnel houses of the whole rural population.'

In the end, owing to the obvious inability of the workhouses themselves to cope with the demands made on them, a system of 'outdoor relief' was introduced, and in this way about 800,000 victims of the famine were given relief in their own homes.

It was this system of workhouse and outdoor relief that was expected to deal with the consequences of the final disastrous potato harvest in 1848 and its aftermath, until better conditions returned at the end of 1849. In effect, Ireland was left to its fate: 'I do not think that any effort of this house', Russell told the Commons in May 1849, 'would, in the present and unfortunate state of Ireland, be capable of preventing the dreadful scenes of suffering and death that are now occurring in Ireland.'

Effects of the Poor Law system

The operation of the Irish Poor Law system during the later years of the famine had one other indirect consequence. The burden of paying the local poor rate was particularly onerous for a number of landlords and farmers. Landlords were liable to pay the rates of any tenant whose rent was £4 or less a year. This fact, together with the difficulties in collecting rent, led some of them to evict their tenants and turn the land over to **pastoral farming**, consolidating the tenancies into larger units with higher rents. This trend was accentuated by some smallholders voluntarily giving up their land in order to obtain poor relief.

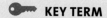

KEY TERM

Pastoral farming Rearing of livestock rather than growing crops.

Eviction in the midst of starvation produced some of the most heartrending scenes during the whole history of the Great Famine, and desperation sometimes led to violence and intimidation and even some cases of landlords being murdered. The exact number of evictions is difficult to establish since no official records were kept prior to 1849. After that, the police kept records and these show 250,000 official evictions from 1849 to 1854. Historians have disagreed about the extent of evictions during the famine itself. It has been estimated that as many as 500,000 tenancies were ended during the famine. However, many of these can be classed technically as 'voluntary', but even this produces controversy. It can be argued that many so-called 'voluntary' arrangements were in fact the result of pressure from landlords. Tenants could be persuaded to leave by the promise of relief in the workhouses or with small sums of cash. They were so desperate in some cases that any change in their circumstances could be made to seem for the better.

The impact of the government's response

The Treasury spent a total of about £8 million on Irish relief, much of it in the form of loans to the Irish Board of Works or Poor Law authorities. About half of the loans had not been repaid by 1850, and the money was written off by the Treasury three years later. The British government congratulated itself on what it had done financially for Irish relief. Trevelyan wrote, characteristically, that 'too much has been done for the people'.

Ireland spent considerably more than £8 million on its own relief if we add together the rates collected by the various Irish agencies and private contributions from landlords and others. One authority has argued that British government relief expenditure was, in fact, small in relation to its resources, amounting to no more than two to three per cent of public expenditure in the 1840s. Other historians, however, have stressed the difficulties that would have faced any government dealing with famine conditions in Ireland at this time:

- lack of good communications
- a primitive system of retail distribution
- an ineffective system of local government
- wide social, regional and religious differences.

They have therefore adopted a more sympathetic attitude towards the efforts of Peel and Russell.

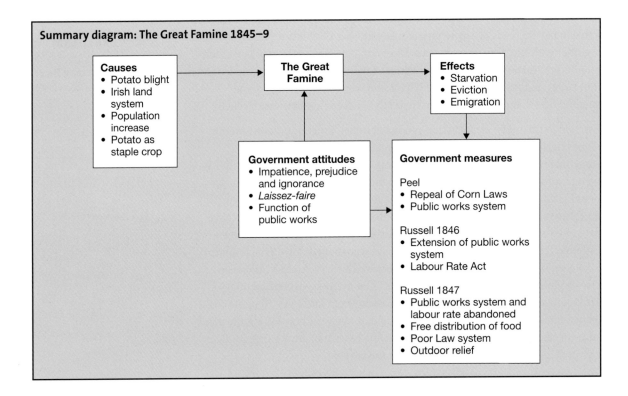

Summary diagram: The Great Famine 1845–9

Causes
- Potato blight
- Irish land system
- Population increase
- Potato as staple crop

The Great Famine

Effects
- Starvation
- Eviction
- Emigration

Government attitudes
- Impatience, prejudice and ignorance
- *Laissez-faire*
- Function of public works

Government measures

Peel
- Repeal of Corn Laws
- Public works system

Russell 1846
- Extension of public works system
- Labour Rate Act

Russell 1847
- Public works system and labour rate abandoned
- Free distribution of food
- Poor Law system
- Outdoor relief

The results of the Great Famine

▶ *What were the economic and demographic effects of the Great Famine?*

Population and the economy

The most dramatic consequence of the Great Famine was on the population of Ireland. About 1 million Irish men, women and children died between 1845 and 1850 as a result of starvation and disease, and a further 1.5 million emigrated. Hence, the Irish population declined by about a quarter during this period: from roughly 8 million (according to the 1841 census) to about 6 million (according to the 1851 census). Furthermore, the decline continued. This was mainly due to a reduction in the birth rate owing to later and fewer marriages in the post-famine epoch, and the continuation of emigration. As a result, the Irish population in 1900 was about half what it had been in 1845.

Consolidation of land holdings

Inevitably, these demographic changes had a powerful impact on the pattern of landholding. The cottier class of smallholders was almost completely wiped out as a result of death or emigration. This encouraged the consolidation of holdings, with the cottiers' plots being taken over by the larger farmers, many of whom had survived the famine in reasonable circumstances. In this way, about 200,000 smallholdings – one farm out of every four – disappeared. Thus, whereas before 1845 only just over one-third of farms were over fifteen acres in size, by 1851 about one-half were.

At the other end of the social scale, members of the old landlord class were also badly affected economically by the famine. This was the result of the extra financial burdens imposed on them by labour and poor rates – often on top of mortgages and debts – at a time when it was obviously difficult to collect rents. About ten per cent of landlords went bankrupt. For legal reasons, they often found it difficult to dispose of their estates easily.

As a result, the Whig government passed the Encumbered Estates Act of 1849 to speed up the sale of land, hoping, in addition, that this would lead to the emergence of a new, more enterprising landlord class, prepared to invest money in their estates. In this way, about 3000 estates were sold in the 1850s, amounting to about 5 million acres. But in fact most of the new landlords turned out to be either speculators, who raised rents to extortionate heights (rack-renting), or those members of the old landlord class who had survived the recent crisis with enough spare capital to buy up cheaply the estates now thrown on the market.

Farming

The aftermath of the Great Famine also saw the emergence of a more balanced farming system with less concentration on **tillage**, and especially potato cultivation, and more on pastoral farming. The move to pastoral farming, which had been discernible after 1815 (as a result of the general slump in grain prices), increased considerably after 1850, especially in the form of dairy farming and the export of live cattle.

By 1870, the acreage devoted to grain and potatoes had halved compared with pre-famine days, although the potato still remained an important food staple in the west of Ireland, where the old rural economy changed extremely slowly. During these years too, farmers and landlords expanded the area of cultivation by well over a million acres, a development which vividly reveals how much useful, productive work could have been carried out in pre-famine Ireland.

Living standards

The decline in population, by reducing the pressure on resources in Ireland, also led to a rise in average living standards:

- Labourers' wages rose, helped by a considerable drop in their numbers from 1.2 million (1845) to 700,000 (1861).
- Housing standards improved; the old one-room cabin began to disappear in the countryside.
- Ireland became a more literate and a more urbanised society. This was the result of the building of more schools, and the growth of Irish towns at the expense of the countryside; and both of these developments were signs of the relative prosperity of Ireland in the third quarter of the nineteenth century.

What all these changes in land ownership and farming practice meant was that the medium-sized (by Irish standards) family farm of five to 30 acres, devoted to **mixed farming**, became the norm. It was this middle-class farming group, many of whom had done relatively well during the famine years, who now became the key group in the Irish countryside. Their domination was encouraged by their continuing prosperity as a result of the expansion of Irish agriculture, especially pastoral farming, during the years between the 1850s and the 1870s, when farmers' income rose by about 77 per cent. It was helped also by the 1850 Reform Act which, by enlarging the Irish county electorate, gave many of these farmers the vote. Thus, in the aftermath of the Great Famine and the fiasco of the 1848 rebellion, the farmers' demands over land became the most important theme in Irish politics in the 1850s.

Irish nationalism and politics

The failure of Daniel O'Connell's repeal campaign and the death of the Liberator himself in 1847 paved the way for the emergence of a more extreme group of Irish nationalists associated with the 'Young Ireland' movement.

They held the British government responsible for the Great Famine and began to toy with the idea of armed rebellion.

The role of John Mitchel

The key figure here was John Mitchel, the son of a Presbyterian minister. In 1847, he formed his own newspaper, *United Irishmen*, to espouse his views, aided, notably, by Fintan Lalor, Gavan Duffy, William Smith O'Brien and James Dillon, all of whom were middle-class literary and professional men. Mitchel's political views were summed up in his notorious cry – which links him with the rebels of 1798 and echoes down the years – 'Give us war in our time, O Lord'. He argued that 'legal and constitutional agitation in Ireland, is a delusion … every man ought to have arms and to promote their use'; and he called for a war of vengeance against England in order to achieve 'an Irish Republic, one and indivisible'.

Mitchel was also influenced by the important writings of his colleague Fintan Lalor on the land question. Lalor wanted to sweep away the landlord system on the grounds that, morally, the land belonged to the Irish people, and replace it with a nation of independent peasant proprietors. The Irish people's 'full right of ownership' over their land 'ought to be asserted and enforced by any and all reasons which God has put into the power of man'. A truly independent Ireland, Lalor argued, could be achieved only on the basis of a free peasantry.

The move towards rebellion in Ireland was encouraged by the contemporary **Chartist movement** in Britain. Irish influence in the Chartist movement was strong. Feargus O'Connor, originally from County Cork, was the son of a well-known Protestant nationalist in the 'United Ireland' movement and became a leading figure in Chartism. He became an MP and owned the main Chartist newspaper, the *Northern Star*. However, O'Connor was a controversial figure, erratic and often divisive. He clashed bitterly with William Lovett, a more moderate Chartist leader, who wanted to ensure that the movement remained peaceful, by frequently appearing to advocate violence. James 'Bronterre' O'Brien was another radical Irish Chartist leader, who worked as a journalist. His violently worded articles and speeches – he argued that the aristocracy should have their property taken and then be exterminated – landed him in prison, after which he moderated his approach. A revolution in France in February 1848 which successfully overturned the French monarchy helped to encourage radicals across Europe, including Ireland, to attempt rebellion.

'We must resist, we must act … if needs be we must die, rather than let this providential hour pass over us unliberated', proclaimed Gavan Duffy. It was the British government, however, which acted first. In May, Mitchel was arrested, condemned on a charge of treason, and **transported** for fourteen years. Nevertheless, his followers began an abortive rebellion in Ireland in July 1848. It was a hopeless affair from the start; among the reasons for its failure were:

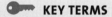 **KEY TERMS**

Chartist movement
The Chartists took their name from the 'People's Charter', drafted in 1838. The Charter made six demands: votes for all men; equal electoral districts; abolition of property qualifications for MPs; payment for MPs; annual general elections; and secret voting. It was presented in petitions to the House of Commons in 1839, 1842 and 1848 – and rejected each time. After 1848 the movement quickly declined.

Transport To send abroad to a penal colony.

- It was badly led and badly organised.
- There was no mass support from a half-starved and demoralised peasantry.
- The Roman Catholic Church was against it.

The Irish Rebellion of 1848 ended within a few weeks in a tragi-comic affray between a handful of peasants led by members of Young Ireland and the police, at a remote farmhouse – 'the battle of the Widow McCormack's cabbage patch', as it is derisively known. It was followed by the subsequent arrest of the leaders. Dillon escaped, but O'Brien was tried and transported.

'The rebellion', according to the historian F.S.L. Lyons (1971), 'exhibited all the classical symptoms of romantic idealism totally out of touch with the world of reality'. Nevertheless, he suggests that the 'men of 1848' bequeathed at least two important ideas to their nationalist successors:

- First, the ideal of an independent Irish Republic, to be fought for and, if necessary, died for.
- Second, the notion of a land war of tenants versus landlords as a fundamental part of this process of liberation – as discussed and justified in Lalor's writings on the Irish land system. This became a grim reality in Ireland in the 1870s.

The tenant right movement

During the 1850s, popular interest in politics declined and, for the middle-class farmers at least, this expressed itself in a concern with their immediate social and economic interests rather than the more abstract doctrines of nationalism. Hence their support for the tenant right movement.

Irish tenant leagues emerged at the end of the Great Famine on a local basis, partly in response to the evictions that were being carried out by some landlords, but also as an expression of the new power of the larger farmers based on their now dominant social, economic and political position in rural Ireland. The leagues demanded 'tenant right': that is, fair rents and compensation from the landlords for improvements carried out by the tenants if they were evicted. The Whig government had promised some reform in this direction, but in the end nothing was done.

The local groups combined together to form an All-Ireland Tenant League in 1850; and they were supported (after the general election of 1852) by a small group of Irish MPs of all political persuasions, calling themselves the 'Independent Irish Party'. But not even the ideal of 'tenant right' was strong enough to overcome social and religious differences, particularly between Ulster Protestants and the rest of Ireland; and this, together with the general **political apathy** of the time and a temporary slump in farming prices in 1859, led to the collapse of the tenants' movement at the end of the 1850s. Nevertheless, it did succeed in making 'tenant right' an important part of any future Irish reform programme.

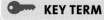 **KEY TERM**

Political apathy A lack of interest in or concern with politics.

The decline of the Irish Party

For similar reasons, the separate Irish Party instigated by O'Connell collapsed about the same time. It is notable that in the general election of 1859 the Conservative Party actually won a majority of Irish seats (55 out of 105), a result which is linked with the hardening of unionist sentiment in Ulster. Indeed, one historian sees this as evidence of something like a 'Conservative revival' in Irish politics in the post-famine period. Certainly, no great Irish national movement emerged during the years immediately following the Great Famine, and the political *status quo* in Ireland remained relatively undisturbed until the rise of the Irish Home Rule Party in the later 1870s, which is discussed in the next chapter.

The Irish Franchise Act 1850

Even before the Great Famine, the political system in Ireland had been seriously out of step with developments in the rest of the UK. The change to the county freeholder voting qualification which accompanied the Catholic Emancipation Act of 1829 had reduced the Irish electorate to around 37,000 from the previous figure of around 217,000. The impact of the 1832 reforms increased the number of borough voters to some extent but it was marginal compared to the fact that the county franchise remained the same. By the eve of the famine, even with the effect of rapid population growth, the total number of qualified voters had only risen to 121,000, still far below the 1829 figure. The effect of the famine was to cause the near collapse of the Irish electorate, which fell by 1850 to just 45,000. The British government responded to this by passing the Irish Franchise Act of 1850. This Act introduced a new lower franchise qualification based on occupation of property in relation to its Poor Law valuation. As a result, the electorate rose again to around 164,000. Even so, Ireland remained proportionately well behind the rest of the UK in terms of the percentage of the adult male population entitled to vote. This remained the situation by the time of the next round of Irish parliamentary reform in 1868.

Emigration

In what ways did the Great Famine change the nature of emigration?

- Between 1815 and 1845 about 1.5 million Irish people emigrated.
- About the same number left Ireland between 1845 and 1850, the period of the Great Famine.

About a quarter of these emigrants went to England and Scotland, where industrialisation provided plenty of work and where settled Irish communities had existed since the early eighteenth century. However, the majority of them went overseas, principally to the United States.

Despite the impression of continuity given by these emigration figures, there were important differences between the character of Irish emigration before, during and after the period of the Great Famine.

For most Irish families before 1845, emigration was not something to be welcomed. The ties of kinship, locality and land were still powerful enough to overcome the sound, practical reasons for leaving a poverty-stricken, overpopulated island to settle in countries overseas with more abundant opportunities. Those who did emigrate in the eighteenth and early nineteenth centuries were generally single, landless young men, mainly from Ulster, who were well enough off to be able to afford the fare to the **New World**.

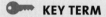

KEY TERM

New World The American continent and associated Caribbean islands reached by Columbus in 1492.

Emigration during the Great Famine

During the Great Famine, however, the motivation and pattern of emigration changed. The key year here is 1847 when, following the disasters of that winter, something like 'panic and hysteria' gripped many Irish families, especially the cottiers and labourers, and led to a mass flight from Ireland. 'All we want', said one of them, 'is to get out of Ireland … we must be better anywhere than here.' Hence, whereas in 1846, 106,000 emigrated, the figure for 1847 leapt to 230,000, and most of these emigrants went to Canada and the United States. The catastrophic impact of the famine in 1847 broke the psychological barrier that had previously held many Irish peasants back from emigration in favour of remaining in the land they knew regardless of the difficulties they faced. The famine made mass emigration a real, acceptable alternative. The emigration figure for 1848 was about the same as for 1847; between 1849 and 1852 about 200,000 left Ireland annually; and in 1851 – another key year – some 250,000 emigrants left for North America alone.

In the earlier years of the famine, although the majority of emigrants were from the poorest groups, some were from higher up the social scale as even the better-off farmers were faced with the consequences of higher rates and taxes, the decline of commerce, the disintegration of social life, and, above all, the loss of hope for the future. After 1850, however, it was the smallholders and labourers who were mainly responsible for the high emigration figures. Thus, in all, about 2 million left Ireland during the decade 1845–55. It was now whole families rather than individuals who departed; the very poor predominated; and, although all parts of Ireland were represented among the emigrants, the majority now came from the poverty-stricken south and south-west, rather than, as earlier, from Ulster and the north.

However, emigration was no easy option. It is true that the cost of passage across the Atlantic was relatively cheap by modern standards, varying between £2 and £5 according to the port of arrival. Even so, it was too much for some potential emigrants; and a number were assisted by their landlords – anxious to clear their estates of smallholders – or borrowed the money, or obtained money or prepaid tickets from friends or relations who were already resident in the 'New World' of North America. Virtually nothing was done by the British government to sponsor emigration.

SOURCE C

'**The causes of emigration from Ireland**', from *The Lady's Newspaper*, **1849.**

Study Source C. How influential might a source such as this have been in 1849?

For many emigrants the 40-day journey across the Atlantic was almost as hazardous as famine conditions in Ireland, and they were exploited unmercifully. Many of the ships – the notorious '**coffin ships**' – were barely seaworthy, and conditions aboard were primitive in the extreme. About twenty per cent of emigrants perished on board or soon after landing. One monument to the dead at Grosse Isle in Canada, put up by their descendants, reads: 'Thousands of the children of the Gael were lost on this island while fleeing from foreign tyrannical laws and an artificial famine in the years 1847–8. God bless them. God save Ireland!'

🔑 **KEY TERM**

Coffin ships Ships that carried Irish immigrants escaping the effects of the famine. These ships, crowded and disease ridden, with poor access to food and water, resulted in the deaths of many people as they crossed the Atlantic.

KEY TERMS

'Old Country' The country
of origin of an immigrant; in
this case Ireland.

Fenian movement
Revolutionary society
organised in 1858 in the
USA and called the 'Fenian
Brotherhood', aiming to
achieve Irish independence
from England by force. Its
counterpart in Ireland was
officially known as the Irish
Republican Brotherhood
(IRB) but the term Fenian
became the umbrella term.
The IRB was a forerunner of
the Irish Republican Army,
which emerged after the
1916 Easter Rising.

It was this hatred of England, based in part on the above view of the Great
Famine, that most Irish emigrants took with them to the New World. With the
rise of a large and politically influential Irish community in the United States in
the second half of the nineteenth century – linked in all sorts of ways with the
'Old Country' – these perceptions were bound to influence the history of the
Irish question. It is no coincidence, then, that the **Fenian movement** – the most
important Irish revolutionary group in the 1860s (see pages 88–9) – emerged
out of and gained some of its most fervent recruits within the American Irish
community. It is the Fenian outrages in England in 1867 that form part of the
background to Gladstone's adoption of his mission 'to pacify Ireland' – the major
theme of the next chapter.

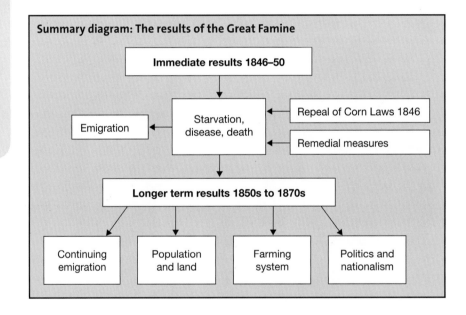

Summary diagram: The results of the Great Famine

Chapter summary

The Great Famine created an entirely new situation in Ireland. Up until 1845, the population, despite all the difficulties faced by ordinary Irish people, was growing steadily. In the census of 1841 it stood at around 8.2 million and by 1845 was probably around 8.5 million. The total population of the UK as a whole in 1845 was around 27.2 million. The famine altered this demographic balance permanently. By the time of the next census in 1851, over 1 million Irish people had died and more than 1 million others had emigrated. The Irish population stood at 6.5 million in 1851 and it continued to fall under the impact of the pattern of emigration established by the famine. In 1901, Ireland's population was less than 4.5 million, out of a total UK population of 41.6 million. The long-term impact was to create a potent image of national suffering that sustained and motivated the nationalist argument for decades. The myth that the British government had deliberately allowed the famine to depopulate Ireland or had even somehow created it, however misconceived and irrational, became widely believed well into the twentieth century and is still given credibility by people some today.

Refresher questions

Use these questions to remind yourself of the key material covered in this chapter.

1 How did the land system make life precarious for so many in Ireland?

2 How did Robert Peel achieve some measure of success in dealing with the early days of the famine?

3 Why were poor people in Ireland so dependent on the potato crop for their subsistence?

4 How did the British government respond to the distress in Ireland?

5 How did Irish nationalists respond to the crisis?

6 What impact did the Young Ireland rebellion have?

7 To what extent should the loss of life be seen as the responsibility of the British government?

8 What were the consequences of the famine for Ireland's relations with Britain?

Question practice

ESSAY QUESTIONS

1 'The British government was entirely responsible for the catastrophe of the Irish famine in the years 1845–9.' How far do you agree with this judgement?'

2 'The Young Ireland movement was a complete failure.' Discuss the validity of this verdict.

3 'Government legislation during the famine years 1845–50 was largely irrelevant to its effects.' Discuss the validity of this verdict.

4 To what extent were Irish radicals the main beneficiaries of the famine?

SOURCE ANALYSIS QUESTION

1 Assess the value of Source 1 for revealing the impact of the famine years on Ireland and the part played by the British government in responding to the Irish distress. Explain your answer, using the source, the information given about its origin and your own knowledge about the historical context.

SOURCE 1

From Jeremiah O'Donovan Rossa's *Personal Recollections*, published in 1898. He was born in 1831 and lived in Ireland during the famine years. He died in the United States in 1915 and his body was sent back by Irish nationalists there to be buried in Dublin.

The year 1845 was the first year of the great blight of the potato crops in Ireland. The landlords of Ireland made a raid upon the grain crops and seized them and sold them for their rents, leaving the producers of those crops to starve or perish or fly the country. Thousands of families were broken up; thousands of homes were razed; I am one of the victims of those bad times. People now allude to those years as the years of the 'famine' in Ireland. That kind of talk is nothing but trash. There was no 'famine' in Ireland; there is no famine in any country that will produce in any one year as much food as will feed the people who live in that country during that year. In the year 1845 there were 9,000,000 people in Ireland; allowing that the potato crop failed, other crops grew well, and the grain and cattle grown in the country were sufficient to sustain three times 9,000,000 people. England and the agents of England in Ireland seized those supplies of food, and sent them out of the country, and then raised the cry that there was 'famine' in the land. There was no famine in the land, but there was plunder of the Irish people by the English Government of Ireland; and Coroners' juries, called upon to give judgment in cases of people found dead, had brought in verdicts of 'murder' against that English government. England cared nothing for that; her work was going on splendidly; she wanted the Irish race cleared out of Ireland – cleared out entirely, and now something was doing for her what her guns and bayonets had failed to do. She gave thanks to God that it was so; that the Irish were gone – 'gone with a vengeance' – 'that it was going to be as hard to find a real Irishman in Ireland as to find a red Indian in New York – that Ireland was nothing but a rat in the path of an elephant, and that the elephant had nothing to do but to squelch the rat.'

What wonder is it if the leading Irishman today, in New York or anywhere else, would do all that he could do to make a return of that 'vengeance' to England? We adopt the English expression and call those years the 'famine years'; but there was no famine in the land. There is no famine in any land that produces as much food as will support the people of that land if the food is left with them. But the English took the food away to England, and let the people starve.

CHAPTER 5

Gladstone and Irish reform 1868–82

The period 1868–82 is of immense significance in the history of the Irish question. You need to understand:

★ the policies pursued by Gladstone's governments, particularly on the issue of land

★ the growth of Irish nationalism, under men like Butt, Davitt and Parnell

★ the reasons for the extensive violence that broke out, particularly in 1879–82

But be certain to keep in mind two important overall questions. First, whether moderate reform could possibly fulfil Irish needs and aspirations. Second, whether Irish nationalism would aim at reform within the Union or at independence, using peaceful or violent tactics. This chapter examines these issues under the following themes:

★ Gladstone and Ireland 1868–74

★ Home Rule and the rise of Parnell

★ Parnell and the Land League

★ Gladstone and Parnell 1880–2

Key dates

1858		Irish Republican Brotherhood (Fenians) founded by James Stephens in Dublin	
1867		Fenian outrages in Ireland and England	
1868	Dec.	Liberal victory at general election: Gladstone formed his first ministry	
1869		Irish Church Act	
1870		Gladstone's first Irish Land Act	
1872		Ballot Act introduced secret voting	
1873	March	Defeat of Irish Universities Bill	
	Nov.	Home Rule League founded by Isaac Butt	
1874		Conservative victory at general election: 60 Home Rulers elected	

1877		'Obstructionism' in the House of Commons	
1879		Foundation of Irish National Land League	
1880	April	Liberal victory at general election: Gladstone's second ministry	
	May	Parnell elected leader of the Irish Parliamentary Party	
1881	March	Coercion Act	
	Aug.	Gladstone's second Irish Land Act	
	Oct.	Parnell arrested, Land League outlawed	
1882	May	Kilmainham Treaty between Parnell and Gladstone	
		Phoenix Park murders	

Gladstone and Ireland 1868–74

▶ *Why did Gladstone decide to take up the Irish question in 1868?*

In the spring of 1866, the Liberal government headed by Earl Russell, the former Lord John Russell, who had become a peer in 1861, introduced a new Parliamentary Reform Bill into the House of Commons. The leading Liberal MP William Gladstone – a recent convert to the idea of further reform – took charge of the bill. However, not all Liberals supported this and the party split over the issue and the bill was defeated in the House of Commons, leading to the resignation of the government. The Conservative leader, Lord Derby, came into power at the head of a minority (in the House of Commons) Conservative administration, and it was they who pushed through a Reform Bill in the summer of 1867. The Conservative Bill was, ironically, a much more democratic measure than the original Liberal proposal – which aimed to enfranchise only a small minority of the urban working class – since it was based upon the principle of '**male household suffrage**'. The new Act was seen as a major achievement for Benjamin Disraeli – Derby's second-in-command as leader of the House of Commons and chancellor of the exchequer – who carried out the task of bringing the Act through the House of Commons despite the lack of a majority. The Second Reform Act of 1867 added over a million new voters to the electorate, most of them working men, who now became a majority of the voters in urban areas. About one in three adult men could now vote, as opposed to one in five previously. However, the 1867 Reform Act applied only to England and Wales. Early in 1868, Lord Derby retired and Disraeli succeeded him as prime minister.

Reform Acts 1868

During 1868, two further Reform Acts were passed in order to extend further parliamentary reform to Ireland and Scotland; this had been promised during the previous year. However, the Reform Act for Ireland did not give all male householders the vote as had been done in England and Wales and was also done in Scotland. In Ireland, the borough property franchise valuation was reduced to £4 rather than being removed altogether. Limited extensions to the county franchises introduced for England and Wales and Scotland also were not introduced in Ireland. As a result, the impact of parliamentary reform in Ireland was much more limited than elsewhere in the UK. Consequently, the percentage of adult male voters in Ireland fell further behind that of the rest of the UK.

In the spring of 1868, Gladstone – who was now leader of the Liberal Party following the retirement of Lord Russell – introduced a series of resolutions into the House of Commons in favour of the disestablishment of the Church of Ireland, one of the pillars of the Protestant Ascendancy. They were passed by comfortable majorities against the protests of Disraeli's government. Opposition to religious privilege was a subject on which all Liberals could unite. With the Conservative government's minority status clearly underlined, and the electoral registers ready, the dissolution of parliament was inevitable and a general election was held in November 1868.

In his election campaign, Gladstone made Irish reform one of the major issues. He was particularly frustrated by what he saw as the failure of the Anglican Church in Ireland, with its corruption and self-interest, to live up to his high standards of conduct. Gladstone believed that Anglicanism was the most highly developed and valid form of Christianity. To his mind, its obvious virtues were being undermined in Ireland. Gladstone saw the Irish Church as a pillar of the Protestant Ascendancy which had poisoned the atmosphere of Ireland in the past and was continuing to do so. He had no hesitation in making his feelings public during the campaign.

SOURCE A

Adapted from a speech by Gladstone at Wigan in October 1868, quoted in W.E. Gladstone, *Speeches of the Right Hon. W.E. Gladstone, M.P., delivered at Warrington, Ormskirk, Liverpool, Southport, Newton, Leigh and Wigan, in October 1868*, Simpkin, Marshall & Co., 1868, p. 85.

The Church of Ireland forms one of the many branches from one trunk, and that trunk is the tree of what is called the Protestant ascendancy ... We therefore aim at the destruction of that system of ascendancy which ... is still there like some tall tree of noxious growth, lifting its head to heaven and poisoning the atmosphere of the land so far as its shadow can extend ... But now at last the day has come when, as we hope, the axe has been laid to the root. It is deeply cut round and round. It nods and quivers from top to base. There lacks but one stroke more – the stroke of these elections. It will then, once for all, topple to its fall, and on that day the heart of Ireland will leap for joy.

> Study Source A. In what way was Gladstone taking a risk in speaking this way about the Irish Church and the Protestant Ascendancy?

Gladstone's 'mission'

The result of the general election of 1868 was a triumph for Gladstone: the Liberals were swept into power with a majority of over 100. Gladstone heard the news by telegram while he was at the family estate at Hawarden Castle in North Wales, engaged in his favourite hobby of felling trees. 'Very significant', he replied, leaning on his axe, and then, turning to his companion, he uttered the famous words, 'My mission is to pacify Ireland.' Why, then, did Gladstone decide to take up the Irish question in 1868?

Gladstone's action in that year was not the inevitable outcome of a long and consuming interest in Irish affairs. The famous letter he wrote to his sister in 1845 is often quoted: 'Ireland, Ireland! That cloud in the west, that coming storm, the minister of God's retribution upon cruel ... injustice. Ireland forces upon us these great social and great religious questions.' Yet Gladstone paid little attention to that country over the next 21 years. His one practical action was his introduction of income tax in Ireland in 1853, during his period as chancellor of the exchequer, and he made only one visit there throughout his long life, in 1877 for around three weeks, during which he stayed almost exclusively with aristocratic Anglican families. Nor were conditions in Ireland exceptionally bad in 1868. Farming remained prosperous, and the figures for agrarian crime and violence were relatively low. His renewed interest in Ireland after 1867 was partly a response to the Fenian outrages of that year.

Fenianism

The Fenians were members of a secret revolutionary organisation established in Ireland (under the name of the Irish Republican Brotherhood) and the United States in 1858, and committed to the forcible overthrow of British power and the establishment of an independent Irish republic. (The movement drew its name from the ancient Irish warriors, the *Fianna*.) They gained a fair amount of support in the 1860s, and even had their own newspaper, *The Irish People*, run by the movement's Irish founder and leader, James Stephens.

In 1865, the British government responded by suppressing *The Irish People* and arresting leading Fenians throughout Great Britain. The Brotherhood planned an armed outbreak in Ireland early in 1867, but this was a total failure for two reasons:

- The authorities were well informed about Fenian plans and so well prepared.
- There was a lack of any widespread popular support for their rebellion in Ireland.

The Fenians then transferred their activities to the English mainland, carrying out two attacks which made them notorious but earned them massive publicity:

- The first incident took place in September 1867 at Manchester when, in carrying out the successful rescue of two leading Fenians from a prison van, Police Sergeant Charles Brett, who was inside the van, was killed when the attackers fired at the van's lock in an attempt to open it.
- The second incident occurred in London in December, where the terrorists destroyed part of the wall of Clerkenwell Prison with explosives in a failed attempt to secure the release of a Fenian prisoner being held prior to trial. The bomb was so powerful that it damaged houses nearby. As a result of the blast, twelve bystanders died and 120 others were injured, many of them children.

The combined impact of these incidents, especially the prison attack, which became known as the 'Clerkenwell Outrage' owing to the loss of innocent civilian lives, caused a serious anti-Irish backlash and may well have affected the public view of Irish reforms and the issue of Home Rule in later years.

In England, the outrages were greeted with horror and anger. Yet in Ireland, three Fenians – William Philip Allen, Michael Larkin and Michael O'Brien – who were arrested and executed in November 1867 for the murder of the policeman, became known as the 'Manchester Martyrs'. Two others were tried

SOURCE B

A contemporary engraving showing the explosion at Clerkenwell in 1867.

with them, one of whom was pardoned when evidence against was found to be false, and the other, an American citizen, was pardoned on the appeal of the United States government. It was argued by a small minority of English Liberals that Sergeant Brett was shot unintentionally and therefore it was not murder. From the Fenians' viewpoint, Brett was simply a casualty of war. Speaking in the House of Commons a decade later, the Irish leader Charles Stewart Parnell told the House: 'I wish to say as directly as I can that I do not believe, and never shall believe, that any murder was committed in Manchester.'

Gladstone later denied that the Fenian activities had any direct influence on his Irish policy, although he did argue that 'they brought home to the popular mind … the vast importance of the Irish controversy'. As a devout Christian, Gladstone was appalled by violence in any form but the Fenians' activities helped to confirm his growing conviction that Ireland had genuine grievances which must be dealt with if the Union was to be maintained in peace and prosperity. It also made the British public, he believed, more amenable to Irish reform, although this idea was very dubious. In a speech at Southport, only a few days after the Manchester outrage, he outlined a programme of Irish reform which covered religion, land and university education.

> How do you think that the event portrayed in Source B may have influenced Gladstone? **?**

Gladstone's Irish reforms

Gladstone was fully aware that proposing Irish reform carried potential political advantages and disadvantages. He knew that the Liberal Party had been outmanoeuvred and divided by Disraeli in 1867 over parliamentary reform. However, the Liberals still had a majority in the House of Commons and the Conservatives could only continue in power if they won the next election, which had to be held once the new voter registers were completed at the end of 1868. Gladstone's support for the disestablishment of the Church of Ireland, which he made clear in the spring of 1868, would be attractive to **nonconformist** Liberals but far less so to the small but highly influential aristocratic Whig group of the party. This was equally true of land reform and university reform. Gladstone believed that with the enlarged electorate created by the Second Reform Act, Irish Church reform would appeal not only to Roman Catholics but also to working men throughout Great Britain whom he had come to believe had, through better education, become willing to accept great causes based on principle rather than self-interest.

On the whole, Gladstone's expectations were apparently fulfilled. The 1868 elections produced a majority of 112 for the Liberals in the House of Commons and Gladstone duly became prime minister for the first time. Significantly, the Liberals improved their electoral position in Ireland (where they won 66 seats in 1868 compared with 50 in 1859) and Wales and Scotland, where nonconformity was strong, as well as in many of the industrial areas of the north of England. Gladstone had certainly placed reform in Ireland into a central position in politics, but how far his victory was the result of this or in spite of it is unclear.

The Irish Church Act 1869

The disestablishment of the Church of Ireland had played an important part in the Liberal Party's electoral campaign and was bound to be top of the new government's agenda. The case for reform was virtually unanswerable. Although the Church of Ireland had been the Established Church since the late seventeenth century, it had never represented more than a tiny minority of the Irish people. The point was driven home emphatically by the census of 1861, which showed that out of a population of 5.75 million, the Catholics numbered 4.5 million and the members of the Church of Ireland less than 750,000. Even the Conservatives now realised that the position of the Church of Ireland was unacceptable as it stood. As prime minister in 1868, Disraeli had tried, unsuccessfully, to find a measure of reform which, while stopping short of disestablishment, would be acceptable to all sections of his party. Gladstone had no such inhibitions. He was a devout Anglican and believed Anglicanism to be the best form of Christianity. He believed and argued that the Irish Church Bill he now produced, based on the simple principle of disestablishment and disendowment, would purify the Irish Church, raising it to the status it should have to attract converts.

KEY TERM

Nonconformist Member of those Protestant Christian Churches who did not 'conform' to the teachings of the Anglican Church of England. Examples would be Presbyterians, Methodists and Baptists.

Disestablishment

The first part of the bill was comparatively straightforward: the disestablishment clauses meant that the link between Church and State was to be broken and the Church of Ireland was to become a separate, voluntary organisation from 1 January 1871. This meant, for example, that tithes no longer had to be paid to the Church by all Irishmen and that Irish Anglican archbishops and bishops would no longer sit in the House of Lords.

Disendowment

The problem of disendowment – that is, the disposal of the properties belonging to the Church of Ireland – proved more difficult. Gladstone was faced with demands from the Anglicans that all the funds should be used to help the dispossessed members of their Church. On the other hand, the Catholics wanted most of the money to be used for secular (non-religious) purposes in Ireland. In the end, a compromise was produced which was reasonably fair and acceptable: £10 million was to be granted to the Church of Ireland for pensions to their clergy and compensation for loss of office; £13 million was to be granted for secular purposes, mainly the relief of poverty and the promotion of education in Ireland.

In order to bring the other Churches in Ireland into line with the new status of the Anglican Church, the State grants to the Catholic Maynooth College and the Presbyterian Church were abolished, although compensation was provided. Another significant clause in the bill facilitated the purchase of the lands of the Church of Ireland by their tenants, and about 6000 farmers took advantage of this.

The significance of the Irish Church Act

The bill easily passed through the House of Commons. The Conservative majority in the Lords, however, hesitated to agree to full disestablishment and disendowment. The potential scale of opposition there made the outcome uncertain and prompted Gladstone to ask Queen Victoria to use her influence to make sure that the bill passed. Victoria accepted Gladstone's constitutional right to ask her for this – and complied – but she deeply resented his action in involving her. The Irish Church Act of 1869 was one of the more successful pieces of Irish legislation passed by Gladstone, since it solved once and for all the major religious grievance of the Irish Roman Catholics. However, in practice it made little difference to the lives of the majority of the Irish people. Roman Catholics obviously welcomed it but considered it to be no more than the situation had required for decades and their gratitude was limited.

The First Irish Land Act 1870

The subject of land reform was much more difficult than Church reform owing to the complexities of the Irish land system and the wider range of interests involved. Gladstone concluded that the main problem was the landlord–tenant relationship, and that what was needed was to give more economic security to the tenant. To some extent, therefore, Gladstone was prepared to go along with the demands of the supporters of tenant right, as they had developed since the 1850s (see page 78). He also had the findings of the Devon Commission of 1843–5, which had been set up by Peel, to consult. Gladstone put forward a land bill that had three major parts.

The terms of the Act

The first part of Gladstone's bill concerned those lands – mainly in the north – which were rented in accordance with what was known as the 'Ulster custom'. In these areas, tenants could not be evicted so long as they continued to pay their rent. In addition, such tenants possessed the right of 'free sale'; that is, if a tenant gave up his holding, he had the right to 'sell' his interest in it to an acceptable incoming tenant by claiming compensation for the work he had put into it. Both these rights were based on 'custom', not law. What the Land Bill now proposed was that these customary rights should be given the force of law.

The second part of the bill dealt with those tenants who did not have the protection of Ulster custom, which was the overwhelming majority. These tenants now received greater security through:

- An entitlement to compensation for any improvements made to a farm if they surrendered their lease. These had previously been accredited to the landlord so that tenants had no incentive to make improvements.
- A right to compensation for what was termed 'disturbance' (damages), for tenants evicted for reasons other than non-payment of rent.

Gladstone's aim was, as he explained, 'to prevent the landlord from using the terrible weapon of undue and unjust eviction, by so framing the handle that it shall cut his hands with the sharp edge of pecuniary damages'.

The third part of the Land Bill, known as the 'John Bright Clauses', after the veteran radical who proposed them, dealt with land purchase. This enabled a tenant wishing to purchase his holding from a landlord who was willing to sell, to obtain two-thirds of the purchase price as a mortgage from the State. The mortgages ran for 35 years at a rate of five per cent interest.

To prevent landlords forcing evictions by simply increasing rents to impossible levels and so avoiding paying compensation to tenants, the bill said that rents must not be 'excessive'. It was left to the courts to define what this meant in individual cases. However, in the House of Lords an amendment to the bill removed the word excessive and substituted 'exorbitant' in its place. This gave landlords greater scope to raise rents above what tenants could pay, and then to evict them for non-payment without giving any compensation. Gladstone opted not to try to restore the original meaning.

Gladstone intended his Land Bill to be a one-off, distinctly Irish measure, with no implications for the rest of the UK. He did not regard it as in any sense an attack on the rights of property. On the contrary, since so much of the bill was concerned with upholding customary rights, he argued that it could be regarded as a 'conservative' measure. Similarly, the Land Bill was meant not to undermine the position of the Irish landlord class but to improve it by removing some of the obstacles to a good relationship with their tenants. In effect, what Gladstone wanted was to make Irish landlords more like English landlords; in his words, to offer them 'a position marked by residence, by personal familiarity, and by sympathy with the people among whom they live'.

The impact of the Act

Gladstone's Land Bill passed through both houses of parliament with little opposition. As one English peer noted shrewdly, 'the great mass of the English people would sacrifice the Irish landlords tomorrow if they knew that by doing so they could tempt the Irish populace into acquiescing in their rule'. However, the Irish Land Act was not very successful and was counterproductive in the following ways:

- The problem of defining legally where the 'Ulster custom' existed was complicated and in some cases led to disputes where none had existed previously.
- The 'Bright Clauses', too, were a largely a failure. Most landlords had no wish to sell. Few tenants could afford the one-third of the purchase price needed to buy their holding – fewer than 1000 tenants took up the mortgages offered.
- Above all, the eviction clauses had little impact. There was still no real means of controlling unfair rents, and tenants on long leases were in any case outside the provisions of the Act.

It can be reasonably argued that as a cure for the ills of rural Ireland the Act was almost totally irrelevant. Irish poverty was not ultimately due to the greed of the landlords, but to the lack of economic growth and, in the west of Ireland particularly, to the shortage of cultivable land. Rents were moderate in the 20 years following the Great Famine; evictions were few; and agricultural improvements were carried out, often jointly by landlords and tenants. In effect, the situation was rather different in 1870 from that which had prevailed at the time of the Devon Commission in the 1840s.

On the other hand, it can be argued that Gladstone's aims were essentially political: to bind Ireland to the Union and its institutions by proving that the Westminster parliament was prepared to legislate for what the mass of the Irish people considered to be their legitimate grievances. The Land Act, therefore, can be seen as having a symbolic significance for, whatever its defects in strictly economic terms, it could be regarded as a further blow against the traditional power of the Protestant Ascendancy. It was noticeable that Gladstone's reform legislation of 1869–70, together with the release of Fenian prisoners, which he secured at the end of 1870, was followed by a greater harmony between English Liberals and Irish Catholics. At the same time, it spread alarm and despondency among Irish Protestants.

All this seemed to Gladstone to justify his policies, particularly over land, and in the 1870s he remained supremely optimistic about the future of Ireland within the Union. Some politicians, however, were less starry-eyed. Lord Kimberley, the colonial secretary, wrote in his journal on 21 February 1870 that no measure of any kind would satisfy the Irish: 'Gladstone now lives in the happy delusion that his policy will produce a speedy change in the temper of the Irish towards this country. He will soon find out his mistake.' Nevertheless, Gladstone remained confident. 'There is nothing that Ireland has asked and which this country and this parliament have refused', he proclaimed in a public speech in 1871, except for the 'simple grievance' of university education. To this he now turned.

The Irish Universities Bill 1873

University reform was badly needed since the Catholics of Ireland, although they controlled a number of small colleges, had no major degree-awarding institutions of their own. Trinity College, Dublin, was an Anglican foundation, and the 'godless colleges' established by Sir Robert Peel in the 1840s as non-denominational institutions were denounced by the Catholic clergy. Gladstone now proposed the establishment of a national, non-denominational University of Dublin, which would embrace both Trinity College and the present and future Catholic colleges. But the project was fraught with difficulties. Quite apart from the practical problems of teaching 'controversial' subjects such as history and theology, Trinity College had no wish to be involved in such an institution. Another significant stumbling block proved to be the proviso that any new Catholic college would get no financial help from the State. The Irish Universities Bill was defeated in the Commons in March 1873 by three votes because of abstentions or opposition votes by Irish Liberal MPs. Gladstone resigned. Disraeli, for tactical reasons, refused to assume office or ask Queen Victoria to dissolve parliament. He had no wish to head another weak minority government and he was not ready to fight a general election since he believed that Gladstone was already unpopular with the public and would become more so. Gladstone was furious and insisted that since the government had resigned following a defeat in the House of Commons, Disraeli had a constitutional obligation to take office. Disraeli, however, was having none of it and Gladstone therefore had no option but to come back into office.

Nevertheless, increasing disunity and acrimony within the parliamentary Liberal Party meant that the government's days were numbered. Although there was general agreement in the Liberal Party that the situation in Ireland could not be ignored and that reform was needed, this did not mean that Liberals in parliament or in the country were unanimous or unequivocal in their support for all his ideas. The aristocratic 'Whig' element in the party was concerned about the interference with landowners' rights involved in the Land Act. The strong nonconformist element of the party resented the fact that Gladstone was prepared to disestablish the Anglican Church in Ireland but not in England or in Wales, which to them represented much higher priorities. Radical Liberals were dismayed that Gladstone was focused on Ireland but not on more far-reaching social reforms in Britain. All this meant that while Gladstone's prestige and authority allowed him to carry through much of what he intended, there was going to be a limit to what these elements in the party might accept over Ireland in the future. Moreover, in Ireland a newly organised Home Rule Party had already arisen to challenge the power of the established parties. The 1874 general election confirmed what the Irish Universities Bill had foreshadowed: the Liberal Party's strength in Ireland would soon to be a thing of the past.

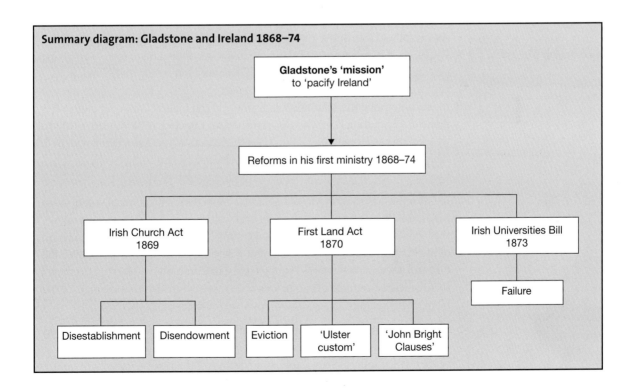

Summary diagram: Gladstone and Ireland 1868–74

Home Rule and the rise of Parnell

▶ *Why was the rise of Parnell so important for Irish politics?*

Even while Gladstone was promoting his Irish reforms, a new movement for constitutional change in Ireland had arisen. The leading figure was Isaac Butt, an Irish Protestant lawyer. Butt had begun his political career as a staunch unionist, and indeed sat in the House of Commons as a Conservative MP from 1852 to 1865. But his growing disillusionment with the House of Commons as a vehicle for dealing effectively with Irish affairs, together with the personal experiences of the Fenian political prisoners whom he defended in the courts after 1865, led him to become an Irish nationalist. He had no sympathy with the Fenian ideal of armed rebellion and Irish independence, but he now believed that some form of self-government for Ireland, based on an elected Irish parliament to deal with domestic affairs, was the best solution for the difficulties which surrounded the Anglo-Irish relationship.

The Home Rule League

KEY TERM

Non-sectarian Not limited to or associated with a particular religious denomination.

As a result of Isaac Butt's initiative, the Home Rule Association was formed in Dublin in 1870 as a **non-sectarian** organisation, appealing to men of all political persuasions, and committed to the single aim of Home Rule for Ireland. In its early days the Association won little support from Irish Catholics, since most of them still pinned their faith on Gladstone and the Liberal Party, although a few members, including Butt who was returned for Limerick in 1871, were elected at by-elections as Home Rulers. But when the leaders of the Association widened their programme to include such popular issues as tenant right (see page 78), they began to build up more support among the Irish electors.

In 1873, the Association was replaced by a more distinctly political organisation, the Home Rule League. The moment was well chosen, for, at the beginning of that year (as we saw in the previous section), Gladstone had incurred the wrath of the Roman Catholic Church and many Irish Liberal MPs over his Universities Bill, and it was in fact rejected by the House of Commons in March. This meant that the Irish electorate began to look with more sympathy on the claims of the Home Rule League.

The organisation of the League had hardly established itself before it was faced by a general election early in 1874. Nevertheless, the League won 59 seats: a verdict which reflected the astonishing decline of the Liberal Party in Ireland from 66 seats in 1868 to twelve seats in 1874. This remarkable result was partly helped by the 1872 Ballot Act which, by introducing secret voting at elections, undermined the electoral pressure normally exerted by the landowning classes.

The impact of the 1872 Ballot Act

Prior to this Act, all voting at UK parliamentary elections was done in public and recorded openly. Results, including the names of voters and their choice of candidate, were published in poll books and usually in the local press as well. This meant that those dependent on others for employment or land they rented were often expected to vote for a candidate of the landowner's choice. The freedom to vote freely in secret was of particular importance in Ireland, where landowner pressure of this kind was very common. The Act, however, was not introduced with Ireland directly in mind. It was mainly the result of instances of landowner abuse of tenants in Wales and certain parts of England that came to light during and after the 1868 general election which forced the British government to agree to reform the voting system. The Act itself was not a government bill. It was introduced with government agreement by a Liberal backbench MP in 1870 and took two years of debate to pass, despite the fact that it was supported by the Conservatives as well as the government.

The Home Rule Party

When parliament reassembled in February 1874 after Disraeli's triumph at the polls, Isaac Butt and his followers constituted themselves into an independent Home Rule Party with their own officials and organisation. This was something even O'Connell's Irish group had not set up in the 1830s. The Home Rule Party, however, had little impact on the House of Commons or English public opinion generally. Part of the fault lay with the character of the party itself: apart from the general commitment to Home Rule, it lacked any real unity in ideas, organisation or membership. Moreover, even the commitment to Home Rule itself did little to bind the party together. In reality, only about a third of the members were genuine Home Rulers in the spirit of Butt: some were Fenians and many were really crypto-Liberals who had only jumped on the Home Rule bandwagon in 1874 in order to ensure their election as MPs.

All these faults were worsened by the weak leadership of Isaac Butt himself. He lacked the necessary single-mindedness and ruthlessness, nor did he have the ability to inspire his followers with his speeches. Often, he was away from the House of Commons pursuing his legal career; and, even when present, his innate conservatism made him deferential to the established practices of parliament and conciliatory towards the traditional parties and their leaders. Thus, Butt was unable or unwilling to impose his own leadership and discipline on the Home Rule Party in order to weld it into a powerful, cohesive instrument for forcing the House of Commons to consider seriously Irish claims.

Unsurprisingly, Butt's leadership was soon challenged by a group of more militant Home Rulers. In 1875, J.C. Biggar and John O'Connor Power, both Fenians, began to apply the tactics of '**obstruction**' in the House of Commons. This involved interminable speeches on Irish affairs, whatever subject was being debated at the time, in order to disrupt parliamentary business and focus

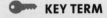 **KEY TERM**

Obstruction Causing a delay in the running of the business of parliament, usually by continuing talking at great length and organising a series of speakers to immediately replace each other and keep the delay going. Since the House of Commons operated on the premise that members were 'gentlemen' and would behave appropriately, there was no official procedure to deal with this abuse of the system.

the attention of the House on Irish grievances. Biggar and Power were soon joined by a more charismatic figure: Charles Stewart Parnell, a young Protestant landowner.

Parnell's aggressive attitude and contempt for English opinion soon made him a popular hero for militant Irish nationalists everywhere, and in 1877 he was elected president of the Home Rule Confederation of Great Britain. This was a bitter blow to the prestige of Isaac Butt, whose power was clearly waning. Parnell also had private contacts with a number of leading Fenians in 1877–8, and although he refused to commit himself to their revolutionary programme, they were impressed and prepared to cooperate. 'He has many of the qualities of leadership', wrote one Fenian leader to a colleague, 'and time will give him more.'

Parnell made no attempt as yet to challenge directly Butt's position as leader of the Home Rule Party. However, the whole situation was completely transformed by the start of agricultural depression in Ireland in 1879. The Irish national cause now became linked with the agrarian crisis.

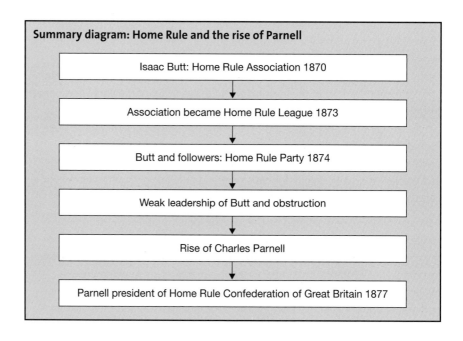

Summary diagram: Home Rule and the rise of Parnell

Isaac Butt: Home Rule Association 1870

↓

Association became Home Rule League 1873

↓

Butt and followers: Home Rule Party 1874

↓

Weak leadership of Butt and obstruction

↓

Rise of Charles Parnell

↓

Parnell president of Home Rule Confederation of Great Britain 1877

Parnell and the Land League

▶ *How did the emergence of the Land League affect Anglo-Irish relations?*

After the years of relative prosperity following the end of the Great Famine, Irish farmers found themselves faced with agricultural depression at the end of the 1870s. This was the result of:

- a series of poor harvests in 1877–9
- the reappearance of famine in the west of Ireland owing to the failure of the potato crop
- the importation of cheap grain from the United States, which also affected England.

All this was followed by a slump in food prices, including the prices of Irish cattle and dairy produce. The Irish smallholder also suffered from the drying up of opportunities for migratory work in England owing to the impact of the depression there. The overall effect of the agricultural depression in Ireland was a drastic fall in farmers' incomes. They responded by demanding the reduction or the remittance of rents. Although many landlords were prepared to agree initially, in the end non-payment by tenants led to evictions. In 1879, about 1000 families (6000 people) were turned off the land. Since the tenants had been demanding 'fair rents' for many years (a topic virtually untouched by the 1870 Land Act), and farmers' organisations existed in many parts of the country, all the material was now present for the creation of a popular agrarian movement directed against the landlords. What was needed was organisation and leadership on a national scale, and this was soon forthcoming. So too was violence, which never lay far below the surface in rural Ireland. Thus began the so-called 'Land War' of 1879–82.

The Land War

The key figure in this was Michael Davitt. Davitt's family had been evicted from their smallholding in the west of Ireland in 1851 and emigrated to Lancashire, where, as a boy, young Davitt worked in the cotton mills. All this left him with a burning hatred of the landlord class in Ireland and of English domination. Later, he joined the Fenians and was arrested in 1870 for arms trafficking and served seven years in prison. On his release, Davitt rejoined the Fenians, although unlike the hard-liners he now believed in cooperation with the **Constitutional Nationalists**. In 1878, he visited the United States, where he met the American Fenian John Devoy, whose views were similar to his own, and Devoy encouraged him to work for land reform and self-government in Ireland.

Davitt, meanwhile, was determined to place the land question at the centre of Irish politics. He believed that agrarian agitation by itself could force the

 KEY TERM

Constitutional Nationalists Nationalists who rejected the use of physical force as a means of achieving Home Rule. Instead, they supported means within the rule of law.

Charles Stewart Parnell

1846	Born in County Wicklow
1875	Elected to parliament as a member of the Home Rule League
1877	Elected president of the Home Rule Confederation of Great Britain
1879	Became president of the Irish National Land League
1880	Elected leader of the Irish Parliamentary Party
1881	Suspended and expelled from parliament
	Arrested and imprisoned
1882	Released from prison
1886	Joined with the Liberals to defeat the Tory government
1890	Replaced as leader of the Irish Parliamentary Party
1891	Died

Early life

Parnell was born in June 1846 into one of the greatest families of the Protestant Ascendancy, which had been established in County Wicklow since the later seventeenth century. Its members had held high office in the Irish government in the eighteenth century and had sat in the House of Commons after the Union. He was educated at schools in England and at the University of Cambridge, although he left without taking a degree. He then returned to Ireland and lived the life of a typical Anglo-Irish country squire. It was not until 1874 that he began to consider seriously a career in politics, partly out of a growing awareness of himself as an Irish nationalist. His mother was an important influence here, since she was American with a family tradition of anti-English feeling, and had been responsible for her son's upbringing since the early death of her husband when her son was only thirteen. Parnell's mother had some sympathy with the Fenians in the 1860s. Parnell, however, regarded their commitment to force as futile and, although he was prepared to accept their support later, he remained convinced throughout his life that real change for Ireland could only come through the Westminster parliament.

Member of parliament

Parnell was elected as a Home Ruler for the Irish constituency of Meath at a by-election in 1875, aged 29. He was tall, handsome, proud and reserved, and already possessed a commanding personality. In his early days he was a poor speaker – hesitant and highly strung. However, through sheer force of will and determination, he turned himself into an effective MP and a capable orator, particularly to mass audiences. As one of his followers later wrote: 'the strength of Parnell was character rather than intellect'. Within the House of Commons his support for obstruction meant that he identified himself with the militant section of the Home Rule Party which was critical of Butt's leadership. 'What did we ever get in the past by trying to conciliate?' he asked.

Irish leader

Later, Parnell established himself as the greatest Irish leader since O'Connell, the Protestant leader of a Catholic nation. He was known as 'the uncrowned King of Ireland' before disaster struck, with the O'Shea divorce (see pages 124–5). He died in 1891, having failed to achieve Home Rule. Yet he had succeeded remarkably in his campaign for land reform, and, despite what his opponents and some supporters said, had pursued a constitutional path that rejected violence. 'He talked daggers', commented a colleague, 'but used none'.

government to yield to Irish demands for constitutional change as well as land reform. In the spring of 1879 he therefore threw himself into the smallholders' struggle in County Mayo (where he had been born) against the landlords, and began organising meetings and demonstrations in opposition to evictions and in favour of 'fair rents' and land reform. He also encouraged Parnell, whom he recognised as the up-and-coming leader of the radical section of the Irish Parliamentary Party, to support the agitation. After some hesitation, Parnell agreed to speak at the great demonstration at Westport in June 1879, where he appealed to the smallholders to 'hold a firm grip of your homesteads and lands'. More importantly perhaps, this was part of Parnell's calculated preparation for the leadership struggle within the parliamentary party, following Butt's death in the previous month.

The 'New Departure'

In an attempt to use the land agitation as a battering ram for the Irish nationalist cause, Davitt followed up these early successes by arranging the famous meeting between himself, John Devoy and Parnell, at Dublin in June 1879. There the three men – symbolically representing agrarian radicalism, revolutionary nationalism and constitutional nationalism – came to an informal agreement in support of the tenants' demands and Irish self-government. This agreement marks the beginning of what is known in Irish history as the 'New Departure'. It can be seen as the point where all the elements of Irish protest and grievance became unified in one national movement.

The Irish National Land League

The tenants' movement now spread from the west to the more prosperous south and east and began to win support from the larger farmers. In October 1879, Davitt formed the Irish National Land League – with the watchword 'the Land for the People' – largely funded by money donated by Irish-Americans. Parnell agreed to become president.

What were Parnell's motives in supporting the tenants' agitation? Although he did agree with their immediate demands for the '**Three Fs**', and, eventually, the buying out of the landlords, Parnell was never as radical a land reformer as Davitt, who supported, ultimately, land nationalisation. He was, after all, a considerable landowner himself and therefore had a degree of sympathy with the Irish landlords. His motives were primarily political. Support for a popular agrarian movement would, he believed, encourage the cause of constitutional nationalism in Ireland and give leverage to the Home Rulers at Westminster, and thus help to wrest Home Rule from parliament. 'I would not have taken off my coat', he proclaimed, 'and gone to this work if I had not known that we were laying the foundation in this movement for the regeneration of our legislative independence.'

Parnell also argued that the agitation would force the British government to introduce land reform, and that this would help to bring to an end to the conflict between tenants and landlords and encourage the latter to throw their weight behind the Home Rule movement. 'Deprive this [landlord] class of their privileges', he said in Liverpool in November 1879, 'show them that they must cast themselves in with the rest of their countrymen … [and] the last knell of English power … in Ireland has been sounded.'

This emphasis on the possibility of winning the landlord class for the nationalist cause forms the most original part of Parnell's views on land reform.

 **KEY TERM**

Three Fs A series of demands issued by Irish nationalists in their campaign for land reform. The 'Fs' were fair rents, free sale and fixity of tenure.

It marks off Parnell from the outlook of Davitt, who aimed at the elimination of, rather than cooperation with, the landlords. But Parnell was enough of a landed gentleman himself to hope that a self-governing Ireland would be ruled by men of position and influence – an outlook not dissimilar from Gladstone's later views. Furthermore, Parnell believed that support for the Irish tenantry would strengthen his own position against the moderates within the Irish Parliamentary Party. Following the death of Isaac Butt in May 1879, another colourless moderate, William Shaw, had been elected temporary leader, but he proved incapable of uniting the party.

Aims of the Land League

The aims of the Land League were as follows:

- to put an end to oppression by landlords in the form of unfair rents and evictions
- to radically change the land system in Ireland so as to put it in the power of every Irish farmer to become the owner, on fair terms, of the land he worked.

The means proposed to effect these aims were stated to be:

- organisation among the people and tenant farmers for the purpose of self-defence
- the cultivation of public opinion by persistent exposure of the monstrous injustice of the present system
- a resolute demand for the reduction of the excessive rents which had brought the Irish people to a state of starvation
- temperate but firm resistance to oppression and injustice.

This manifesto was, of course, largely propaganda. No reputable historian now regards the Land War as a simple clash between a rapacious landlord class and a downtrodden, exploited peasantry. Indeed, it can be argued that the real motive of the League's members in attacking the landlords and demanding the 'Three Fs' was to enable them, and more particularly the larger pastoral farmers, to inflate their dwindling incomes by obtaining rent reductions (that is, 'fair rents', in their eyes). The landlord was thus made the scapegoat for the effects of the agricultural depression.

Tactics of the Land League

Under the leadership of Davitt and his supporters, the Land League became a weapon of popular protest against the landlord class and, in day-to-day terms, concerned particularly with the problems of eviction. Between 1879 and 1883 some 14,600 tenants were turned off the land – more than in the previous 30 years. The League did the following:

- It urged tenants to offer landlords lower rents or no rents.
- It offered help to tenants who were evicted.
- It cared for the families of those who were imprisoned.

- It applied a **boycott** against farmers who attempted to take over the holding of an evicted tenant. In Parnell's famous words in County Clare in September 1880, such a man should be dealt with, he urged, 'by putting him into a moral Coventry, by isolating him from the rest of his kind as if he was a leper of old'.
- It applied a boycott against the evicting landlords themselves, such as the famous Boycott whose name now became used to denote such practices.

Despite the public commitment of the tenants' leaders to peaceful protest, it was virtually certain that violence would erupt given the emotions aroused by eviction and the inflammatory language used in the Land League's propaganda. 'Outrages' against the landlords and their supporters became the characteristic feature of the Land War: 2590 incidents were reported in 1880. This meant murders (there were 67 in the years 1879–82), as well as assaults, intimidation, threatening letters, and attacks on property and animals.

All this placed the authorities in an intolerable position in 1879–80. The Land League was a legal organisation and could not easily be prosecuted. Police and troops were used to protect persons and property; but the sporadic and varied nature of the outrages – generally perpetrated at night by 'moonlighters' – and the silent acquiescence of the local populace made the whole situation difficult to control.

Violence also raised problems for constitutionalists such as Parnell, since it was difficult to dissociate the outrages completely from the activities of the Land League of which he was president. Parnell, however, was away in America during the early months of 1880 raising money for the League and spreading the gospel of Irish nationalism. It was also an important move in his personal campaign for the leadership of the Irish Parliamentary Party. The US trip was an enormous success, financially and personally. Parnell addressed audiences in 62 cities and appealed deliberately and effectively to every section of Irish-American opinion.

The general election 1880

Parnell cut short his US tour to return home and fight the general election of April 1880. The election resulted in victory for the Liberals and the formation of Gladstone's second ministry with an overall majority in the House of Commons of 51. At the same time, 61 Home Rulers were returned to parliament, including many new members sympathetic to Parnell. On 17 May 1880, at a meeting at the City Hall in Dublin, Parnell was elected leader of the Irish Parliamentary Party, receiving 23 votes to William Shaw's 18. The result showed that although his abilities were recognised, there was still much resentment against him by the moderates because of his association with agrarian radicalism and the Fenians. The problems of unity in the party, therefore, still remained. Nevertheless, after only five years in politics, and at the age of 34, Charles Stewart Parnell had become leader of the Irish Parliamentary Party. The rise of Parnell, in the words of one historian, 'constitutes the most brilliant political performance in Irish history'.

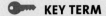

KEY TERM

Boycott The word came into the language after Captain Boycott, a land agent in County Mayo, was isolated – without servants, mail delivery or service in shops – as a result of the Land League's policies because he refused to charge lower rents and evicted tenants.

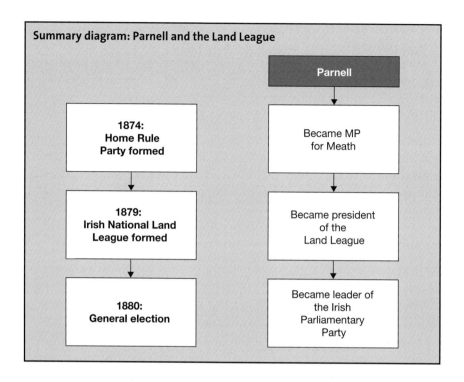

Summary diagram: Parnell and the Land League

Parnell

1874:
Home Rule
Party formed

Became MP
for Meath

1879:
Irish National Land
League formed

Became president
of the
Land League

1880:
General election

Became leader of
the Irish
Parliamentary
Party

 4 # Gladstone and Parnell 1880–2

▶ *What happened with Gladstone and Parnell from 1880 to 1882?*

The general election of 1880 was not fought by Gladstone on Irish issues. His main focus was on Disraeli's record in foreign and imperial affairs. Indeed, it was his outrage at what he saw as the 'immorality' of Disraeli's Eastern policy (which involved diplomatic support for the Turks despite their brutal repression of Christian rebels in their Balkans territories) which had led Gladstone to re-enter politics after his retirement from the Liberal leadership in 1875. Apart from this, the only other issue he raised regularly in the campaign was Disraeli's handling – or mishandling as he saw it – of financial and economic policy. Gladstone had no plans for further Irish reform and had barely mentioned Ireland during the election campaign. In fact, apart from a vague commitment to parliamentary and local government reform, the Liberals came into power in 1880 with no definite programme at all.

Nevertheless, Ireland soon emerged as a major problem. As Gladstone admitted frankly in 1884: 'I did not know, no one knew, the severity of the crisis that was already swelling upon the horizon, and that shortly after rushed upon us like a flood.' What changed his attitude was his belief that Ireland now faced a social revolution as a result of the activities of the Land League and the outrages which seemed to accompany them. Violence increased substantially in the second half of 1880, exacerbated by the Lords' rejection of a bill to protect tenants who were in arrears with rent from eviction. Gladstone therefore concluded that the only long-term solution to this crisis was further land reform.

The Coercion Act

The prime minister eventually accepted that exceptional powers of arrest and imprisonment must first be granted to the authorities, as W.E. Forster, the Irish secretary, had been urging for some time. Early in 1881, the government therefore introduced a tough new Coercion Bill which temporarily suspended *habeas corpus* so that those people suspected of committing an offence could be detained without trial. This was delayed in the House of Commons by the Irish Party led by Parnell for 41 hours (from 31 January to 2 February) using the by now familiar tactics of obstruction, until, on his own initiative, the speaker brought the debate to an end by using the unprecedented device of the '**guillotine**'. Once this was done, the bill was soon passed. Since the Commons subsequently approved the new procedure, Irish obstruction using delaying tactics became almost impossible. Then, on 3 February, Michael Davitt was arrested and imprisoned under the new Act, an event that soon led to uproar in the House, followed by the suspension and expulsion of 36 Irish MPs, including Parnell.

These events played into the hands of the new Irish leader. The vigour displayed by the Irish MPs in their opposition to the Coercion Bill, as well as the outrage aroused by the expulsions, helped to unify and strengthen the Irish Parliamentary Party and increased the personal prestige and authority of its leader. This was emphasised by Parnell's deliberate refusal to support a 'No Rent' campaign, or to authorise the withdrawal of the Irish Party from the House of Commons, in response to the militants' demands in protest at the government's repressive policies.

The Second Land Act 1881

Coercion was followed a few months later by Gladstone's Second Land Act, which introduced the 'Three Fs':

- 'Fair Rents' for tenants, which were to be fixed for fifteen years by Land Courts.
- 'Fixity of Tenure' throughout Ireland, which meant that tenants could not be evicted providing they paid their rents.
- 'Free Sale', which was the recognition of the tenant's 'interest' in his holding and his right to compensation when he relinquished it.

In addition, the government again included a land-purchase scheme. This time it was rather more favourable to the tenant since it raised the State's proportion of the purchase price from around 60 per cent to around 75 per cent.

 **KEY TERM**

Guillotine A parliamentary procedure whereby debate on specific clauses of a bill could be terminated.

Despite his masterly performance in pushing the complicated Land Bill through the Commons in the summer of 1881 (followed by the agreement of the Lords), recent historians have argued that Gladstone again failed to face up to the economic realities of rural Ireland. In the west of Ireland in particular, it was the lack of cultivable land rather than the problem of rents that was the fundamental problem for the smallholders, hence the emphasis on land reclamation and improvement by some land reformers.

But the Second Land Act has been described as 'less an economic policy than … a political stroke'. Gladstone's intention was both to destroy the appeal of the Land League and the excuse for violence by granting the tenants their major demands. To a large extent he succeeded, thanks to the work of the Land Courts, which, it soon became clear, intended to set genuinely fair rents. Because of their decisions, over the next few years, a twenty per cent reduction in rents gradually occurred. This harsh economic fact, together with their rapidly declining morale as a result of their general unpopularity, finally led more of the landlord class in Ireland to consider seriously selling off their estates, although the land-purchase clauses of the Second Land Act were still regarded as insufficiently generous by most tenants to induce them to consider buying their holdings. Within the Liberal Party, the Second Land Act aroused further concern among the Whig aristocrats about Gladstone's radicalism on landowners' rights, while radicals and nonconformists – often one and the same – continued to protest over the lack of new social reforms and Anglican disestablishment in England and Wales. Gladstone's president of the Board of Trade, Joseph Chamberlain, was the leading radical in the government, and his personal ambitions and political opposition to the direction Gladstone was taking over Ireland would eventually prove critical.

Parnell's arrest

The passage of the Second Land Act presented Parnell with a real dilemma. As Irish leader he had to maintain the support of both the militants and the moderates inside his own party and within the wider Irish communities in the UK and USA. If he supported the Land Act he would be denounced by the militants for currying favour with the Liberals and abandoning the struggle for fundamental land reform; if he opposed it, he might lose the support of the moderates and antagonise those tenants who saw tangible benefits in the Act. Parnell therefore played for time: he criticised aspects of the Act (such as the exclusion of tenants in arrears from its provisions) without absolutely rejecting it, but refused to cooperate with the working of the Land Courts. However, Parnell was soon rescued from his dilemma by the obtuseness of the government.

In October 1881, Gladstone warned Parnell and the leaders of the Land League in a public speech that continued violence would not be tolerated: 'If … there is to be fought a final conflict in Ireland between law on the one side and sheer lawlessness on the other … then I say … the resources of civilisation are not yet exhausted.' Parnell replied by denouncing the Liberal leader as 'a masquerading knight errant, the pretending champion of the rights of every other nation except those of the Irish nation'. Shortly afterwards, on the grounds that Parnell was deliberately wrecking the working of the Land Act, Forster had him arrested and imprisoned in Kilmainham Gaol in Dublin. It was, as Parnell himself admitted, the best thing that could have happened to him. It switched attention from his indecisiveness to the hard-line attitude of Gladstone and Forster, and for all nationalist Irishmen it turned Parnell into a martyr for the cause. It also gave him time to reflect on the changing character of the 'Irish question', especially as his own imprisonment was soon followed by the banning of the Land League. 'Politically', he wrote to his mistress, Mrs Katharine O'Shea, 'it is a fortunate thing for me that I have been arrested, as the [national] movement is breaking fast and all will be quiet in a few months when I shall be released.'

The Kilmainham Treaty 1882

Paradoxically, Parnell's arrest was the prelude to better relations between the Irish leader and the British government. Gladstone realised that the imprisonment of Parnell solved nothing: violence inevitably worsened rather than improved during his six-month incarceration. Only the 'uncrowned King of Ireland', it appeared, could control the level of law and order in his domain. Parnell on his side accepted that the situation in Ireland had now changed dramatically. The Land Act had defeated the Land League. Significantly, the tenants had earlier ignored the League's call for a 'No Rents' campaign, and were now busily using the new Land Courts to get their rents reduced legally. The Land War was effectively grinding to a halt. In these circumstances might it not be better for the cause of Irish nationalism to recognise facts and come to terms with the dominant Liberal Party? For Parnell this would also mean that he could reassert his essential role as the leader of a constitutional Irish Party, committed to obtaining Home Rule through the parliamentary process. By the early months of 1882, Parnell also had personal reasons for wishing to be released from prison, since Kitty O'Shea was pregnant with their first child and he wished to be with her.

Thus, all the conditions were present for an agreement between Gladstone and Parnell. With Joseph Chamberlain, the outstanding Radical in the government, and Captain O'Shea (Katharine's husband!) acting as intermediaries, what became known as the 'Kilmainham Treaty' was rapidly concluded in April 1882. By its terms (these were verbal – nothing was actually written down), Gladstone agreed to release Parnell and other Land League detainees, relax the Coercion Act, and also amend the Land Act so as to help those in arrears with their rent. In turn, Parnell agreed to use his influence against violence and to accept and support the carrying out of the recent Land Act, and especially the work of the Land Courts. He also agreed, if the government carried out its side of the bargain, 'to cooperate cordially for the future with the Liberal Party in forwarding Liberal principles and measures of general reform'. Forster's response to the Kilmainham Treaty, concluded without his knowledge or agreement,

SOURCE C

What point is the cartoon in Source C making about Irish nationalist violence?

"THE HIDDEN HAND."

This cartoon, 'The Hidden Hand', from 1883 shows an Irish anarchist, armed with knife and pistol, surreptitiously accepting a bag of gold. This is a reference to the murder of the new chief secretary for Ireland and his colleague, who died after being attacked in Dublin's Phoenix Park. Published in *Punch*, 3 March 1883.

was to resign. It was Parnell who called the agreement a 'Treaty', a term which implied a written agreement between two equal parties. To the Irish, this gave him and Ireland an implied status that Gladstone had never intended.

The Phoenix Park murders

The new accord between Gladstone and Parnell was shaken by the brutal murder of Lord Frederick Cavendish, who had been moved from his position as financial secretary to the Treasury to replace Forster as Irish secretary. Cavendish was Gladstone's nephew by marriage as well as formerly his private secretary, and their relationship was closer to father and son than uncle and nephew. He was murdered along with T.H. Burke, the permanent under-secretary at the Irish Office, in Phoenix Park, Dublin, on 6 May, by an Irish revolutionary terrorist group known as the **Irish National Invincibles**. They had plotted several times without success to kill Forster. Burke was now the intended target; he was a Catholic Irishman and, therefore, in the eyes of the attackers, a traitor. The assassins had no idea who Cavendish was but bravely he tried to defend Burke using only his umbrella. He died along with Burke – stabbed to death with the surgical knives carried by their attackers. The shock and horror displayed by Parnell in response to the murders created a good impression in the House of Commons and he even expressed an intention to resign, although how serious he was about this is open to doubt.

The Phoenix Park murders were followed by a general reaction against political violence in the UK and, to a lesser extent, the USA. The new Irish secretary, G.O. Trevelyan, unsurprisingly felt compelled to impose new security measures. Ultimately, five of the conspirators were hanged, having been denounced by two of their comrades who gave evidence against them. Others less directly involved received long prison sentences. Several of the main leaders escaped to the United States. The Kilmainham Treaty looked worthless in so far as Parnell clearly could not deliver an end to violence from extremists. The events of 1882 drove home to Parnell and all political observers the basic fact that the agrarian struggle belonged to the past and had been superseded by the need for a political solution. Once again, the fate of Ireland was centred on the House of Commons, but the shadow of the Phoenix Park murders cast a long shadow over future attempts to resolve the Irish question.

 **KEY TERM**

Irish National Invincibles
A terrorist splinter group of the Irish Republican Brotherhood usually known simply as 'the Invincibles'.

Summary diagram: Gladstone and Irish reform 1868–82

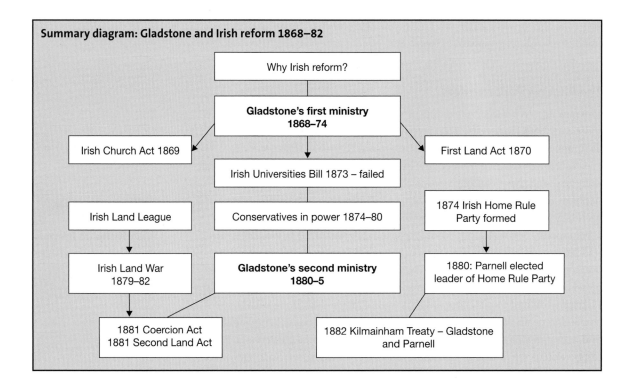

Chapter summary

Gladstone's record as a reformer of conditions in Ireland is mixed at best. He deserves credit for tackling the anomalous and provocative position of the corrupt and intolerant Irish Anglican Church's domination of Ireland, in which its adherents were very much a minority. His Land Act of 1870 probably did more harm than good, although Gladstone was breaking new ground by even attempting to regulate the relationship between landlords and tenants. His Second Land Act was quite a different matter. It effectively solved the land question. Critically, however, it came at a time when sensible concessions could easily be construed as weakness in the face of violence. Gladstone saw Ireland's problems almost entirely in terms of how they reflected on Britain. He believed that the continual crises in Ireland and the oppressive way in which Ireland was governed were a moral reproach to Britain, which he saw as having a duty to set an example of enlightened government to the world. He visited Ireland only once, for three weeks in the autumn of 1877. He stayed in County Wicklow and Dublin enjoying the hospitality of aristocratic families, although his diary records that he visited 'farms and cottages'. Apart from that, he relied on extensively reading academic studies of different aspects of Irish history and life from his extensive library.

Refresher questions

Use these questions to remind yourself of the key material covered in this chapter.

1 Why did Gladstone focus so much on reforming Ireland when he came to power in 1868?

2 With what success did Gladstone introduce a series of reforms to remedy Irish grievances and ensure the stability of the Union?

3 What factors led to the growth of the Home Rule movement in Ireland?

4 In what ways did Gladstone face a different set of circumstances in Ireland when he returned to power in 1880?

5 What factors led to the formation of the Land League?

6 How did the activities of the Land League help Parnell's rise?

7 What effect did the Coercion Act have on Parnell and his party?

8 How did the Second Land Act lead to the demise of the Land League?

9 Why were Gladstone and Parnell able to reach an agreement by 1882?

10 Was Gladstone more or less effective as a reformer in Ireland in 1880–2 as compared to 1868–74?

Question practice

ESSAY QUESTIONS

1 'Gladstone failed completely in his mission to pacify Ireland in the years 1868–82.' Assess the validity of this verdict.

2 To what extent were Gladstone's Irish reforms 1868–82 a case of 'too little, too late'?

3 'It was the pressure of Irish nationalism, rather than Gladstone's sense of a "mission" that did most to bring about reform in Ireland in the period 1868–82.' Assess the validity of this verdict.

SOURCE ANALYSIS QUESTION

1 Assess the value of Source 1 (page 112) for revealing the tactics of the Irish Land League and the attitude of the British government towards the situation in Ireland. Explain your answer, using the source, the information given about its origin and your own knowledge about the historical context.

SOURCE I

From the manifesto of the Irish Land League, 18 October 1881.

NO RENT MANIFESTO

'FELLOW-CITIZENS: The hour to try your souls and to redeem your pledges has arrived. The executive of the National Land League, forced to abandon its policy of testing the Land act, feels bound to advise the tenant farmers of Ireland from this day forth to pay no rents under any circumstances to their landlords until Government relinquishes the existing system of terrorism and restores the constitutional rights of the people. Do not be daunted by the removal of your leaders. Do not let yourselves be intimidated by threats of military violence. It is as lawful to refuse to pay rents as it is to receive them. Against the passive resistance of the entire population military power has no weapon. Funds will be poured out unstintedly for the support of all who may endure eviction in the course of the struggle. Our exiled brothers in America may be relied upon to contribute, if necessary, as many millions of money as they have contributed thousands to starve out landlordism and bring English tyranny to its knees. You have only to show that you are not unworthy of their boundless sacrifices. One more crowning struggle for your land, your homes, your lives – a struggle in which you have all the memories of your race, all the hopes of your kindred and all the sacrifices of your imprisoned brothers.

Stand together in face of the brutal,
cowardly enemies of your race!

One more struggle in which you have the hope of happy homes and national freedom to inspire you, one more heroic effort to destroy landlordism, and the system which was and is the curse of your race will have disappeared forever. Stand together in face of the brutal, cowardly enemies of your race! Pay no rent under any pretext! Stand passively, firmly, fearlessly by, while the armies of England may be engaged in their hopeless struggle against the spirit which their weapons cannot touch, and the Government, with its bayonets, will learn in a single Winter how powerless are armed forces against the will of a united, determined, and self-reliant nation.

[signed] Charles Stewart Parnell. Thomas Brennan. A.J. Kettle. Thomas Sexton. Michael Davitt. Patrick Eagan. John Dillon.

CHAPTER 6

Gladstone, Parnell and Home Rule

Two Home Rule Bills were introduced by Gladstone, first in 1886 and then in 1893. Both of them failed to secure acceptance by parliament. You need to understand the reasons for both their introduction and their failure. This will involve examining the policies and motives of Gladstone, as well as appreciating the realities of political power in Britain during this period. The other key figure is Parnell, and his importance as a parliamentarian and nationalist. This chapter will consider these issues through the following themes:

★ Parnell and the Irish Parliamentary Party 1882–5

★ The First Home Rule Bill 1886

★ The fall of Parnell

★ The Second Home Rule Bill 1893

Key dates

1882	Oct.	Formation of the National League
1884	Dec.	Third Parliamentary Reform Act passed – standardising the voting qualifications throughout the UK
1885	June	Parnell supported Conservatives: Gladstone resigned
		Conservatives in power under Lord Salisbury
	Nov.	General election: Irish Party won 86 seats and held the balance of power
	Dec.	Herbert Gladstone flew the 'Hawarden kite'
1886	Jan.	Parnell supported Liberals: Gladstone formed his third ministry
1886	April	First Home Rule Bill introduced – defeated in the Commons
1889	Dec.	Captain O'Shea sued for divorce, citing Parnell as co-respondent
1890	Nov.	Divorce granted, Gladstone opposed Parnell as Irish leader
	Dec.	Irish Party split over leadership
1891	Oct.	Death of Parnell
1892	July	General election: Gladstone formed fourth ministry, with Irish support
1893	Sept.	Second Irish Home Rule Bill passed by Commons but rejected by Lords

Parnell and the Irish Parliamentary Party 1882–5

▶ *How did Parnell come to dominate the party?*

After the Kilmainham Treaty (see page 107), Parnell was determined to turn the Home Rule group in the House of Commons into a powerful, unified Irish Party, subject completely to his personal authority – a party which could really make its weight felt in British politics. At the same time, he intended to make the Irish Parliamentary Party the dominant nationalist organisation in Ireland.

The National League

The latter aim was forwarded by the creation of the National League in October 1882. Unlike the Land League (which had not survived its banning by the British authorities, see page 101), the National League was essentially a political organisation; its first aim was 'national self-government', and it intended to win support among all classes of Irish society and not just the farmers. The National League's central organisation was dominated by Parnell and his followers, and the League became in effect the electoral arm of the Irish Parliamentary Party. It soon possessed over 1000 branches throughout Ireland. The League's electoral role was helped enormously by the passage of the Third Reform Act of 1884. This increasing identification between the Irish Parliamentary Party and the cause of Irish nationalism was reflected – after years of mutual suspicion – by the unofficial alliance between the Irish Catholic Church leaders and Parnell in 1885–6. The Church now came out definitely in support of Home Rule, and in return Parnell was prepared to go along with the Church's policies on education, although relations between the two sides were never very close.

Third Reform Act of 1884

This was the first reform of voting qualifications to deal with the whole of the UK as a single entity rather than in separate units of England and Wales, Scotland, and Ireland. The effect was to standardise voting qualifications across the UK in both county and borough seats. This had a tremendous impact in Ireland, where the percentage of adult males with the right to vote was far behind the rest of the UK: the Irish electorate quadrupled. Following this Act, it is estimated that around 70 per cent of adult males in England and Wales had the vote compared to 60 per cent in Scotland and 50 per cent in Ireland. So Ireland still lagged behind, but the gap had been substantially reduced. By granting the vote to the rural householders within the UK, the Act enabled the Irish Party to dominate the county vote throughout Ireland, outside Protestant Ulster.

Parnell's influence

As far as the Irish Party at Westminster was concerned, Parnell now imposed greater discipline and centralisation, a task which was made somewhat easier by the increasingly homogeneous, middle-class character of the party's membership, compared with the days of Isaac Butt. Parliamentary candidates were now chosen in practice by the party's leadership, and, if elected, they were required to sign a 'pledge' that they would act and vote only with the Irish Parliamentary Party. If they failed to do so, they would resign.

By the mid-1880s, therefore, Parnell completely dominated the Irish Party. Acknowledged by all members as 'the Chief', his power was, as one of his protégés later admitted, 'irresponsible and more or less despotic'. Parnell's personal traits of pride, coldness and arrogance had hardened over the years, and he was now viewed by his followers with a mixture of awe, respect and something akin almost to fear. His attitude towards them was, in the words of Paul Bew in his 1980 biography, 'comparable to that of a feudal magnate towards his band of retainers: a curious blend of hauteur, autocracy and condescension'. In a subsequent 2011 biography, Bew portrays Parnell as the greatest enigma in Irish political history. Yet, whatever the Chief's personal faults, by 1885 his efforts on behalf of the Irish Parliamentary Party and the national cause generally seemed to have been extraordinarily successful. Now he really was 'the uncrowned King of Ireland', and was also acknowledged by everyone as an outstanding parliamentary leader. He was courted by both Liberals and Conservatives, since both groups recognised that his Irish Party might well hold the balance of power in the Commons after the next general election, due in 1885.

The first move was made by Joseph Chamberlain, who was anxious to ensure not only a Liberal government after the election but also the strengthening of his own personal position within the Liberal leadership. In order to obtain Parnell's support, he proposed to him a 'Central Board' scheme for Ireland which would have given the Irish wide-ranging powers of internal control: in Chamberlain's words, 'the widest possible self-government … consistent with the integrity of the Empire'. Chamberlain conceived this as an alternative to Home Rule; but on those terms it had no possible chance of being accepted by Parnell. The scheme was in any case rejected by the Cabinet, despite Gladstone's support. Parnell's speeches meanwhile were making it clear that Home Rule was the minimum requirement to satisfy Ireland's sense of nationality and he frequently seemed to suggest that it might not be enough or would only be the start of a road towards complete independence.

In what way do Parnell's comments in Source A undermine the case for Home Rule?

SOURCE A

From a speech by Parnell in January 1885, quoted in Alan O'Day, *Irish Home Rule, 1867–1921*, Manchester University Press, 1998, p. 96.

I do not know how this great question will eventually be settled. I do not know whether England will be wise in time, and concede to constitutional arguments and methods the restitution of that which was stolen from us towards the close of the last century ... We cannot ask for less than the restitution of Grattan's Parliament ... But no man has a right to fix the boundary to the march of a nation. No man has a right to say to his country, 'thus far shalt thou go and no farther'.

Parnell and the Tories

Parnell now drew nearer to the Tories, hoping to get more from a Conservative government than from the Liberals. Nor was Parnell in principle opposed to a Conservative settlement of Ireland. As the Radical Henry Labouchère correctly said, 'Home Rule apart, he was himself a Tory'. On 9 June 1885, therefore, the Irish Party switched their votes from Liberals to Conservatives; and as a result of numerous Liberal abstentions – a reflection of growing divisions within the party – Gladstone was outvoted and resigned. Lord Salisbury then formed a Conservative caretaker government until the results of the forthcoming general election were known.

The new government showed its good intentions by dropping coercion, and passing the Ashbourne Act – the first really effective land purchase scheme for Ireland, since it provided for 100 per cent State loans to tenants at a low rate of interest. For the moment, therefore, Parnell stood by the Tories, and, since Gladstone refused to commit himself publicly over Home Rule, in the general election in November 1885 he called on the Irish voters in Great Britain to vote Conservative. Parnell demanded Home Rule – with powers as wide as possible for an Irish parliament – but insisted that it did not mean a complete separation from Great Britain.

The 1885 general election

In the election, the full extent of the impact in Ireland of the Third Reform Act was clearly seen. The Irish Parliamentary Party won every seat in Ireland south of eastern Ulster (with the exception of Trinity College, Dublin), and ended up with 86 seats. The Liberals won 335 seats and the Conservatives 249; however, fifteen of the Liberal MPs had been elected as 'Independent Liberals' and their attitude to Gladstone's government was potentially unclear. The real victor in the election was Parnell, who had utterly destroyed the power of the Liberal Party in Ireland. The result meant that neither the Liberals nor the Conservatives could govern with complete confidence without his support. If he chose Gladstone, the Liberals would have a big majority; if he chose Salisbury, the Conservatives could form a government but it would struggle to maintain majorities. Which of them he now decided to back would depend on the attitude of Salisbury and Gladstone towards Home Rule. The political situation was therefore highly confused when parliament reassembled in December 1885.

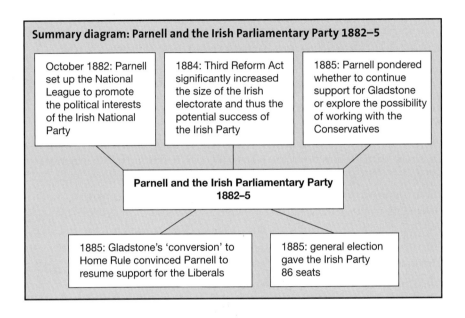

Summary diagram: Parnell and the Irish Parliamentary Party 1882–5

October 1882: Parnell set up the National League to promote the political interests of the Irish National Party

1884: Third Reform Act significantly increased the size of the Irish electorate and thus the potential success of the Irish Party

1885: Parnell pondered whether to continue support for Gladstone or explore the possibility of working with the Conservatives

Parnell and the Irish Parliamentary Party 1882–5

1885: Gladstone's 'conversion' to Home Rule convinced Parnell to resume support for the Liberals

1885: general election gave the Irish Party 86 seats

② The First Home Rule Bill 1886

▶ *What was the impact of the First Home Rule Bill?*

Neither during the election campaign itself nor in its immediate aftermath would Gladstone commit himself publicly over Home Rule. Nevertheless, during the summer months of 1885, while brooding at home at Hawarden Castle on the realities of the Irish problem, he appears to have become convinced that Home Rule was the only solution. He now believed, despite his earlier optimism, that his programme of religious and agrarian reform had failed to reconcile the Irish to the continuance of English rule; and further reform was bound to be just as unsuccessful. Moreover, he became convinced of the reality of Irish nationalism. How then on moral grounds could he oppose what a majority of the Irish people wanted? Indeed, Gladstone came to believe that it was his obligation to lead a great moral crusade on behalf of the Irish people which would culminate in Home Rule and the solution of the Irish problem. Home Rule, he said, was based on 'the first principles of religion'.

During the run-up to the election in November 1885, however, Gladstone kept quiet about his conversion to Home Rule. Why was this? He seems to have been moved by several considerations:

- In the first place, if he spoke out publicly in favour of Home Rule, the Liberal Party would inevitably be divided over the issue.
- In addition, he could be accused of counterbidding for the Irish vote (a charge to which he was particularly sensitive).
- Also, as J.L. Hammond argued in the 1930s in his sympathetic study of Gladstone's Irish policy, the Liberal leader believed, sincerely if naively, in achieving a non-party approach to the Irish problem.

The Conservatives had come into power in June 1885 as a result of Parnell's conviction that he could get more from them than from the Liberals. Gladstone realised the enormous advantages of a Home Rule policy introduced by Lord Salisbury, with his mastery of the House of Lords, backed up by the majority of Liberals. 'Every step he took between June 1885 and January 1886', wrote Hammond, 'was a deliberate effort to obtain a solution by passionless co-operation among the leading statesmen.' It was these considerations that led Gladstone to keep silent, even during the election campaign at the end of 1885 effectively refusing to contest Irish support for the Conservative Party. The strategy was fundamentally flawed since Salisbury had no intention whatever of agreeing to Home Rule. The outcome of the election was a disappointment for Gladstone in so far as it failed to provide either of the English parties with a majority independent of the Irish members. On the other hand, the fact that the Irish Party won every seat in southern Ireland (bar one) clinched his support for Home Rule.

'I consider that Ireland has now spoken', Gladstone wrote to Lord Hartington on 17 December, 'and that an effort ought to be made by the government without delay to meet her demands for the management by an Irish legislative body of Irish as distinct from imperial affairs. Only a government can do it, and a Tory government can do it more easily and safely than any other.'

Gladstone's third ministry 1886

Gladstone's hope, however, was utterly destroyed by the publication in the press on the very same day of the news of his support for Home Rule, as a result of the deliberate action of his son. Herbert Gladstone believed that Chamberlain and his Radical friends were planning to take over the Liberal Party, and the only way to forestall them was by encouraging Parnell to join with the Liberals and oust the Conservatives, and thus force his father to re-enter the political arena. Herbert Gladstone's action in 'flying the Hawarden kite' (as it was dubbed) was successful. Since it soon became clear that Lord Salisbury had no intention of supporting Home Rule, on 26 January 1886 the Irish deliberately supported a Liberal resolution on land reform, and the Conservatives were defeated by 331 votes to 252, although 76 Liberals abstained, and a few, led by Lord Hartington, actually voted with the government. The Liberal Party was clearly very divided. Nevertheless, Gladstone now became prime minister for the third time, at the age of 77, committed to the introduction of Home Rule.

These events led John Vincent and A.B. Cooke, in their major study of English parliamentary politics in 1885–6, *The Governing Passion* (1974), to argue that, for Gladstone, 'Ireland was viewed in a context of deep party calculation'. They suggest that Gladstone's support for Home Rule was due to opportunism rather than conviction: it was primarily an attempt to reunite the Liberal Party under his own leadership and thus put paid to the ambitions of Joseph Chamberlain. 'The Home Rule Bill', they wrote, 'was meant to unite the Liberal Party by committing it to the principle of Home Rule and to prepare it for further protracted struggle in which there would be only one possible leader.' However, although we can accept that Gladstone was inevitably concerned with the future of the Liberal Party in 1885–6, there is abundant evidence that he was committed to Home Rule before the general election of November 1885; and, more recently, a number of historians have argued powerfully that it is impossible to understand Gladstone's politics without constant reference to his moral and religious outlook.

Following his return to power in January 1886, Gladstone, determined 'to grasp the Irish nettle', proceeded with a Home Rule Bill swiftly and boldly. Earlier he had hoped to have time to educate the electorate and his party; now he believed, incorrectly as it turned out, that the potentially revolutionary situation developing in Ireland brooked no delay. In that sense he was, in Lord Randolph Churchill's words, 'an old man in a hurry'. The task was undertaken in the worst possible circumstances since nearly all his colleagues, as well as Parnell, had been left completely in the dark about his change of attitude. Hartington and most of the more conservative-minded 'Whigs' refused to join the government. Other Liberals, such as Chamberlain and Trevelyan, despite their doubts, joined but later resigned when the details of the Home Rule Bill became known. Gladstone refused to consult with anyone over the proposals and even his Cabinet did not see them until shortly before they were to be presented to the House of Commons.

The Home Rule proposals 1886

Gladstone finally presented his proposals to his Cabinet in March 1886. They consisted of two closely related bills which aimed to solve the political and the social problems of Ireland together.

The first bill proposed the establishment of Irish Home Rule on the following basis:

- An Irish 'Assembly' would be created to take over internal affairs in Ireland; Gladstone deliberately did not use the term 'parliament' because he did not want to imply that the union was being repealed and the old Irish parliament of the eighteenth century restored.

- The Assembly would consist of two 'Orders' which could meet either together or separately.
- The first Order was to consist of the 28 Irish peers traditionally elected by all Irish peers to sit in the House of Lords plus 75 members elected by substantial property owners and with a very high property qualification to be eligible for election. This Order could delay the passage of laws for three years.
- The second Order would consist of 204 members elected from the existing Irish constituencies.
- There would be no Irish MPs in the Westminster parliament.
- Britain would still retain control over issues of war, peace, national defence, treaties with other countries, trade and currency, and – initially – the Royal Irish Constabulary.
- From the Assembly would be drawn an Irish 'Executive' (or government), which was to be responsible to the Assembly for internal affairs and to the British government for other matters.
- Royal authority (in effect that of the British government) would continue to be exercised by the lord-lieutenant of Ireland.
- Ireland would contribute one-fifteenth to the Imperial Treasury, but would receive back its share of customs revenue and income tax.

The second bill consisted of a land purchase scheme by which the British Treasury would buy out the landlords at a cost of some £50 million. Gladstone believed this was essential in order to prevent the new Irish legislature being burdened at the outset with the problems of the Irish land system. He also hoped that this would lead eventually to the former landlord class reasserting its influence in the social and political affairs of Ireland – a view with which Parnell was sympathetic.

Gladstone presented his Home Rule Bill to the House of Commons on 8 April 1886 in a great three-and-a-half hour speech. The Land Purchase Bill was soon abandoned when it became apparent that it was unpopular with all sections of opinion in the House, although Gladstone hoped to reintroduce it later. The debates which followed centred therefore on the provisions concerning the government of Ireland. Gladstone explained in more detail the main reasons which had led him to adopt Home Rule, and the solutions he proposed. He touched briefly and dismissively on the problem of objections from Ulster, which, he made clear, he did not take very seriously. He ended his speech with an appeal to the House of Commons, asserting that his bill represented probably the last chance for solving the Irish question peacefully:

SOURCE B

From Gladstone's speech in the Commons 8 April 1886, quoted in W.E. Gladstone, *Speeches on the Irish Question in 1886*, Andrew Elliot, 1886, p. 14.

While I think it is right to modify the Union in some particulars, we are not about to propose its repeal … The fault of the administrative system of Ireland … is simply this – that its spring and source of action … is English and not Irish … what we seek is the settlement of that question; and we think we find that settlement in the establishment … of a legislative body sitting in Dublin for the conduct of both legislation and administration under the conditions … defining Irish as distinct from Imperial affairs … We stand face to face with what is termed Irish nationality which vents itself in the demand for local autonomy … Is that an evil in itself? … I hold that it is not … The Irishman is profoundly Irish, but it does not follow that because his local patriotism is keen he is incapable of Imperial patriotism … Think, I beseech you; think well, think wisely, think not for the moment, but for the years that are to come before you reject this bill.

> **?** What assumption is Gladstone making about the Irish reaction to Home Rule in Source B?

Reaction to the bill

The bulk of the members of the parliamentary Liberal Party supported Gladstone. This was not because they accepted his arguments over Irish nationality or had much enthusiasm for Irish self-government, but out of loyalty to the 'Grand Old Man' and because they could see no alternative to Home Rule but perpetual coercion – and they no longer had any stomach for that. Parnell had doubts about some of the details, particularly the financial provisions, which he believed were unfair to Ireland, but he supported the Home Rule Bill. 'I accept the Bill', he pronounced in the House of Commons, 'as a final settlement of our national question and I believe the Irish people will accept it as such.'

The bill was bitterly attacked by the Conservatives. Many leading Liberals were also opposed, from both wings of the party. Lord Hartington represented the conservative-minded Whig aristocrats while Joseph Chamberlain spoke from a radical viewpoint. Although there was some crude anti-Irish feeling displayed in the debates, many of the points made against the bill were reasoned and cogent. Three major criticisms were directed against Gladstone's proposals:

- First, it was argued that Irish self-government would lead inevitably to complete separation and therefore the break-up of the UK, especially as Ireland was not to be represented at Westminster.
- Second, critics questioned whether the members of the future Irish legislature could be trusted to protect even-handedly the lives and property of all Irishmen, and especially Protestants, when many of those MPs would inevitably be nationalists who had been associated with illegality and agitation in the past.
- Third, it was argued that Irish nationality and unity (the rock on which Gladstone appeared to rest his case) could not really be said to exist when all classes in Protestant Ulster were so violently against Home Rule.

Towards the end of the debates, on 27 May, Gladstone called a meeting of his supporters in the parliamentary Liberal Party to rally support. Hartington and Chamberlain refused to attend. In the meeting, Gladstone indicated that he might possibly reconsider the exclusion of the Irish MPs from Westminster but he gave no commitment. His attitude was angry and uncompromising. Four days later, Chamberlain called a meeting of the Liberal anti-Home Rulers and they decided to vote against the bill. On 8 June 1886, when the vote was finally taken on the Second Reading of the Home Rule Bill, 93 Liberals voted against, and it was defeated by 343 votes to 313.

SOURCE C

? How does Source C illustrate the significance of the Home Rule Bill in Gladstone's defeat?

'The Finish', published in *Punch*, 1886. Lord Salisbury, the Leader in the Lords of the Conservative Party, comes through the tape a good head in front of the Liberal prime minister, Gladstone.

The second general election of 1886

Parliament was then dissolved and the parties squared up for the second general election within a year. The Conservatives, united and confident, fought a vigorous campaign and relied heavily on the anti-Irish sentiments of the majority of the English voters. They also worked effectively to produce a unionist victory by making sure that the anti-Home Rule 'Liberal Unionists', as they were now called, were unopposed by Tory candidates. The new Liberal Unionist Party was composed of an unlikely alliance of those Radicals who supported Chamberlain's position and the Whig Liberals headed by Lord Hartington. Although these two elements had been effectively on opposite wings of the Liberal Party, they agreed that resisting Home Rule in Ireland transcended their other differences.

The Liberal Party was now weak and divided. It had lost some of its most able leaders. During the election campaign it relied mainly on Gladstone's prestige. This still had credibility in the 'Celtic fringe' (Wales and Scotland) where the Liberals did reasonably well. The Irish Party was inevitably tied to the Liberals as the only English party now committed to Home Rule. Yet the outcome of the election in the summer of 1886 was a resounding victory for the Unionists. They won 394 seats (316 Conservatives, 78 Liberal Unionists); the Gladstonian Liberals were reduced to 191 MPs, backed up by the Irish Party of 85 members. Clearly, for the moment, Home Rule was a lost cause: Ireland – in Lord Salisbury's phrase – was to face nearly twenty years of 'resolute government' under the Unionists.

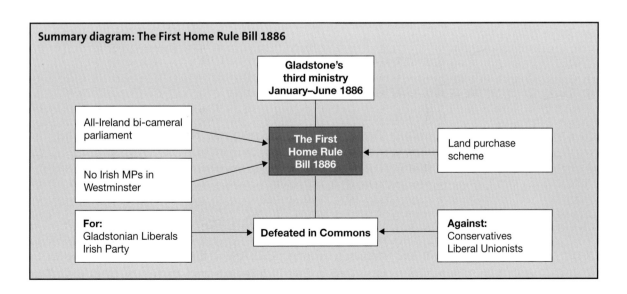

Summary diagram: The First Home Rule Bill 1886

The fall of Parnell

▶ *What led to Parnell's political eclipse?*

After the general election of 1886, the Irish Parliamentary Party still dominated the representation of Ireland outside Protestant Ulster, and Parnell remained determined to stick to the constitutional path in securing Home Rule. This meant, he believed, maintaining the alliance with the Liberal Party which, under its aged and obstinate leader, was still committed to the same ideal. Parnell therefore refused to support the new phase of agrarian agitation in Ireland known as the 'Plan of Campaign', which aimed at reducing rents still further by collective action by the tenants. Both the Liberals and the Irish were at one, however, in condemning the harsh, coercive measures introduced by the new Conservative Irish secretary, A.J. Balfour, in 1887, in order to break the power of the Campaign.

'Parnellism and Crime'

That same year, *The Times* published a damaging series of articles, 'Parnellism and Crime', which accused the Irish leader of complicity in violence in Ireland, and, in particular, of approval of the Phoenix Park murders. In 1889, however, a judicial investigation revealed that the articles were based on forged letters. The editor of *The Times*, who had paid £2500 for the letters, had believed them genuine because he wanted them to be. The forger blew his brains out in a Madrid hotel. The ignominious collapse of the case against Parnell led to a wave of public sympathy for the Irishman. In December 1889, Gladstone, in a gesture of support, invited him to visit Hawarden Castle. Just days after his visit, however, his career began to unravel. Within a year, Parnell's personal reputation and his political career were in ruins.

The O'Shea divorce

In the same month as Parnell's visit to Harwarden, Captain O'Shea sued his wife for divorce, naming Parnell as co-respondent on the grounds of her adultery with him. The case came to court in November 1890. Katharine O'Shea and Parnell offered no defence other than stating that Captain O'Shea had known of their relationship for many years and had not objected. This did not convince the court and O'Shea was granted his divorce. He was also awarded custody of Katharine's two surviving daughters, born in 1883 and 1884, both of whom had been fathered by Parnell (their first daughter, born in 1882, had died shortly after her birth). At first, the divorce seemed to have no political repercussions, and the Irish Parliamentary Party stood by its leader. But Gladstone soon found himself under pressure from the powerful nonconformist element in the Liberal Party, who refused to accept alliance with a party whose leader was a confessed adulterer. Gladstone felt he therefore had no alternative but to urge the Irish to repudiate Parnell as their leader if the alliance – and therefore the cause of Home Rule – was to be maintained. In a letter to Justin McCarthy (Parnell's second-in-command) he spelled out the position:

SOURCE D

From a letter by Gladstone to Parnell's second-in-command Justin McCarthy, quoted in R. Barry O'Brien, *The Life of Charles Stewart Parnell*, Harper & Brothers, 1898, p. 248.

The conclusion at which … I had myself arrived … was that notwithstanding the splendid services rendered by Mr. Parnell to his country, his continuance at the present moment in the leadership would be productive of consequences disastrous in the highest degree to the cause of Ireland … the continuance I speak of would not only place many hearty and effective friends of the Irish cause in a position of great embarrassment, but would render my retention of the leadership of the Liberal Party, based as it has been mainly upon the prosecution of the Irish cause, almost a nullity.

Why did Gladstone take such an uncompromising attitude to Parnell in Source D?

When this letter was eventually published in the press at the end of November, Parnell reacted furiously. He not only refused to resign the leadership – even temporarily – but in an extraordinary manifesto to the Irish people attacked Gladstone personally, denounced the Liberal alliance and reaffirmed the independence of the Irish Party. Thus, he appeared to throw overboard the whole political strategy he had cultivated so assiduously over the previous five years. Irish Nationalist MPs were now faced with a cruel dilemma: if they stood by Parnell they would lose Liberal support and, apparently, any further possibility of Home Rule. They had to choose, as one contemporary put it, 'between Parnell and Parnellite principles'. At the historic meeting of the Irish Parliamentary Party at the House of Commons on 1 December 1890, the party split: 45 MPs (led by McCarthy) repudiated Parnell's leadership, 37 supported him. As Timothy Healy, one of Parnell's bitterest opponents, insisted: 'I say that the necessities of Ireland are paramount'. A few days later – another nail in Parnell's coffin – the leaders of the Irish Catholic clergy called on the Irish people to repudiate him.

Parnell reacted to his critics with characteristic defiance. In the summer of 1891 he fought one last campaign in Ireland at a series of by-elections. His language became more and more extreme and at times he even seemed to endorse violence in the pursuit of Irish freedom. In all these by-elections, however, the anti-Parnellites triumphed. Parnell's health had always been fragile and he was now ill and worn out. He died of stomach cancer on 6 October 1891 at Brighton in the arms of Katharine, whom he had married four months previously. He was only 45.

How valid is the assessment of Parnell in Source E?

SOURCE E

From Michael Davitt, *The Fall of Feudalism in Ireland*, Harper & Brothers, 1904, pp. 651–2.

Parnell's claim to greatness no Irish nationalist and few Irishmen will ever deny … Like all the world's historic characters, there were marked limitations to his greatness, not counting the final weakness which precipitated his fall … He was unlike all the leaders who had preceded him in his accomplishments, traits of character and personal idiosyncrasies … In fact he was a paradox in Irish leadership … bearing no resemblance of any kind to those who handed down to his time the fight for Irish nationhood … What, then, was the secret of his immense influence and popularity? He was above and before everything else a splendid fighter. He had attacked and beaten the enemies of Ireland in the citadel of their power – the British Parliament.

Parnell's achievements and failures

Charles Stewart Parnell was a controversial figure in his lifetime, and he has remained so ever since. Most historians are now agreed on the nature of his contribution to Anglo-Irish history. Although Parnell was associated with the Land League, and, at the height of his power, was regarded as the embodiment of Irish nationalism, he was pre-eminently a practical politician rather than an agrarian reformer or an agitator or even a romantic nationalist. In the political field his achievement was significant. He turned the question of Home Rule from a vague ideal into practical politics. He 'set it on its legs', as Gladstone said, by his belief that it must be worked for and could be achieved constitutionally through the British parliament by the exercise of political skill and judgement. Like Gladstone, however, he underestimated the enormous problems that surrounded the whole conception. In particular, he showed no understanding of, or sympathy with, the attitude of the Ulster Protestants, which was remarkable considering that he was one of them.

Parnell was also able to convince the majority of the Irish people that Home Rule was both a just and a feasible solution to the problem of Irish government. Moreover, it was his determination in pursuing a new political settlement for Ireland in the Commons – and his party's success in elections – that finally convinced Gladstone to adopt Home Rule as Liberal Party policy. By throwing the weight of the Irish Parliamentary Party on to the Liberal side in January 1886, Parnell assumed he was making the passage of Gladstone's First Home Rule Bill in the Commons a reasonable expectation. Both he and Gladstone completely failed to anticipate the scale of the Liberal revolt that followed.

One of Parnell's greatest achievements was his creation of a united, disciplined Irish Parliamentary Party backed up by an efficient electoral machine in Ireland itself. In some ways this was all the greater as an achievement in that Parnell was by no means an ideal party leader. He was ultra-sensitive to any form of criticism. He was arrogant and aloof. His attitude to some of his colleagues was often one of contempt. His frequent absences from parliamentary business to stay with Katharine O'Shea caused confusion for his colleagues as they often had no idea how to get in touch with him. All this helps to account for the reaction against him at the fateful party meeting on 1 December 1890. Had Parnell been a different character then Gladstone's rather arrogant demand to the Irish Party that Parnell be removed, might have provoked a sympathetic counter-reaction, but this did not happen.

The Irish Party under Parnell's leadership played a key role in British politics and in the history of the Irish question during the 1880s, largely as a result of his political skill and grasp of the workings of the British party system. After Parnell's death in 1891, the Irish Parliamentary Party was left divided and was only a shadow of its former self. Its problems were exacerbated by the defeat of the Second Home Rule Bill in 1893 and the subsequent domination of the Conservatives and Liberal Unionists working together. Nevertheless, the Irish Parliamentary Party survived. Although divided, it still won 81 seats in the 1892 general election and in 1895 it won 82 under the nominal but disputed leadership of McCarthy. Reunited under the leadership of John Redmond, in 1900, it would re-emerge as an important factor in British politics during the Liberal governments after 1906 (developments discussed further in Chapter 7).

 # The Second Home Rule Bill 1893

▶ *Why did Gladstone persist with, and ultimately fail to achieve, Home Rule?*

Despite grumblings from many party members anxious to free themselves from the Irish burden and turn their attention to social and economic reform, Gladstone remained firmly committed to Home Rule as his major objective. The Liberal Party, with its natural alternative leaders such as Chamberlain and Hartington gone, had no alternative but to follow where he led. In the 1892 general election, the Liberals made a considerable recovery and gained 80 seats. With 273 MPs the Liberals were still in a minority compared to the Conservatives with 269 MPs and the support of 46 Liberal Unionists. The 81 Irish Nationalists elected were still bitterly divided between the majority who had abandoned Parnell and those who had supported him. However, with their support the Liberals could form a government with a majority of 40 in the Commons. Gladstone was now aged 82 and he remains the oldest British politician to form a new government – a record he now seems unlikely to lose!

Gladstone's fourth ministry 1892–4

As in 1886, Gladstone refused to discuss his proposed new Home Rule Bill with his Cabinet colleagues. His chancellor of the exchequer, Sir William Harcourt, complained that he had been excluded even from consultation on the financial arrangements, a point made more significant by the fact that Gladstone then made a serious miscalculation in his figures which had to be corrected during the bill's passage. The most important difference from 1886 was Gladstone's reluctant decision that 80 Irish MPs should be retained at Westminster, where they were to be allowed to debate and vote on all subjects. He remained, however, unmoved on the question of any separate treatment for Ulster.

The Second Home Rule Bill was introduced by Gladstone in the House of Commons in February 1893. The debate that followed was as furious as in 1886 and the arguments were much the same on either side. In the end, the bill was passed on its third reading in September by 34 votes: 301 to 267. 'Too small, too small', was Gladstone's reaction, although why he would have expected anything much larger given the balance of seats in the Commons is unclear. He was perhaps belatedly and reluctantly recognising that the majority was too narrow to put any pressure on the House of Lords to accept it. Within less than a week, the Lords rejected it by the massive majority of 419 to 41. The Lords justified their action by pointing to the lack of an English majority in favour of Home Rule, since (excluding the Irish MPs) the supporters of Home Rule in the House of Commons were in a minority. Gladstone carried on as prime minister for another seven months, increasingly at odds with his Cabinet colleagues. They refused their support for another general election aimed at securing greater Commons support for Home Rule. There was also increasing division over other policy matters, particularly over the question of naval expansion, which Gladstone opposed and all his colleagues supported. Gladstone finally retired in March 1894. He died four years later.

Reasons for the bill's rejection

Gladstone's personal and obsessive commitment to Home Rule after the summer of 1885 led him to underestimate – indeed to ignore – the problems involved in getting such a measure accepted. Not only was there a great deal of anti-Irish and anti-Catholic feeling among the English electors, there was considerably more opposition to his policy within the Liberal Party than the prime minister expected. Yet the signs had been there for some time. By the early 1880s, many Whigs were already worried by the implications of Gladstone's Irish land policy for the rights of property generally, and a number had already abandoned the Liberal Party. For some Radicals, such as Joseph Chamberlain, Home Rule seemed the very antithesis of their commitment to strong, efficient, progressive government within an imperial framework.

An even more formidable obstacle to Home Rule was the House of Lords with its built-in unionist majority, as Gladstone himself had realised by his willingness in 1885 to allow Salisbury to initiate Home Rule (see pages 116–17). As the fate of his own 1893 bill showed, it was virtually certain that any Home Rule Bill would be destroyed by the House of Lords. To continue with it under those circumstances seemed to many Liberals – even those devoted to Gladstone – sheer perversity. It meant the sacrifice of the unity and future prospects of the Liberal Party to an old man's pride and stubbornness. One result of the bill's failure, however, was to convince Gladstone and most Liberals that reform of the House of Lords was a necessary prelude to any future radical programme.

It can be argued that an opportunity for settling the Irish question was lost when parliament rejected Home Rule. On the other hand, implementing Home Rule in either 1886 or 1893 would have raised serious difficulties:

- the complexity of the financial provisions of the bills
- the difficulties involved in the division of powers between the Irish and the Imperial parliaments
- the persistence of extremist forms of nationalism
- above all, the opposition of Protestant Ulster to rule from Dublin.

Despite Gladstone's failure, the commitment to Irish Home Rule officially remained an integral part of the party's programme. However, as will be seen in the next chapter, when the Liberals returned to power in 1905, Home Rule was far from being the first priority for them and, when they finally introduced a Third Home Rule Bill in 1912, it was in circumstances which left them little option if they wished to remain in government.

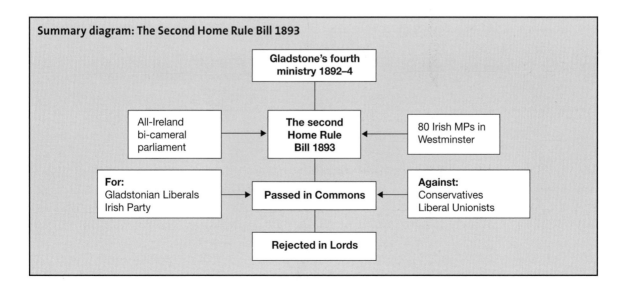

Summary diagram: The Second Home Rule Bill 1893

Chapter summary

Gladstone's decision to introduce a Home Rule Bill for Ireland in 1886 was controversial at the time and has remained so. Equally controversial was – and is – his decision to try again in 1893. Gladstone's motives are also debatable. So far as his 'conversion' is concerned, it is clear that he began to contemplate the possibility of Home Rule as a final solution for Ireland well before his son leaked the information at the end of 1885. Once committed, he took no account of the consequences. He was prepared to accept the split in the Liberal Party; arguably, he actually welcomed the departure of Chamberlain, whom he detested. Very significantly for the future, he completely ruled out any separate status or treatment for the Protestant majority in Ulster. His commitment to Home Rule as an all-Ireland solution remained Liberal Party policy even after his retirement and death. What motivated Gladstone? His acceptance of the advent of Parnell and the rise of the Irish Party's strength at Westminster was a key factor. He also clearly believed that it was best if Irish representation was removed altogether from the House of Commons, as he proposed in 1886. His decision to allow Irish representation in his 1893 bill was taken reluctantly and only because he supposed that it would make the bill easier to pass.

Refresher questions

Use these questions to remind yourself of the key material covered in this chapter.

1 How successful was Parnell in making the Irish Parliamentary Party a significant political force?

2 What factors brought Gladstone to the conclusion in 1885 that Home Rule was the best solution for Ireland's problems?

3 What was the main reason that Gladstone failed in his bid to pass Home Rule in 1886?

4 Would you agree that Parnell did more harm than good to the cause of reform and progress in Ireland?

5 Why did Gladstone's Second Home Rule Bill fail?

6 Were Gladstone's policies towards Ireland in 1882–93 a case of too little, too late or too much, too soon?

7 Was the attitude of the Conservatives and Liberal Unionists towards the problems in Ireland entirely negative in 1886–93?

CHAPTER 7

The Ulster problem

In 1912, the Liberals introduced another Home Rule Bill. But, rather than solving the Irish question, it threatened to unleash civil war. It is essential for you to understand why Home Rule was anathema to the Protestants of Ulster, why there was no simple 'solution' to which the Liberal government could turn, and why the outbreak of the First World War in 1914 merely postponed the crisis in Ireland. This chapter will examine these issues through the following themes:

★ The industrialisation of Ulster

★ The origins of Ulster unionism

★ The Liberals and Home Rule 1906–12

★ Ulster resistance

★ 1914: The year of crisis

Key dates

1886	Jan.	Loyalist Anti-Repeal Union set up
1900		Reunion of Irish Parliamentary Party under John Redmond
1903		Wyndham's Land Act
1905		Ulster Unionist Council formed
1906	Jan.	Liberal landslide victory at general election
1907		Liberals' Irish Councils Bill dropped
1910		General elections wiped out Liberal majority
1911		Parliament Act
1912	April	Third Home Rule Bill introduced
1912	Sept.	Solemn League and Covenant signed
1913	Jan.	Ulster Volunteer Force (UVF) set up
	Nov.	Irish Volunteers formed
1914	March	Curragh 'Mutiny'
	April	Larne gunrunning incident
	May	Home Rule Bill passed
	July	Home Rule Amending Bill rejected by Lords
		Buckingham Palace Conference
		Howth gunrunning incident
	Aug. 4	Britain entered First World War

The industrialisation of Ulster

 ► *How did industrialisation affect Ulster in the nineteenth and twentieth centuries?*

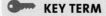 **KEY TERM**

Linen cloth A cool and very durable textile made from the fibres of the flax plant. Its manufacture is documented as far back as written records exist. When the tomb of the Egyptian Pharaoh Ramses II – who died in 1213BC – was discovered in the 1880s, the linen wrappings were found to be perfectly preserved.

Until late on in the seventeenth century, Ulster was the poorest province of Ireland. From around the 1680s this began to change. The reason for the transformation was the growth of the **linen cloth** industry, which became the dominant economic influence on the province throughout the eighteenth century and into the nineteenth century. By the early nineteenth century, Ulster – or to be more precise the eastern part of Ulster where the industry was primarily located – was the most prosperous part of Ireland. From this time, the pace of industrialisation in east Ulster increased rapidly and the scale of industrial development began to distinguish east Ulster from the rest of Ireland, including the western part of the province. This industrial development meant that east Ulster had far more in common with the neighbouring parts of north-west Britain than with the rest of Ireland, and links between Belfast, Liverpool and Glasgow became increasingly strong as the nineteenth century went on. The other essential difference between Ulster and the rest of Ireland was, of course, the presence there of a Protestant majority population. This factor had a significant impact on the economic, social and political evolution of the province.

The linen industry

By the middle of the eighteenth century, exports of linen cloth from Ireland had reached around 11 million yards (10,000 km) – almost all of it produced in Ulster. By 1815, the figure had risen to 43 million yards (40,000 km). By the 1830s, the 50 million mark had been topped. The significance of this can be seen when it is taken into account that by the early nineteenth century the value of linen exports from Ireland was greater than that of either of the two other major export items, corn and cattle. In terms of exports, Ulster had become a manufacturing rather than a food-producing province. Originally, the linen industry was a domestic one, that is to say essentially carried out in domestic homes by small-scale producers, in a similar way to the well-established woollen cloth industry of mainland Britain. From the 1820s, however, the industry underwent a phase of rapid modernisation similar to that which had been underway in the British woollen cloth industry for the previous 50 years. The establishment of a factory system transformed the industry. The legions of small-scale domestic producers, who usually combined their weaving with some kind of agricultural activity, were either redundant or their incomes from weaving were much reduced.

The decline of Irish woollen cloth and cotton production

The supremacy of linen production in Ireland and the rapid mechanisation of the British woollen cloth and cotton industries in the late eighteenth century left the

Irish woollen and cotton industries at a serious disadvantage. Even before this, however, the woollen cloth industry faced a problem.

In 1698, under pressure from the English government, the Irish parliament imposed high taxes on the export of woollen cloth. The following year, as a result of pressure from the English woollen merchants who feared competition due to the lower costs of Irish production, the English parliament (after the 1707 Act of Union with Scotland this would become the British parliament) passed an Act prohibiting the export of Irish woollen goods. However, the argument once put forward by Irish nationalist historians that this was a conspiracy to favour the linen industry and, as such, the origin of the eventual collapse of the industry has long since been disproved.

It was the export market that was the target. The domestic Irish market for woollen goods was, and remained, unaffected throughout the eighteenth century, and from time to time efforts were even made to encourage it. Sometimes these efforts were macabre, for example in 1733 an Act was passed making it obligatory for corpses to be buried in a woollen shroud! Consequently, the industry continued to grow, supported by the home market. Given the rapid development of the British woollen industry and subsequently the impact of the industrial revolution, it is doubtful whether the Irish woollen industry could have competed effectively with the British manufacturers anyway. Indeed, so competitive did the British woollen cloth industry become that its exports began to dominate the Irish market. Economic historians now argue that what happened to the Irish woollen cloth centres simply paralleled what was happening to traditional centres in Britain such as Norwich and the south-west, which declined in the face of competition from the mass production of the Yorkshire towns.

The impact of cotton production elsewhere

In the late eighteenth and early nineteenth centuries, an Irish cotton industry prospered for a short period. Cotton started to be produced in Ireland around 1750. From the late 1770s, the Irish parliament gave increasing financial support to the development of Irish industry, and, encouraged by the Linen Board, cotton was established in Counties Dublin, Kildare, Meath, Carlow, Waterford and Cork before 1782.

Water-powered spinning factories began to appear in a number of towns and from 1790 to 1830 the cotton industry flourished, particularly in and around Belfast, where its expansion threatened the linen industry's dominance. However, in the 1820s, the pressure of competition from much larger cotton producers in Glasgow began to tell. Between 1824 and 1840, over half the cotton spinning mills in Belfast closed. Outside Ulster, in other cotton-producing provinces of Leinster and Munster, the collapse was even more rapid and complete. The decline of cotton therefore reflected the same process as had affected the woollen industry. The concentration and expansion of the cotton industry in Lancashire and Glasgow was simply too competitive. In Ulster, however, the collapse of the cotton industry was accompanied by increased mechanisation in linen production. Many of the Belfast cotton mills that closed in the 1820s and 1830s converted to linen production. A classic example of this transformation was the business of Andrew Mulholland. Mulholland was originally a cotton manufacturer who opted to convert his business to linen in 1830 after a fire destroyed his cotton mill. His new venture became one of the biggest mills of its kind in the world.

Railways

The initial development of the railway in Ireland followed quickly the progress of its counterpart in Britain. Three companies were formed:

- Dublin and Kingstown Railway in 1834
- Dublin and Drogheda Railway in 1836
- Ulster Railway, also in 1836.

A rail link between Dublin and Belfast was completed by 1852, and all three companies merged to form the Great Northern Railway (Ireland) in 1876. The Great Northern became the most profitable railway in all Ireland and continued as the second largest railway in Ireland well into the twentieth century, surviving even the partition of Ireland in 1921, which resulted in a border being created across its lines. But, in the meantime, railway development continued with new companies setting up to develop new lines all over the rest of Ireland. In Ulster the most important was the Belfast and Ballymena Railway, which opened in 1848. This was followed by further extensions to the original line and new companies opening up to cover other areas of Ulster. In 1860, the Belfast and Ballymena Railway was wound up and replaced by a new company called the Belfast and Northern Counties Railway, which went on to take over almost all the other Ulster railways during the rest of the century before itself being taken over by the British-based Midlands Railway in 1903.

Shipbuilding

By 1800, Belfast was already an important industrial centre. In addition to textiles, it was noted for commercial shipbuilding from the late eighteenth century. Over the course of the nineteenth century, as iron and steam ships increasingly took over from wood and sail, Belfast emerged as one of the world's greatest shipbuilding centres. Belfast was an important port as well as a centre of textile production but it was the success of the shipbuilding industry that was to transform it into an industrial giant of global significance. Even in 1800, Belfast and the Ulster counties in proximity to it were already significantly different from the rest of Ireland. By the time Belfast was granted city status in 1888, this difference had already translated into the political arena in the shape of the campaign in Ulster against the first Irish Home Rule Bill of 1886.

The rise of Belfast as a shipbuilding centre was initially the work of a Scot, William Ritchie. He had transferred his shipbuilding business from Scotland in 1791, at that time the shipbuilding industry in Belfast was in a steep decline. Ritchie, along with his brother Hugh as his partner, brought men and equipment to Belfast, and the business prospered. When Hugh Ritchie died in 1807, John, another brother, took over. In partnership with his son-in-law Alexander McLaine – another Scot – John set up the firm of Ritchie & McLaine and they built their first steamship in 1824. Other successful ventures in shipbuilding followed, such as Charles Connell & Sons and Thompson & Kirwan, the latter being the first shipyard to open on Queen's Island in 1851. Queen's Island would become a centre of shipbuilding lasting into the early twenty-first century. Originally known as Dargan's Island (after an engineer who began the industrial development of the site), Queen's Island was renamed in honour of Queen Victoria following her visit to Belfast in 1849. Charles Connell came from Scotland to work for William Ritchie's original company in 1815 and ended up taking it over as his own company and further expanding the business. Charles Connell & Sons launched their first vessel in 1825 and went on to produce ships for a global market. Their ship *Aurora,* launched in 1838, was the largest ship ever built in Belfast up to that time.

These firms, although successful, were still operating on a small scale. Taken together, they launched only 50 ships in the period 1820–50 and most of these were relatively small, wooden ships. However, another engineering entrepreneur, Robert Hickson, a successful ironmonger originally from Liverpool, unconsciously paved the way for breaking new ground. Hickson branched out into shipbuilding, setting up a yard to build iron ships on Queen's Island in 1853, which he sold in 1858 to his yard manager Edward Harland for £5000 (equivalent in modern terms to around £12 million). At the same time, Harland also bought another local firm, the Belfast Shipbuilding Co. In 1861, Harland entered a partnership with a German, Gustav Wolff, so creating Harland & Wolff, which would become one of the largest shipbuilding concerns in the world over the next decades. Harland & Wolff established a close relationship with the White Star Line from 1867 and would go on to build the ill-fated RMS *Titanic* and her sister ships *Olympic* and *Britannic* in the early twentieth century.

Belfast as a port

In 1785, the Irish parliament passed an Act recognising the growing importance of Belfast as a port. As a result, a new body was set up, called the Corporation for Preserving and Improving the Port and Harbour of Belfast. Despite its obvious importance and potential, Belfast as a port had serious disadvantages. There were problems of shallow water, bends in the channel approach and inadequate quays. These problems, along with the ever-increasing amount of trade, led the British government to introduce an amending Act in 1837. This gave the port authority increased powers to improve the port, through the development of a new channel. Initial work on straightening the river started in 1839 and by 1841 the first bend had been eliminated. This was the beginning the creation of what was to become known as the Victoria Channel. In 1847, the Belfast

Harbour Act repealed the earlier Acts and led to the formation of the Belfast Harbour Commissioners. This new body was granted much wider powers and completed the second stage of the new channel two years later. From that time, the Commissioners continued to develop and improve the port.

As the industrialisation of Ulster – or more specifically Belfast – progressed, more and more Roman Catholics were attracted to the prospect of employment there. Sectarian rivalry and their minority status meant that they were generally confined to the lower paid work and consequently the worst housing. By the time of the first Home Rule Bill of 1886, about a third of the population of Belfast were Roman Catholics and resentment between Catholics and Protestants was dangerously intense.

Belfast, however, was increasingly the most prosperous part of Ireland. General environmental conditions in Belfast, although dangerously insanitary by later standards, were significantly better than in Dublin, for example. It is noticeable that when Asiatic cholera, which reached the UK from Europe during 1831–2, hit Ireland the death rate in Belfast, although severe, was lower than in Dublin, Cork and other major urban areas. When cholera returned in 1848–9, the result was the same: Belfast suffered but to a lesser extent than other urban centres in Ireland. The nature of the spread of cholera through contaminated water supplies and general insanitary and unhygienic conditions did not begin to be properly understood until the 1850s. In 1831–2 and again in 1848–9, experts argued as to whether the disease spread through direct contagion or through the air. Such misconceptions hampered the battle against the disease in Belfast and elsewhere. The supposition by many medical practitioners and scientists that diseases such as cholera spread through 'bad' air by 'miasmatic theory' remained popular well into the 1880s.

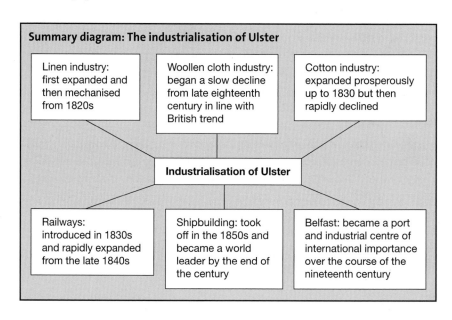

Summary diagram: The industrialisation of Ulster

Linen industry: first expanded and then mechanised from 1820s	Woollen cloth industry: began a slow decline from late eighteenth century in line with British trend	Cotton industry: expanded prosperously up to 1830 but then rapidly declined

Industrialisation of Ulster

Railways: introduced in 1830s and rapidly expanded from the late 1840s	Shipbuilding: took off in the 1850s and became a world leader by the end of the century	Belfast: became a port and industrial centre of international importance over the course of the nineteenth century

2 The origins of Ulster unionism

▶ *What were the origins of Ulster unionism?*

Ever since they had come to Ireland, centuries before, the Protestants had been marked off by religion and culture from the Catholic majority. Nowhere was this sense of a separate identity stronger than in Ulster, where the majority of Protestants were concentrated. Although they represented only about a quarter of the total Irish population around 1900, the Protestants in Ulster formed about 57 per cent of the people of that province. Protestant separatism in Ulster was sustained not only by the fervour and rabidly **anti-papal** attitude of the dominant Presbyterian Churches, but also by the nature of the Ulster economy. Ulster was the only segment of Ireland where a truly industrial economy had developed. Thus, Ulster became not only the most progressive and prosperous province in Ireland but, owing to its dependence on British markets and raw materials, an area which looked eastwards to Great Britain rather than southwards to the rest of Ireland.

KEY TERM

Anti-papal Opposition to the Pope and/or Roman Catholicism more generally.

In these circumstances it was understandable that the Ulstermen should have become stalwart defenders of the Union after 1801. After the collapse of the repeal and revolutionary movements in the 1840s (see pages 56–9), there seemed to be no outstanding threat to the *status quo* during the relatively quiet years of the mid-nineteenth century. Hence, there appeared to be no need for them to take special measures to defend their position. It was not until the 1880s that the Ulster Protestants began to organise in defence of the Union and as a result Ulster unionism was born. This was due to:

- the re-emergence of Irish nationalism
- the rise of the Home Rule Party in Ireland
- the Home Rulers' swift capture of the Roman Catholic vote
- the introduction of Gladstone's Home Rule Bills in 1886 and 1893.

By raising the spectre of self-government for the whole of Ireland, centred on a Dublin parliament, these developments seemed to threaten the very existence of the Ulster Protestant way of life.

The Loyalist Anti-Repeal Union

One response to this threat was the revival of the Protestant Orange Order. But political organisation among the Ulster Protestants to defend the Union emerged only slowly. In the key election of 1885, for example, Liberals and Conservatives in northern Ireland still opposed one another, and as a result the Nationalist Party under Parnell won seventeen Ulster seats (out of 33) compared with only three in the general election of 1880. The Nationalist Party also swept the board in southern Ireland. The shock of these results, together with the introduction of Gladstone's First Home Rule Bill which soon followed, brought members of

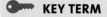
the most influential Protestant groups in Ulster – landowners, businessmen, churchmen – together in January 1886 in the Loyalist Anti-Repeal Union, in opposition to Home Rule. The movement grew rapidly. It was strengthened by the visit of the prominent Tory politician, Lord Randolph Churchill, to Belfast in February. He was a younger son of the Duke of Marlborough and father of Winston Churchill. While in Belfast, Lord Randolph decided, in his own famous phrase, 'to play the **Orange card**' to use Ulster unionism to weaken Gladstone's position and advance the interests of his own party. At a large and enthusiastic public meeting he called on Ulstermen to organise in opposition to Gladstone and Home Rule, and hinted, ominously, that such resistance would receive support in England: 'Ulster will fight, and Ulster will be right'.

Why were the Ulster Unionists so vehemently opposed to Home Rule?

The introduction of the First Home Rule Bill in April 1886 led virtually all the Ulster Liberals to break with their party and join with the Conservatives to denounce the proposal to hand them over 'to their inveterate nationalist foes'. This Conservative–Liberal unionist alliance was maintained firmly at the general election in the summer of 1886 following the defeat in the Commons of the Home Rule Bill. This time, the unionists won just a majority of the Ulster seats – 17 out of 33. Politics in Ulster was now completely polarised between the unionists and the nationalists. The tensions created there by the Home Rule crisis were illustrated by the sectarian riots in the Belfast shipyards that spring, which led to 32 deaths and scores of injuries.

Following the 1886 general election, the unionists worked hard to consolidate their forces in Ulster and justify their stance. Unionist clubs were formed throughout the province, links were established with the unionists in the south and with the Conservative Party on the mainland, and a propaganda campaign was carried out in Great Britain on behalf of the Ulster unionist cause. An Ulster Defence Association was also formed – a portent of what was to come.

Economic reasons

The Union was defended, in the first place, because it was believed that there were sound economic reasons for doing so. Ireland, it was argued, had prospered under the Union: the British connection had helped to produce thriving industries in Ulster on which the prosperity of the whole region was based. That prosperity would be threatened if the link with Britain was broken; especially if, as seemed likely, an Irish parliament introduced a system of protective duties against British goods and raw materials. 'All our progress has been made under the Union', the Belfast Chamber of Commerce told Gladstone in 1893; 'why should we be driven by force to abandon the conditions which have led to that success?' But southern Ireland, it was insisted, had also benefited from the British connection, as revealed by the reforms introduced by successive governments.

Political reasons

Politically too, the Irish unionists were fearful of what the results of an Irish parliament would be. It would, they believed, be dominated by extreme nationalists, radicals and Fenians, who possessed little respect for persons or property and whose ultimate goal was a completely independent Ireland. By opposing Home Rule, therefore, the unionists were at the same time defending the integrity of the British Empire.

Religious reasons

In the famous unionist phrase, 'Home Rule is Rome Rule'. The Protestants' image of the Roman Catholic Church – based on historical memory and the contemporary links between Irish Catholicism and Irish nationalism – convinced them that their religious and civil liberties would be threatened by a Dublin parliament which would represent an overwhelming Catholic majority. Irish nationalists were not prepared to accept that unionist fears about the consequences of Home Rule had any validity. But, equally, the unionists underestimated the emotional force of an Irish nationalism which aimed at unity and freedom for the whole island. Thus, as the twentieth century dawned, there was no real dialogue between the two sides.

Irish nationalism 1893–1905

The prospect of Home Rule receded after the defeat of the Second Home Rule Bill in 1893 and lifted the immediate danger to Ulster. Gladstone retired in the following year, and the Irish Parliamentary Party split into two hostile factions following the death of Parnell in 1891. Irish nationalism temporarily became more cultural than political, as with the founding in 1893 of the Gaelic League, which aimed to 'de-Anglicise' Irish culture and revive the use of the Irish Gaelic language. Furthermore, the Conservatives triumphed at the general elections of 1895 and 1900. The Conservatives then attempted to 'to kill Home Rule with kindness', by a policy of radical reform in Ireland. The Local Government Act of 1898, which introduced elected county councils, destroyed the waning power of the landed gentry throughout the country, and handed over local political power ever more firmly to the middle-class unionists in Ulster and their nationalist counterparts in Catholic Ireland. Wyndham's Act of 1903 (named after the Irish secretary, George Wyndham) virtually solved the land problem in Ireland by:

- organising the buying out of the landlords by the State at an acceptable price
- allowing their tenants to purchase the land they farmed through State loans at a very low rate of interest extended over a long period.

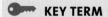

KEY TERM

Devolution A transfer of powers from central government to local government.

The Ulster Unionists and the Conservatives

Yet the relationship between the Ulster unionists and the Conservative government was not all sweetness and light. In 1904, a **devolution** scheme was produced behind the scenes at the Irish Office, which proposed the control of some important aspects of Irish internal affairs, including finance, by a representative Irish Council. This was denounced by the Ulster Unionists when the details leaked out, as 'Home Rule by instalments'. It led to their increasing distrust of the government, even though the scheme was repudiated by the prime minister, A.J. Balfour, and George Wyndham was forced to resign.

The eventual outcome of this political storm in a teacup, however, was vitally important and represents (in the words of the historian George Boyce) 'one of the most significant events in the political history of modern Ireland'. It led directly to the formation of the Ulster Unionist Council in March 1905, centred on Belfast: a democratically elected body which now represented every strand of Ulster unionism: the unionist clubs, the Orange Order, the Protestant Churches and the Ulster members of the Commons and Lords. The Council thus became the directing force of Ulster unionism, and therefore in any future political crisis Ulster unionism could speak with one powerful, unified voice. Even more portentously, it also meant that Ulster now possessed the framework of an independent governmental organisation, which could be summoned into life as and when the political situation demanded.

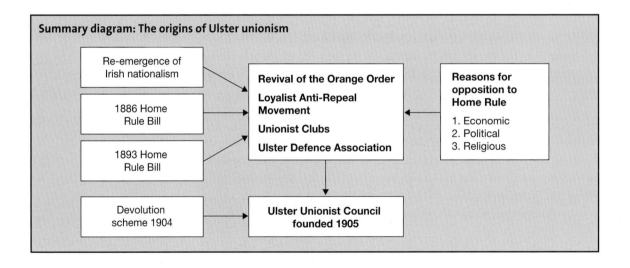

Summary diagram: The origins of Ulster unionism

The Liberals and Home Rule 1906–12

▶ *What were the main concerns of the Liberal Party in the period 1900–10?*

Although the Liberal Party after 1900 remained committed in principle to Home Rule for Ireland, important sections of the party regarded it as an irritating distraction, diverting energies away from more urgent plans for imperial and social reconstruction. The new party leader, Sir Henry Campbell-Bannerman, and his chief whip, Herbert Gladstone, saw their main task as the reorganisation and reunification of the Liberal Party. They were well aware of the lessons of the disastrous general election of 1895 which had given the Tories their greatest electoral victory of the nineteenth century, and they attributed this mainly to the unpopularity in England of Irish Home Rule.

What the party leaders wanted was a more practical and less ideological approach to the issue, especially as they realised that Home Rule was impossible while the House of Lords retained its traditional powers. Moreover, as the decline of the Conservative government under Balfour became more evident in the early years of the new century, the desire for Liberal unity to prepare for the coming general election became paramount. All sections of the Liberal Party therefore accepted Campbell-Bannerman's formula, adopted early in 1905, of a 'step by step' approach to the Irish question. Irish reform, yes; but (in Herbert Gladstone's phrase) 'no pledge either as to method or time' over Home Rule.

The Liberals in power 1906–10

During the election campaign of 1906, the Liberal Party leaders made it clear that while Home Rule remained their official policy, it was no longer a priority and there would be no immediate move to raise it. After the Liberals' landslide victory – which gave them 400 MPs and an overall majority of 270 – all that the Liberal government was prepared to offer was another Councils Bill in 1907 which aimed at introducing administrative devolution. This was merely a revised version of the Unionist Bill of 1904 and proposed a representative Irish Council to deal with some aspects of Irish internal affairs. It was rejected out of hand by John Redmond, the moderate leader of the Irish Parliamentary Party. Apart from his own views, Redmond was under pressure from the extremists within his own party and a new non-violent nationalist organisation, **Sinn Féin** (see pages 170–4), to stand firm over Irish demands. Thus, it was now made clear to the Liberal government that half-measures would not suffice – nothing less than Home Rule would be acceptable.

Yet there was little that the Irish Parliamentary Party could do to bring pressure to bear on the government. The Liberals had a massive parliamentary majority,

 KEY TERM

Sinn Féin Gaelic term meaning 'we, ourselves'. Sinn Féin was founded in 1905. Officially non-violent, it was quickly infiltrated by members of the Irish Republican Brotherhood.

and (especially after Asquith replaced Campbell-Bannerman as prime minister in 1908) most of their time and energy went into promoting the radical social welfare programme which was their major achievement on the domestic front. It is true that the government was determined to deal with the problem of the House of Lords (which had rejected a number of Liberal bills passed by the Commons), but Asquith did not feel that Home Rule was the most popular issue on which to challenge the Lords' powers. For the moment, therefore, the Irish had to bide their time, although Redmond still believed – in opposition to some of his nationalist compatriots – that support for the Liberals offered the best hope for Home Rule.

The whole situation was changed dramatically when the Lords rejected Lloyd George's '**People's Budget**' in November 1909. They objected particularly to proposed new taxes. But by long constitutional practice the Lords had no right to reject a 'money bill' passed by the Commons. The unwise Lords' action – which brought to a head years of Liberal anger and frustration over their blatantly **partisan** behaviour – made the reform of the powers of the Upper House inevitable.

The 1910 general elections

The rejection of the budget was followed by the dissolution of parliament and a general election held in January 1910. For Redmond, the Irish leader, this seemed to offer new opportunities for the cause of Home Rule, for he believed that the Liberals would need Irish support in the election. Redmond also realised that another Liberal victory in 1910 would be followed by the expected reform of the Lords and then there would be no legitimate obstacle to the introduction of a new Home Rule Bill. Redmond conveyed his views in a letter to the Liberal cabinet minister, John Morley, a long-term supporter of Home Rule.

SOURCE A

From a letter by John Redmond to John Morley in November 1909, quoted in Denis Gwyn, *The Life of John Redmond*, George Harrap, 1932, p. 166.

The political conditions in Ireland are such that unless an official declaration on the question of home rule be made, not only will it be impossible for us to support Liberal candidates in England, but we will … have to ask our friends [Irish voters] to vote against them … We cannot acquiesce in the present situation being continued. There is a large majority in the government and in the House of Commons in favour of home rule and yet their hands are tied … We must, therefore, press for an official declaration which will show clearly that the home rule issue is involved in the issue of the House of Lords by declaring that the government shall be free to deal with it, not on the lines of the Council Bill, but on the lines of national self-government, subject to imperial control, in the next parliament.

KEY TERMS

People's Budget The main terms of the budget that the Lords objected to were that the standard rate of income tax was to be raised on annual incomes of up to £3000 and there would be a new 'super tax' on incomes over £3000 a year.

Partisan Biased in support of a particular party; in this case the Conservatives.

? What does Redmond's letter in Source A reveal about the relationship between the Irish National Party and the Liberals?

Although it was not the only factor affecting Asquith's election campaign in 1909–10, the prime minister heeded Redmond's warning. For the Liberal leadership, the election was centred on the major issue of ending the **absolute veto** of the House of Lords over legislation, and to achieve this Asquith needed the support of all the anti-Conservative forces in the country. Hence, in his great speech at the Albert Hall on 10 December 1909, the prime minister made in effect a definite commitment to introduce a Home Rule Bill in the next parliament if the Liberals were re-elected, as well as promising to deal with the grievances of other disaffected groups whose claims had been rejected by the House of Lords.

However, the outcome of the general election of January 1910 was a disappointment for the Liberals in that their majority over the Conservatives was reduced to just two seats. Even so, Asquith was able to carry on as prime minister because he had the support of the Irish MPs, and the Labour MPs, although their support, unlike that of the Irish, was not vital as they only had 40 seats. In June, the Commons passed the government's Parliament Bill by a substantial majority, and the Lords finally agreed to pass the budget. However, it took another general election (in December 1910) before the Lords agreed to bow to the will of the House of Commons and pass the Parliament Bill. This second election of 1910 produced near identical results to the first except that the Liberals and Conservatives now had exactly the same number of seats. The Lords eventually passed the Parliament Act in August 1911. The Act:

- abolished the absolute veto of the House of Lords over legislation
- ensured that the Upper House could only hold up a bill passed formally by the House of Commons for two years (three successive parliamentary sessions).

In this way, the long drawn-out constitutional crisis came to an end. The Irish could now look forward to the introduction of a new Home Rule Bill.

The Home Rule Bill 1912

The Liberal government introduced its Home Rule Bill in the following year. The state of the parties in the House of Commons (following the general election of December 1910) was now as follows:

- Liberals 272
- Unionists 272 (including sixteen Ulster Unionists)
- Irish Nationalists 84
- Labour 42.

It can be argued that introduction of the Home Rule Bill by the Liberals was the result of pressure from the Irish Nationalists on whose votes the government relied to carry the House of Commons. Patricia Jalland, however, in her detailed study *The Liberals and Ireland: The Ulster Question in British Politics to 1914* (1993), has insisted that Liberal policy was, on the contrary, 'the logical consequence of a long-standing commitment'. Liberal leaders since the days of Gladstone's last ministry had consistently supported Irish Home Rule in principle. Augustine Birrell, the Irish secretary, had told Redmond, the Irish Nationalist leader, a year before the elections of 1910 had drastically cut down the Liberal majority, that Home Rule was 'the live policy of the Party without limitation or restriction'. In any case, she argues, the Liberal government was not dependent on Irish votes, since if both Irish Nationalist and Irish Unionist votes were excluded from the reckoning, the government had a small majority of sixteen over the Conservatives, which would normally be increased to over 50 with the support of Labour. Jalland concludes that only an overwhelming belief by the Liberal Party that, for the sake of honour and conviction, it must attempt to secure Home Rule for Ireland, can explain why over the next two years it was prepared to endure the storms and stresses of another and greater Home Rule crisis.

Terms of the third Home Rule Bill

The Home Rule Bill of 1912 was fundamentally the same as Gladstone's 1893 proposal and it was a very moderate measure:

- There was to be an Irish parliament, consisting of a small, nominated Senate (Upper House) and an elected House of Commons.
- The Executive would be responsible to parliament.
- The powers of the Irish parliament were to be even more limited than those proposed in 1893 (see page 127), since the Imperial government (in addition to its retention of the major powers listed in the 1893 bill) was now to have a greater degree of financial control over Ireland and would also be responsible for the new old-age pensions and national insurance schemes.
- Ireland was also to be represented at Westminster by 42 MPs.

The main point about the new bill, however, was that once again Ulster was to be included in a self-governing Ireland. This was due not only to the pull of the past; self-deception and complacency also played a part. There was little real discussion of the Ulster problem among Liberals, whether in Cabinet, the House of Commons or even in the columns of the Liberal press, despite the fact that the Ulster Unionists had insisted for over a year that they would resist the implementation of Home Rule. Many Liberals had convinced themselves that unionist opposition was somehow 'artificial'.

Asquith bears a major responsibility for this. He controlled Irish policy after 1911, and his prevarication and refusal to take hard decisions, as well as the influence of Redmond (who declared that 'Irish Nationalists can never be consenting parties to the mutilation of the Irish nation'), meant that there was no real attempt to face up to the realities of the Ulster situation at the outset, when a compromise solution was perhaps possible. By 1914, the situation had deteriorated so much that almost any compromise scheme was bound to fail. 'This failure to assess the Ulster problem', writes Jalland, 'and to examine the possible methods of dealing with it, is surely a severe indictment of the Government'. On the other hand, it can be argued that Ulster Unionist intransigence and Redmond's need to maintain his credibility as an Irish Nationalist leader made a settlement no more likely in 1912 than in 1914.

SOURCE B

From a speech by Asquith introducing the Home Rule Bill in April 1912, quoted in *The Liberal Magazine*, Liberal Publication Department, 1913, p. 236.

We put this Bill forward as … the embodiment of our own honest and deliberate judgement. What is your alternative? Are you satisfied with the present system? … What do you propose to put in its place? Have you any answer to the demand of Ireland beyond the naked veto of an irreconcilable minority and the promise of a freer and more copious outflow to Ireland of Imperial doles? There are at this moment between twenty and thirty self-governing Legislatures under the allegiance of the Crown. They have solved … the problem of reconciling local autonomy with Imperial unity. Are we going to break up the Empire by adding one more?

In what way is Asquith in Source B seeking to counter the likely challenge to his proposal?

Reactions to the bill

Despite the limited powers granted to the Irish parliament, Redmond and the Nationalist Party gave Asquith strong support. The Conservatives, however, were determined to kill the bill, come what may. They were now led by Andrew Bonar Law, a Scots–Canadian industrialist, who had succeeded Balfour as Conservative leader in November 1911. Bonar Law was (or appeared to be) a much tougher character than the fastidious Balfour; he had grown up in Ulster (where his father had been a Presbyterian minister) and this made him particularly sympathetic to the claims and outlook of the Ulster Unionists.

Bonar Law attacked the Home Rule Bill on the grounds that it was the outcome of a 'corrupt bargain' between Asquith and Redmond. He condemned it as the price to be paid for gaining Irish votes to prop up the government. The Liberals, he argued, had no mandate to introduce Home Rule, as the recent election campaign had shown. These arguments were ignored by the supporters of Home Rule, as were the powerful points produced by the leaders of the Ulster Unionists on behalf of their province. The bill easily passed through the Commons at the end of May 1912 with a majority of about 100.

But the Commons' vote meant little since, as everyone realised, the bill would certainly be rejected by the House of Lords – as it was by an enormous majority – and the Lords' opposition could be overcome only by the application of the 1911 Parliament Act. The bill could not, therefore, become law before the spring of 1914 at the earliest. This two-year wait was bound to increase all the tensions and bitterness surrounding the issue; on one notorious occasion in the House of Commons, Asquith was howled down by the opposition. It also encouraged extremism in Ulster. This meant that the fate of the bill would be decided by events outside parliament, and indeed the Liberal government now found itself opposed by the united, stubborn resistance of the Ulster Unionists. In April 1912, two leading Unionists, Sir Edward Carson and James Craig, set up the Ulster Volunteers – a **militia** force that soon numbered over 100,000 – to defend Ulster from all-Ireland Home Rule.

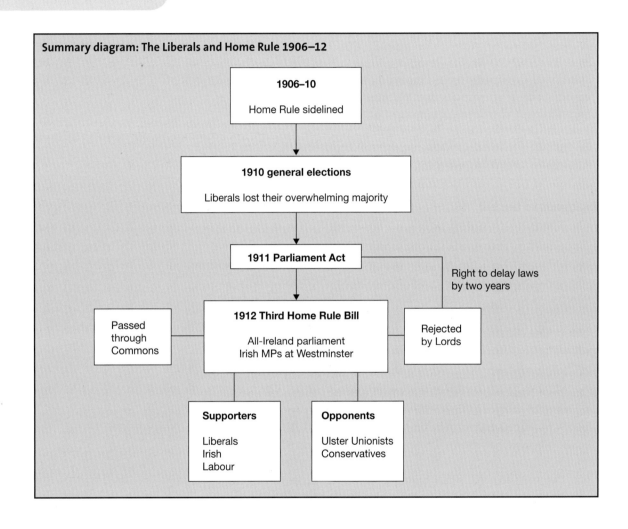

Summary diagram: The Liberals and Home Rule 1906–12

1906–10

Home Rule sidelined

↓

1910 general elections

Liberals lost their overwhelming majority

↓

1911 Parliament Act — Right to delay laws by two years

↓

Passed through Commons — **1912 Third Home Rule Bill**

All-Ireland parliament
Irish MPs at Westminster — Rejected by Lords

Supporters

Liberals
Irish
Labour

Opponents

Ulster Unionists
Conservatives

Ulster resistance

▶ *What were the main events of Ulster resistance?*

Even before the Home Rule Bill was presented to the House of Commons, the Ulster Unionist Council had begun to organise resistance. It also put its case to the British people through its own propaganda and the cooperation of the Conservative Party. Two men now emerged as the main leaders of Irish unionist resistance: Sir Edward Carson and **James Craig**.

Resistance took the form of great meetings and military-type demonstrations embracing all classes and groups in Protestant Ulster, to express their determination to oppose Home Rule. Typical of these actions was the great protest demonstration organised in Belfast's Balmoral grounds on Easter Tuesday 1912, two days before Asquith introduced the Home Rule Bill in the House of Commons. There, an estimated 100,000 Ulstermen marched past the platform where Bonar Law and Carson were present as the main speakers, together with 70 British Conservative MPs. The culmination of this provocative movement to display the solidarity and resolution of Protestant Ulster was the nomination by the Ulster Unionist Council of 28 September 1912 as 'Covenant Day' and a public holiday. Ulster's 'Solemn League and Covenant' (see below) was then signed by about 250,000 men. Carson signed first; some men (it is reported) signed with their own blood. A similar declaration was supported by roughly the same number of women.

SOURCE C

Ulster's Solemn League and Covenant of September 1912, quoted in Marie Coleman, *The Irish Revolution, 1916–1923*, Routledge, 2014, p. 123.

Being convinced in our consciences that Home Rule would be disastrous to the material well-being of Ulster, as well as of the whole of Ireland, subversive of our civil and religious freedom, destructive of our citizenship, and perilous to the unity of the Empire, we, whose names are underwritten, men of Ulster, loyal subjects of his Glorious Majesty King George V, humbly relying on the God Whom our fathers … confidently trusted, do hereby pledge ourselves in solemn Covenant throughout this our time of threatened calamity to stand by one another in defending … our cherished position of equal citizenship in the United Kingdom and in using all means which may be found necessary to defeat the present conspiracy to set up a home rule parliament in Ireland. And in the event of such a Parliament being forced upon us we further and mutually pledge ourselves to refuse to recognise its authority. In sure confidence that God will defend the right, we here to subscribe our names.

 **KEY FIGURE**

James Craig (1871–1940)

A much more provincial and less commanding figure than Carson, although he had fought with distinction in the South African War and had sat in the House of Commons as an Ulster Unionist MP since 1906. He was obstinate and single-minded and determined at all costs to resist any attempt to force Ulster into a self-governing Ireland. Craig's real strength lay in action and administration: it was he who began the organisation of provincial government in Ulster on behalf of the Ulster Council, in order to take over local power if Home Rule became law. It was Craig, too, who first began to speak in terms of armed resistance to Home Rule.

Study Source C. **?** Compare this to Source B on page 145. Which source do you think offers the more convincing argument about the likely result of introducing Home Rule?

Sir Edward Carson

1854	Born in Dublin
1892	Elected as MP for Dublin University
	Appointed solicitor-general for Ireland
1900	Appointed solicitor-general for England
1910	Elected leader of Ulster Unionists
1912	Organised military opposition to Home Rule in Ulster
1915	Attorney-general in Asquith's coalition government
1916–17	Lord of the Admiralty
1917–18	Member of the War Cabinet
1921	Resigned as leader of the Ulster Unionists
1935	Died

Sir Edward Carson was a southern Protestant lawyer, who had been born in Dublin in 1854 and educated there at Trinity College. He had an outstanding career at the Bar in Ireland and England. After his election as Liberal Unionist MP for Dublin University in 1892, he was appointed solicitor-general for Ireland by Lord Salisbury, and later, in 1900, solicitor-general for England. By birth and upbringing Carson had little in common with the Ulster Unionists; but, as he said, the maintenance of the Union 'is the guiding star of my political life', and he was prepared to use Ulster as a base to prevent any Home Rule Bill. In this way, he hoped that the position of the weak and scattered southern Unionists would also be protected. In 1910, he was recognised as the leader of the Ulster Unionists in the House of Commons. At his visit to Belfast in the following year he proclaimed that Ulster's cause was 'the cause of the Empire', and announced solemnly, 'I dedicate myself to your service whatever may happen'. Carson proved to be a redoubtable advocate of Ulster's claims and a determined supporter of its resistance to Home Rule.

SOURCE D

How does Source D help to explain why there was so much opposition to Home Rule in Ulster?

A 1912 postcard, appealing to the British not to sever economic and political ties with Ulster.

The Ulster Volunteer Force

The implication of the Ulstermen's determination to defend themselves was seen shortly after the signing of the covenant. Sporadic drilling and training of volunteer soldiers had been taking place for some time (with the acquiescence of the local Protestant **JP**s), and these men were now organised by the Ulster Unionist Council into the Ulster Volunteer Force (UVF).

In setting up the force, the Council received the advice of Field-Marshal Lord Roberts; and a retired British officer, Lieutenant-General Sir George Richardson, was appointed as commanding officer. The UVF grew rapidly and was organised into county divisions and regiments throughout the province, backed up by supporting corps of nurses, despatch riders and so on. Most of the men in the new force did not possess arms, and those who did were for the moment not allowed to display them. The UVF, however, was almost certainly an illegal organisation, yet it was supported by MPs such as Carson and Craig who soon made it clear that they were prepared to use force to resist subjection to a Dublin parliament.

Reasons for resistance

The Ulstermen took their stand on their established constitutional and legal rights. They argued that they were justified in defying a law which overrode the rights of minorities, especially a minority so united in its resistance to the dictates of the government. Moreover, no safeguards were provided for their religious or civil liberties within the Home Rule Bill to which they were being asked to submit – a bill which many Irish nationalists were already describing as merely 'a provisional settlement'. Irish self-government, therefore, might well lead on to independence. 'We see', said Carson, 'that there can be no permanent resting place between complete union and total separation.' Thus, the integrity of the Empire was also at stake. The unionists concluded, therefore, that their duty to the Crown, as the symbol of imperial unity and constitutional authority, was greater than their duty to the law passed by a particular government.

Bonar Law was sympathetic to these claims. He had spoken at the great Balmoral meeting in Belfast on Easter Tuesday 1912; and at a speech in July of that year at a mass meeting held at Blenheim Palace near Oxford, he appeared to go even further and give full endorsement to any resistance measures planned by the Ulster Unionists.

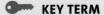

KEY TERM

JP Justice of the peace; a local magistrate.

? How justified was Bonar
Law in Source E in
claiming that this was not
'an ordinary constitutional
struggle'?

SOURCE E

From a speech by Andrew Bonar Law at Blenheim Palace in July 1912, quoted in R. Blake, *Bonar Law – The Unknown Prime Minister*, Eyre & Spottiswoode, 1955, p. 130.

In our opposition … we shall not be guided by the considerations or bound by the restraints which would influence us in an ordinary constitutional struggle … if an attempt were made to deprive these men [Ulster Unionists] of their birth-right – as part of a corrupt parliamentary bargain – they would be justified in resisting such an attempt by all means in their power, including force … if such an attempt is made, I can imagine no length of resistance to which Ulster can go in which I should not be prepared to support them, and in which, in my belief, they would not be supported by the overwhelming majority of the British people.

Such sentiments did not mean that Bonar Law and the Conservative Party supported the Ulster Unionists' claims purely for the sake of Ulster. What also motivated them were imperial and, perhaps more importantly, party considerations. Ulster Unionist resistance would help the Conservatives to destroy the Home Rule Bill and thus preserve the integrity of the UK and the Empire. At the same time, the destruction of the Home Rule Bill might well bring down the Liberal government.

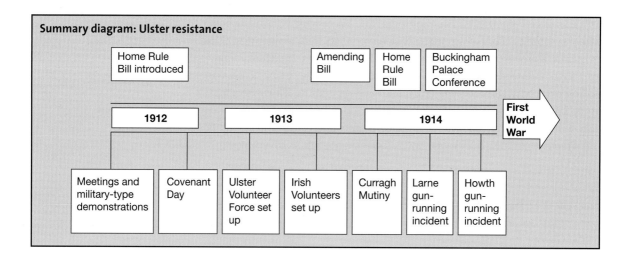

Summary diagram: Ulster resistance

5 1914: The year of crisis

▶ *Why did the crisis worsen during 1914?*

The aggressive speeches of unionist leaders such as Carson and Bonar Law were denounced by Asquith, with his moderate, rational and legalistic approach to politics, as a 'Grammar of Anarchy'. 'I tell you quite frankly', he told a public meeting in Dublin in July 1912, 'I do not believe in the prospect of a civil war.' Redmond, similarly, assured him that the unionists were playing 'a gigantic game of bluff and blackmail'.

It is true that the UVF was intended in the first place to be a powerful pressure group to force the Liberal government to give way peacefully over Home Rule; but all the evidence points to the fact that, if the testing time came, Ulster would fight. Faced then with intransigence and subversion by the unionists both at Belfast and at Westminster, and unable or unwilling to impose a more compromising policy on his Irish nationalist allies, Asquith adopted his usual strategy of 'wait and see'. No action was to be taken against the spokesmen for rebellion. He held to his conviction that the Irish question still remained amenable to a parliamentary solution and hoped to bring his opponents to their senses.

Yet the ultimate effect of the policy of 'drift' was to intensify rather than relieve the growing tensions in Ireland. In November 1913, following the example of the UVF in Ulster, a group of republicans and moderate nationalists in the south founded the **Irish Volunteers** as a defence force. This grew rapidly throughout Catholic Ireland and was eventually supported by Redmond and the Irish Parliamentary Party. By 1914, therefore, the government was faced with opposing private armies in the north and the south; but still Asquith did nothing.

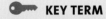 **KEY TERM**

Irish Volunteers A militia force established to try and ensure the passing of the Home Rule Act.

The Curragh Mutiny

The government's position was weakened even further by the so-called Curragh 'Mutiny' in March 1914. This incident arose from the government's decision to reinforce the army depots in Ulster: some 23,000 men were now enrolled in the UVF, faced by only about 1000 regular troops. This led to rumours among the unionists that the army was to be used to 'invade' Ulster and crush the UVF, although the government had no such clear-cut plans.

In this situation, the War Office became worried about the loyalty of officers stationed in Ireland who came from Ulster. As a result, a message was sent to the commanding officer in Ireland, indicating that, in the event of hostilities, officers from Ulster would be allowed to be 'absent from duty' and should 'disappear from Ireland'. On the other hand, if other officers were not prepared to carry out orders they would be 'be dismissed from the Service'. As a result of the War Office's foolishness in posing such hypothetical issues, and the bungling way in which the message was delivered to the officers assembled at the army headquarters at Curragh, in County Kildare, General Gough and 57 officers of the Cavalry Brigade said they preferred dismissal.

The British public was appalled by what the press called a 'mutiny', and as a result of the recriminations that followed, the war minister, Colonel Seely, was forced to resign. The Curragh Mutiny convinced Asquith that it would be impossible to take military action against Ulster. There is no doubt, he wrote, that 'if we were to order a march upon Ulster about half the officers in the Army … would strike … That is the present situation and it is not a pleasant one'.

The Larne gunrunning incident

The shock produced by the Curragh Mutiny had hardly died down, when news came in the following month of the Larne gunrunning incident. On the night of 24–25 April 1914, in a daring and completely successful operation, which defied the ban on importing arms, the UVF obtained 35,000 rifles and 5 million rounds of ammunition from Germany. These were landed at Larne, on the north-east coast, collected by the Volunteers' Motor Car Corps – under the noses of the authorities – and quietly distributed throughout the province. The nationalists were outraged; the government was left demoralised. 'It was no longer a question of our coercing Ulster', said one Liberal minister, 'it was a question of our preventing Ulster from coercing us.' Asquith felt he had little choice but to seek a political settlement which gave at least some recognition to Ulster's claims. As Patricia Jalland commented in *The Liberals and Ireland* (1980), Asquith: 'relied throughout on a high-risk policy of prevarication and delay which had clearly failed by May 1914'. The outlines of such a settlement had already been put forward by a number of Cabinet ministers before the crises in the spring of 1914.

SOURCE F

From a letter by Winston Churchill to John Redmond in August 1914, quoted in Denis Gwyn, *The Life of John Redmond*, George Harrap, 1932, p. 214.

*I do not believe there is any real feeling against home rule in the Tory party apart from the Ulster question, but they hate the government, are bitterly desirous of turning it out, and see in the resistance of Ulster an extra-parliamentary force which they will not hesitate to use to the full … my general view is just what I told you earlier in the year – namely, that something should be done to afford the characteristically Protestant and Orange counties the option of a **moratorium** of several years before acceding to the Irish parliament … Much is to be apprehended from … the fanaticism of these stubborn and determined Orangemen.*

? What were Churchill's possible motives in Source F for writing to Redmond with these ideas?

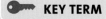 **KEY TERM**

Moratorium A period of delay.

'Exclusion'

This policy of 'exclusion', as it came to be called, that is, excluding Ulster from a self-governing Ireland, had much to commend it to all parties by the spring of 1914. Public opinion in Britain seemed to approve, since such a settlement would recognise the special position of Ulster without denying the Irish majority Home Rule. Carson and Craig too realised by this time that a Home Rule Bill for Ireland could not be stopped, and were therefore prepared to support exclusion in principle, even though Carson accepted, unhappily, that this meant deserting the southern Unionists. Even Redmond, in the end, although it went against the grain, was prepared to consider a temporary exclusion of the distinctly Protestant areas of Ulster.

The application of the policy of exclusion was, however, much more difficult than it seemed, since Ulster was not – despite the rhetoric of the unionists – an entirely Protestant province. Only four counties (see the map on page 3) had definite Protestant majorities: Armagh, Londonderry, Down and Antrim. In Fermanagh and Tyrone, the Protestants and Catholics were almost evenly divided, and in Cavan, Donegal and Monaghan the Protestants were in a minority. The problem therefore arose of which parts of Ulster should be excluded from Home Rule. This was linked with a second question: if exclusion for some counties was agreed on, was it to be temporary or permanent?

Asquith eventually came to accept 'exclusion' as a reasonable compromise plan for both nationalists and unionists, and also as a way out of his difficulties. In March 1914, an Amending Bill to the original Home Rule Bill was drawn up based on the principle of 'county option'. This meant that through a simple majority vote, the electors in each of the counties of Ulster could decide separately either for or against exclusion. In addition (as a sop to the nationalists), those counties which opted for exclusion were only to be excluded temporarily, for six years. Whether they were to be allowed to remain permanently outside the rest of a self-governing Ireland would depend on the verdict of the whole electorate of the UK at a subsequent general election.

The plan was dismissed by Carson as merely 'a stay of execution' for the Ulster Unionists; what he wanted was an immediate 'clean break' for the whole province of Ulster. Asquith's hopes for an early settlement were in any case destroyed by the House of Lords, which rejected his Amending Bill when it was presented to them in June, and replaced 'county option' by their own amendment which insisted (like Carson) on the permanent exclusion of the whole province of Ulster.

Deadlock

Once again, there appeared to be deadlock. Civil war loomed nearer, since in May the original Home Rule Bill had passed through all the parliamentary stages for it to become law. It was likely, therefore, that the Ulster Unionists would carry out their threats to take over the administration of Ulster and defend themselves with the support of the UVF, whose members were now authorised to carry their arms openly. Tensions increased even more when, at the end of July, the nationalist volunteers carried out their own gunrunning operation in broad daylight at Howth, near Dublin. This was less successful than the UVF's earlier coup at Larne, and, partly owing to the confusion of the authorities, there was a clash between the regular troops and the volunteers which led to three civilian deaths.

One last effort was made through the king to bring about an agreement, by inviting all the party leaders to a conference at Buckingham Palace on 21 July to discuss 'exclusion'. Although it was generally accepted there that the four 'Protestant' counties should be excluded, there was no agreement at all over the future of Tyrone and Fermanagh, the two counties where there was no clear-cut religious majority. As a result, the Buckingham Palace Conference broke up in failure after three days without discussing any other problem. Nevertheless, it is fair to suggest that the principle of the **partition** of Ireland had been accepted by all sides – and that was to be important for the future.

With the worsening international situation in Europe, Asquith now agreed, at the prompting of all the other party leaders and in the interests of national unity, to abandon his attempt to introduce a revised Amending Bill. Everything was 'put into the shade' (as he wrote to a friend) by the coming war. For the moment, the Irish problem was to be shelved. If the parties had been forced to continue the negotiations, a constitutional settlement would almost certainly have been reached. In the event, the war enabled all sides to agree to shelve the issue in a way that virtually guaranteed the renewal of the crisis at some later date. The Home Rule Act – officially known as the Government of Ireland Act 1914 – was passed as an all-Ireland measure in September 1914 but its implementation was suspended for the duration of the war and the government promised that amending legislation would be required to meet the Ulster demands, although exactly how was left undefined. This outcome was preferable to a civil war, but it only postponed the crisis for an unknowable length of time. Even more significantly, it created the opportunity for extremists to strike for Irish independence during the great ordeal of war that was to come.

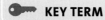

KEY TERM

Partition Division of a country into separate nations or separately governed regions.

Chapter summary

The Ulster Crisis over Home Rule was long in the making and entirely predictable. As far back as the Brunswick Clubs of 1828–9, mobilised (unsuccessfully) to oppose Catholic emancipation, Ulster Protestants had shown their willingness to challenge legislation they saw as offensive and dangerous to their interests. The distinctive social, economic and political position of Ulster, or at least the six counties with clear Protestant majorities, was also beyond dispute. Just as Catholic Ireland could invoke a cultural tradition based in the Irish Gaelic language, Protestant Ulster had its own cultural tradition based in Ulster Scots Gaelic, imported into Ulster in the sixteenth century. This tradition still flourished in the nineteenth and early twentieth centuries through the work of Ulster novelists such as W.G. Lyttle (1844–96) and Archibald McIlroy (1860–1915), who wrote in Scots. It has also enjoyed a revival from the 1990s with the founding of the Ulster Scots Language Society in 1992. Anglican and Presbyterian distrust of Roman Catholicism was deeply woven by historical events into the fabric of Ulster society and still remains so. Gladstone chose to ignore Ulster distinctiveness in 1886 when he argued that Ulster resistance to Home Rule was temporary and would quickly pass away once Home Rule was passed. Ulster opposition to Home Rule was also strongly supported in Britain by the Conservatives and Liberal Unionists.

Refresher questions

Use these questions to remind yourself of the key material covered in this chapter.

1 How and why did Ulster develop along different social and economic lines compared to the rest of Ireland?

2 Why were the Ulster Unionists so vehemently opposed to Home Rule?

3 What impact did the defeat of the Second Home Rule Bill have on Irish nationalism?

4 How did the Conservatives' actions lead to the formation of the Ulster Unionist Council?

5 How committed were the Liberals to the idea of Home Rule when they returned to office in 1905?

6 What opportunities did the 1910 elections offer the Irish Parliamentary Party?

7 Why did the Liberals introduce the Third Home Rule Bill and what were its strengths and weaknesses as a proposal for the future of Ireland?

8 What form did Ulster resistance take?

9 Why were the Ulster Unionists prepared to push their opposition to Home Rule to such lengths?

10 Was the opposition in Ulster the most important element in the campaign against the Third Home Rule Bill?

11 How well did the Liberal government handle the 'Ulster Crisis' of 1912–14?

12 Was civil war in Ireland averted only by the First World War?

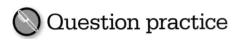
Question practice

SOURCE ANALYSIS QUESTION

1 Assess the value of Source 1 for revealing the impact of the cholera epidemic of 1848 and the methods used to combat it. Explain your answer, using the source, the information given about its origin and your own knowledge about the historical context.

INTERPRETATION QUESTION

1 Evaluate the interpretations in Passages 1 and 2 (page 157) and explain which you think is the more convincing explanation of Ulster's position during the Home Rule crisis of 1912–14.

SOURCE 1

From a Report of the Commissioners of Health in Ireland on epidemics between 1846 and 1850.

With a view to information on the disputed question of the contagion of Cholera, we subjoin extracts on both sides of the question.

'Belfast Union, December 6th 1848. A case of Cholera was admitted into the Fever Hospital in the morning of Monday last, and died in the evening. The patient, Thomas Tiernan, and his family had removed on 28th November, from a part of Edinburgh, in which there had been no case of Cholera, to another part of that city in which this disease had prevailed for some weeks. He arrived at Belfast on Saturday morning suffering from Diarrhoea, and was admitted into the probationary ward of the workhouse in the evening.'

To the supposed contagion of this case, the attack of Cholera in Belfast, in both workhouse and city was attributed. Mr. Phelan was directed to report on this case – the following is an extract from his observations:

'This opinion of contagion seems unfounded. Tiernan was for some hours in the probationary ward and next transferred to the Fever Hospital where he died. The next case, 7 days after, was in the Infirmary – it is stated to me that she had no communications whatever with Tiernan. Although all other cases slept in beds having one, two or three in the same bed, not one other that slept in such beds got Cholera.'

'Armagh Workhouse, 14th April 1849. Respecting the recent outbreak of Cholera – on Saturday last a strong wind blew in a direct line to Armagh from Belfast, forty miles away, where Cholera is now prevalent, and on that evening a girl of 12 years in the female school of the workhouse was suddenly attacked with malignant Cholera which proved fatal. This girl had no communication with any infected person. About the same hour a man was attacked with this disease on the Belfast road and has since died. On Sunday 5 persons in the workhouse were seized with Cholera – and for 3 days the disease continued to increase in frequency and fatality. During this period the wind from Belfast continued but on its shifting towards the west, there was an evident decline in the virulence of the malady proving unquestionably that the poison of Cholera was carried by the atmosphere.

PASSAGE 1

Adapted from Martin Pugh, 'The Triumph of New Liberalism 1899–1914' in Robert Ingham and Duncan Brack, editors, *Peace, Reform and Liberalism: A History of Liberal Politics in Britain 1679–2011*, Biteback Publishing, 2011.

During the 1890s the Liberal commitment to home rule had weakened, so much so that Rosebery had urged abandoning it altogether. However in many urban constituencies the small but well-organised Irish vote was crucial in sustaining the party's majority – and after the 1910 elections the Liberal government became dependent on Irish nationalist support in the Commons. The third Home Rule Bill, announced in the King's Speech in February 1912, had to be passed three times between 1912 and 1914 to overcome the peers' opposition and some Liberals complained that too much time was being devoted to Ireland; but it was not damaging on the mainland. In Northern Ireland the story was different. Led by Sir Edward Carson, the Ulster Unionists used this period to mobilise a violent resistance. Yet despite gaining influential support in Britain, their position was not strong; even in Ulster they had only seventeen seats compared to sixteen for the Nationalists, and one of those was lost at a by-election in Londonderry in 1913. In March 1914 Asquith offered to allow the Ulster counties to opt out of home rule for six years, after which they would join Dublin unless Parliament decided otherwise; but he refused demands to hold yet another general election before the enactment of the bill. Beyond this he declined any further compromise. Although by the summer of 1914 there was a real prospect of the two sides engaging in a civil war, the government was probably correct in thinking that the Tories were damaging themselves by their extremism and irresponsibility.

PASSAGE 2

Adapted from E.J. Feuchtwanger, *Democracy and Empire: Britain 1865–1914*, Bloomsbury, 1985.

The Liberals began to consider at an early stage the exclusion of Ulster from a Home Rule settlement. As the crisis proceeded, the view that Ulster must be offered some separate deal gained ground. On the other hand the violence of Unionist opposition to Home Rule increased Liberal determination to see it through. Nevertheless, among all the uncompromising protagonists Asquith faced over Ireland Redmond was the man in the weakest position. The third Home Rule Bill was in itself a very modest measure of self-government but neither Redmond nor the opponents of Home Rule regarded it as more than a staging post to full separation and independence and therefore the limited nature of the bill in no way mitigated the fierceness of the battle. The signs that the situation might drift into violence convinced Asquith to make concessions. This meant putting pressure on Redmond to accept the temporary exclusion of Ulster from the Home Rule Bill for six years. It was a dangerous concession for Redmond to make but when Asquith announced the proposal in the House of Commons Carson immediately turned it down. When the Great War put Irish affairs into cold storage, Ireland was certainly set for an outbreak of violence. It is impossible to tell how far this violence would have spread and it seems likely that it would have spurred the party leaders into further efforts to find a settlement. Asquith and his colleagues had tried to deal with the Irish problem within the conventions of the British parliamentary system; Bonar Law and the Unionists had taken their stand on the fact that a representative system must take account of a minority as large and determined as the Ulstermen.

CHAPTER 8

The making of the Anglo-Irish settlement

This chapter focuses on the impact of the First World War on Ireland; the bloody Anglo-Irish War of 1919–21 and the Anglo-Irish settlement of 1921–2. The background to these events needs to be carefully investigated, especially the way in which the Easter Rising led to an escalation of nationalism in Ireland. You also need to be aware of the constraints on Lloyd George, especially the fact that his government was dominated by Conservatives who insisted that Ireland should not become a republic and that the position of the Ulster had to be safeguarded. It also should be appreciated how this 'answer' to the Irish question led to further troubles. The chapter will examine these issues through the following themes:

★ The emergence of the 'new nationalists'

★ Ireland and the First World War

★ The Easter Rebellion 1916

★ The transformation of Sinn Féin

★ The Government of Ireland Act 1920

★ The Anglo-Irish War 1919–21

★ The Anglo-Irish Treaty 1921

Key dates

1914	Sept.	Home Rule Bill became law
1915	May	Formation of Asquith's coalition
1916	April 24	Beginning of Easter Rebellion
	April 29	Rebels surrendered
	May	Execution of rebel leaders
	Dec.	Formation of Lloyd George coalition
1917	July	Meeting of Irish Convention
	Oct.	De Valera elected leader of Sinn Féin
1918	April	Conscription proposed for Ireland
	Dec.	Landslide victories for Sinn Féin in Ireland and Lloyd George coalition in Britain
1919	Jan.	Beginning of Anglo-Irish War

1919	April	Dáil Éireann met; de Valera elected president of Irish Provisional government
	Sept.	Dáil declared illegal
1920		Black and Tans recruited
	Nov. 21	'Bloody Sunday' in Dublin
	Dec.	Martial law proclaimed in southern Ireland
1921	June	Opening of Northern Ireland parliament by George V
	July	Truce in Anglo-Irish War
	Dec.	Anglo-Irish Treaty signed
1922	Jan.	Anglo-Irish Treaty accepted narrowly by the Dáil
1923		End of civil war

The emergence of the 'new nationalists'

▶ *Who were the 'new nationalists'?*

In the early years of the twentieth century, new nationalist forces were taking shape in Ireland that would ultimately control Irish destinies and destroy the Irish National Party. These forces, however, were anything but unified in their understanding of what Irish nationalism should be.

The rise of revolutionary trade unionism

A militant new **labour movement** was growing, under the control of James Larkin, an ardent socialist and trade union organiser, and his colleague James Connolly. Ironically, neither was Irish born. Larkin was born in Liverpool in 1876 and Connolly in Edinburgh in 1868, both to Irish immigrant parents and both in poverty. Connolly, however, claimed in the 1901 and 1911 censuses to have been born in County Monaghan. Both men were essentially self-educated with little formal teaching. Larkin founded the Irish Transport and General Workers' Union (ITGWU) in 1909 with Connolly as his right-hand man; the overall aim was to unionise unskilled workers. The two then went on to form the Irish Labour Party in 1912 as the political wing of the Irish Trade Union Congress, which had split from the British TUC in 1894 to set up a purely Irish organisation. The immediate purpose of the Irish Labour Party was to represent workers' interests in the Home Rule crisis that followed the introduction of the Third Home Rule Bill in 1912. Larkin aided by Connolly then led a series of successful strikes in early 1913. This alarmed the Dublin employers and, in particular, the chairman of the Dublin United Tramway Company, William Martin Murphy. Murphy was an Irish nationalist – a former Irish National Party MP – and a newspaper owner, and had once turned down a knighthood offer from King Edward VII because it compromised his nationalist principles.

However, all this served only to demonstrate the huge gulf which could exist between Irish nationalists from vastly different backgrounds and with vastly different ideas. To Murphy, Larkin's desire to unionise workers represented a major threat to his business interests and he was determined to destroy that threat. In August 1913, he sacked 340 workers he suspected of being members of the ITGWU. At the end of August, the tramway workers went on strike in protest. Murphy then organised over 400 Dublin companies in demanding that their employees sign a pledge not to be members of the ITGWU or to engage in 'sympathy' strikes; that is, to support the strikes of other workers. The result was a bitter confrontation in which the employers engaged in a 'lock out', in effect refusing to allow their employees to work for them and employing workers from other parts of Ireland and Britain to replace them. The British TUC sent

 KEY TERM

Labour movement
The organisation of the working classes so that they can achieve better conditions.

limited financial aid to the Dublin workers but rejected the call from Larkin and Connolly to stage sympathetic strikes in Britain. Finally, in January 1914, the union was forced to give in and the workers returned to work agreeing to sign the required pledges. Exhausted, Larkin left for the USA, where he remained until 1923 when he was deported back to Ireland after several years in prison for 'communist subversion'.

James Connolly and the influence of Marxism

Unlike Larkin, who consistently refused to engage in or advocate violence, James Connolly aimed for the revolutionary overthrow of British government in Ireland. He was motivated by the argument of Karl Marx (see the box below) that socialism could be achieved only when a country was sufficiently industrialised for the industrial workers (or the 'proletariat', to use Marx's terminology) to be strong enough to overthrow 'capitalist oppression' in a revolution. Connolly believed that Ireland had remained largely agricultural because it was forced to serve the wider needs of the British economy. To Connolly, Irish independence was essential if Ireland was ever to reach the stage at which a socialist state could be established. Connolly had military experience gained in the British Army, in which had he enlisted aged fourteen, falsifying both his name and age. All his time in the army was spent in Ireland. After seven years' service he deserted because his regiment was being sent to India. Having deserted, he married and returned to Edinburgh. He moved permanently to Ireland in 1896.

However, in 1903 forced by intense poverty and frustration at the lack of progress of revolutionary ideas in Ireland, Connolly emigrated to the USA. He did not return to Ireland until 1910 when he began his trade union work with James Larkin. While in America, Connolly founded an organisation he called the Irish Socialist Federation with around 80 members intended to raise awareness of Irish issues. Connolly managed to publish a magazine *The Harp* in which he developed his ideas about Marxism and it relevance to Ireland.

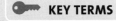 **KEY TERMS**

Socialist Workers' Republic Political system where government is based on the principle of a socialist state controlled by the working classes.

Separatism Principle of separating Ireland from Great Britain.

In aiming for a **Socialist Workers' Republic**, and in linking that idea with trade unionism, Connolly made a major breakthrough in the cause of Irish nationalism. He won over the urban working classes in Dublin to republicanism and therefore, by definition, to **separatism**. This provided a new and important political driving force for independence from Britain. Connolly was an inspirational speaker and, despite being self-taught, a brilliant writer. He set up a newspaper called the *Workers' Republic*. In 1913, aided by his military experience, he set up a new paramilitary force, the 'Irish Citizen Army'. The Citizen Army was well trained but small, never numbering more than 250 men. Connolly's aim was to prepare to fight a revolutionary struggle against British rule and capitalism. His political philosophy was essentially syndicalism (see the box below). In 1910, he published *Labour in Irish History*, in which he argued the Marxist case and dismissed the opposition of Ulster to Irish independence as temporary and irrelevant. In this, he was following Marx's stated view that the distinctiveness of Ulster was superficial and would eventually disappear. Connolly had little time for the leaders of the Irish Volunteers whom he considered middle-class capitalists out of touch with working-class interests.

Marxism

Karl Marx (1818–83) was a German-born philosopher who argued that a struggle between social classes for control of economic resources is the primary driving force in history. He believed that the emergence of a global socialist (or communist) society was an inevitable process that could be advanced more quickly by revolution against any existing ruling elite. Marx claimed that the old agricultural elites of the pre-industrial age had already been overthrown by industrial capitalism and the next stage was for the industrial working class to overthrow the capitalist system in a revolution and establish control of economic resources.

Marx's ideas are contained in two main works: *The Communist Manifesto* (1848) and *Capital* (1867). In these books he aimed to show that the capitalist system is forced to exploit labour in order to make profits and is doomed ultimately to fail. 'Capital' is defined as any form of wealth that can be used to invest in profit-making ventures. So capital might take the form of money, land, buildings, machinery, vehicles for transportation and so on. According to Marx, a worker's capital is his labour – skilled or unskilled.

Marx's ideas are highly controversial and some of his main assumptions can be easily disproved. Marx disliked trade unions, which he saw as conforming to capitalism and dividing workers rather than uniting them. He opposed parliamentary democracy and social reform legislation as attempts to buy off the workers and divert them from revolution. Many of his ideas are vague, especially those which relate to how society is to be administered after the overthrow of capitalism, and thus Marxists do not agree about many issues and there are several different varieties of Marxism. Nevertheless, his ideas, and particularly the ways in which his ideas were subsequently interpreted, had great influence in the twentieth century.

Syndicalism

In 1905, a French socialist, George Sorel, published a book entitled *Reflections on Violence*. In this, he traced the actions of French trade unions, which were generally far more aggressive than their British counterparts, and argued that trade unionism should forget trying to reform existing parliamentary systems and focus on creating an alternative revolutionary society governed on behalf of the workers by trade unions. Syndicalism – based on the French word for trade unions, *syndicats* – developed from this idea. Syndicalists argued for class war and the violent overthrow of the capitalist system. The strategy would be to merge all trade unions into a single revolutionary organisation and use it to start a general strike of all workers in all industries to paralyse the country and destroy the parliamentary system of government.

Sinn Féin

James Connolly's Marxist movement, with its newspaper, the *Workers' Republic*, and its group of activists, the Citizen Army, was opposed by another new nationalist force, Sinn Féin (meaning 'we, ourselves'), founded by Arthur Griffith in 1905. This movement, through its paper the *United Irishmen*, rejected Connolly's ideas of socialism and violent revolution as well as the Irish National Party's constitutional approach. Instead, Griffith wanted a system of peaceful resistance in which a voluntary parliament would be formed to govern Ireland in defiance of the British government. This meant simply carrying on as if Ireland was already independent and ignoring British institutions, such as the British parliament, the courts and civil administration, as though they did not exist.

The essence of Griffith's policy was a federal solution, in which Ireland and Great Britain would have been made equal in status. A similar solution had been used – after years of disputes and hostility – by Austria and Hungary in the 1860s. This had successfully improved their relations as the two strongest powers within the Austrian Empire, which was often referred to as the Austro-Hungarian Empire thereafter. Griffith did not want a republic and he did not want the overthrow of capitalism. He aimed to create conditions in which capitalism could flourish more to the benefit of the Irish people.

Underground groups

Apart from these two open organisations, there remained the underground groups dedicated to the Fenian tradition, such as the Irish Republican Brotherhood (IRB). Although republican, the IRB had no clearly defined political philosophy: it was not Marxist, and it had little natural sympathy with Connolly's movement. On the other hand, its commitment to violence repelled Griffith. The IRB infiltrated other nationalist groups including Sinn Féin, the Irish Volunteers and the Gaelic League. There were, therefore, serious divisions of opinion between the various strands of Irish nationalism and, in these circumstances, the Irish National Party under the leadership of John Redmond faced little in the way of a serious challenge to its continued domination of Irish politics.

Summary diagram: The emergence of the 'new nationalists'

1905: Arthur Griffith formed Sinn Féin as a non-violent nationalist movement

1909: James Larkin and James Connolly formed the Irish Transport and General Workers' Union

The emergence of the 'new nationalists'

1912: Connolly and Larkin founded the Irish Labour Party as a political wing of the Irish trade unions

1913: Connolly founded the Irish Citizen Army as a military force to promote a Marxist revolution in Ireland

Ireland and the First World War

▶ *How did the First World War affect Ireland?*

Ireland's future was to be determined more by the impact of the First World War than by any other factor. Britain's declaration of war on Germany on 4 August 1914 was supported by both the Irish Nationalist Party and the Ulster Unionists. Indeed, Redmond offered to use the nationalist-controlled Irish Volunteers to help defend the shores of Ireland against enemy action. In return for their patriotic stance, both sides hoped to secure some positive response from the British government in support of their Irish claims. Redmond regarded it as a triumph for the nationalists when, in September, Asquith placed the 1914 Irish Home Rule Act on the statute book, although its provisions were to be suspended until the end of the war. No one expected the war to last very long, and so the unionists in the House of Commons and the House of Lords were angry at what they considered to be Asquith's high-handed action. They acquiesced for the sake of national unity and patriotic duty in a war situation, but had no intention of accepting the idea of compelling Ulster into the Home Rule provisions. In any case, the position of Ulster was still to be finally resolved. The government had accepted – as part of the passing of the Act – that there would need to be further amending legislation at the end of the war before the Act was actually put into operation. Exactly what form these amendments would take, however, was unclear.

In Ireland, the early period of the war was marked by massive recruiting for the armed forces, in both the north and the south. By the spring of 1916, around 150,000 Irishmen were in active service. There was also increased prosperity, owing to the stimulus given to the Irish economy by the needs of war – especially the demand for foodstuffs – and the money sent home by Irish servicemen. But for Irish nationalists frustration soon set in. As the war dragged on with no sign of an early victory, the prospect of any rapid change in the constitutional status of Ireland became increasingly remote: Home Rule became 'a cheque continuously post-dated', as the leading nationalist Eoin MacNeill bitterly observed in 1916. Even loyal nationalists were irritated by the insensitivity of the British government. A special division was formed in the British Army for the Ulster Volunteer Force, for example, but not for the Irish Volunteers, and, even more damning, when Asquith formed a wartime coalition government in May 1915, Carson and several other leading Irish Unionists were invited to join.

Many began to feel that the war was no longer Ireland's concern. Redmond's old policy of alliance with the Liberals seemed to have got him nowhere. After the formation of the coalition in the spring of 1915, the purpose of the Irish Parliamentary Party became difficult to discern. All this played into the hands of the more extreme Irish nationalists. The revolutionaries were soon to advance to the centre of the stage.

3 The Easter Rebellion 1916

▶ *What were the events of the Easter Rebellion?*

▶ *Why did the British government punish those involved in the way that it did?*

From the start, the revolutionary Irish nationalists – mainly members of the IRB – had opposed the war and the policies of the Irish Parliamentary Party, and did their best to prevent recruitment and support for the British war effort in Ireland itself. In September 1914, following an incautious public speech by John Redmond, in which he intimated that the Irish Volunteers might be allowed to serve overseas as well as in Ireland, the volunteer movement split.

The overwhelming majority – some 180,000 men – remained loyal to Redmond, and became known as the 'National Volunteers'. A small, anti-war group of about 11,000 men, under the leadership of Eoin MacNeill, set themselves up as a separate organisation called the 'Irish Volunteers'. The leaders of the latter group were mostly romantic revolutionaries, strongly influenced by the literary, historical and religious roots of Irish nationalism – MacNeill was a professor of medieval Irish history – and passionately committed to a free and independent Ireland. Their main aim now was to gain power in Ireland and, with the support of the Irish people, proclaim an independent Irish republic. MacNeill, the Irish Volunteers' chief of staff, was against a premature uprising, believing it could have no possible chance of success against the British forces and would lead to a pointless waste of life. He preferred to hold his force in reserve as a counter in later negotiations with the British.

Planning the rebellion

Despite MacNeill's opposition, a small group of his fellow commanders and other revolutionaries were prepared to go ahead with an armed rebellion, despite the odds. Early in 1916, they began planning for an uprising at Easter. The key figures were Tom Clarke, Sean MacDermott, James Connolly and Patrick Pearse – in many ways the outstanding personality in the Easter Rebellion. For Pearse, questions of military success or failure were largely irrelevant: the 'blood sacrifice' – to die for Ireland – was a noble end in itself and would help to stimulate Irish national consciousness. 'Bloodshed', he had written earlier, 'is a cleansing and sanctifying thing … there are many things more horrible than bloodshed, and slavery is one of them.' Connolly, a Marxist, and the leader of the tiny Irish Citizen Army which he had helped to form to defend the transport workers in the Dublin strike of 1913, was more of a realist. He believed that a successful rebellion was possible if it secured the support of the Irish masses. Initially, it was Connolly who pressed hardest for a revolt. The revolutionaries hoped to obtain arms from Germany, and indeed Sir Roger

Casement, a former British diplomat and a fanatical supporter of the Irish cause, had gone from the United States to Germany in October 1914 (financed by Irish-American funds) to obtain German support for an Irish revolution in the form of weapons and munitions. The German arms shipment, however, was intercepted by the Royal Navy and the Germans scuttled the ship. Casement then returned to Ireland three days before the rebellion in an attempt to prevent it from going ahead, since he now believed it could not possibly succeed. He was captured by the British authorities and sent to London to be charged with treason.

Plans for the rebellion were organised by Clarke, MacDermott, Pearse and Connolly and their tiny band of fellow conspirators in conditions of intense secrecy, both for security reasons and because they were aware that MacNeill was against such action. Their plan was to begin the uprising in Dublin through the Irish Volunteers, under the guise of ordinary field manoeuvres, and at a time when the city would be relatively deserted and the authorities off guard.

The course of the rebellion

On the morning of Easter Monday 1916, a small detachment of Irish Volunteers and members of the Irish Citizen Army, headed by Pearse, Connolly and other leaders, marched into central Dublin – without a shot being fired – and seized control of the General Post Office; there they made their headquarters. Pearse, standing on the steps outside, then read out a proclamation (see Source A) announcing the birth of the Irish Republic to puzzled passers-by. A provisional government was established with Pearse as head.

SOURCE A

From the Irish Proclamation of Independence, 1916 (available at www.anpost.ie/ AnPost/History+and+Heritage/History/1916+Rising/The+Proclamation/).

In the name of God and of the dead generations from which she receives her old tradition of nationhood, Ireland, through us summons her children to her flag and strikes for her freedom … supported by her exiled children in America and by gallant allies in Europe, but relying in the first on her own strength, she strikes in full confidence of victory … We declare the right of the people of Ireland to the ownership of Ireland and to … control of Irish destinies … we hereby proclaim the Irish Republic as a Sovereign Independent State … The Republic guarantees religious and civil liberty, equal rights and equal opportunities to all its citizens … cherishing its children … oblivious of the differences carefully fostered by an alien government, which have divided a minority from the majority in the past. In this supreme hour the Irish nation must, by its valour and discipline and by the readiness of its children to sacrifice themselves for the common good, prove itself worthy of the august destiny to which it is called.

Study Source A. How far was Pearse speaking for the whole Irish people?

SOURCE B

Devastation on Sackville Street in Dublin, May 1916, where it crosses the River Liffey, caused during the Easter Rising. The street later was renamed O'Connell Street and a statue of O'Connell now stands on the left.

> ? Study Source B. Why do you think the failed rising has been commemorated in this way?

By nightfall, many of the key buildings in the city of Dublin were in the hands of the rebels, purely because of the unexpected nature of their actions. However, as a serious military enterprise, the Easter Rebellion was doomed from the start for the following reasons:

- The rebellion was mostly confined to Dublin, and most citizens there were bemused or downright hostile. Indeed, many felt that the rebels were simply traitors, stabbing Britain in the back when so many Irishmen were fighting and dying in France.
- Strategically, the success of the rebellion depended on the participation of the provincial units of the Irish Volunteers; but this did not take place. MacNeill got wind of Pearse's plans and used his authority as chief of staff to ban military activity by the Irish Volunteers over the weekend, and the provincial units obeyed.
- The rebels did not receive the help from Germany that had been expected.
- Once the authorities got organised, the rebels were heavily outnumbered by soldiers and armed police.

The end of the rebellion

It is true that the British authorities, who had never taken the earlier activities of the Irish Volunteers very seriously, were caught unawares by the outbreak of the rebellion in Dublin. But even on Easter Monday the rebels were outnumbered by soldiers and armed police. When reinforcements and artillery were brought into action on the following day, the position of Pearse and his comrades, despite their fervour and bravery, was hopeless. British shelling set the General Post Office ablaze, and the rebel leaders were forced to flee and join their comrades in other parts of the city, where there was fierce fighting and much destruction of property. Then the rebels were hunted down, and within a week it was all over. On Saturday 29 April, Patrick Pearse, on behalf of the rebel forces, surrendered unconditionally to the British authorities. It has been estimated that about 450 Irish people were killed during the rebellion and about 2000 wounded. Most of these casualties were civilians not directly involved in the conflict. On the British side, 116 soldiers and police were killed and 300–400 wounded.

The aftermath

The Easter Rebellion of 1916 was in no sense a **national rising**: only about 1600 men and women participated on the rebel side, most of them supporters of one section of the Irish Volunteers (the National Volunteers remained loyal), and the rebellion was therefore made 'by a minority of a minority'. It was condemned by the Catholic Church, and denounced by Redmond and the moderate nationalists. Public opinion was generally hostile. Yet, within a few weeks, Irish attitudes towards the rebellion began to change. This was mainly due to the policies now adopted by the British authorities.

Prime Minister Asquith handed over the problem of dealing with the aftermath of the rebellion to the army. Martial law had been proclaimed in Dublin and then throughout Ireland at the beginning of Easter Week. As a result, General Maxwell, the British commander-in-chief, applied martial law and instituted a draconian policy of wholesale arrests, followed by imprisonment or **internment**. Fifteen executions then followed as Maxwell pursued the objective of destroying revolutionary nationalism once and for all. In all, the aftermath of the Easter Rebellion was as follows:

- About 3000 Irish men and women were arrested; about half of these were soon released.
- One hundred and sixty people suffered terms of imprisonment and most of the remainder were interned in England and Wales.
- Ninety prisoners were tried and sentenced to death.
- Fourteen leaders, including all seven signatories of the Easter Monday Proclamation, were executed early in May. James Connolly, who had been badly wounded in the fighting and was unable to stand, was shot sitting in a chair. The fifteenth execution was of a man who had shot and killed a police officer while resisting arrest in the aftermath of the rebellion.

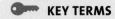

KEY TERMS

National rising A revolt or revolution carried out with the support of a large part of the population of a country.

Internment The practice of detaining persons considered dangerous during a war or a crisis.

- The remaining 75, including Éamon de Valera (see profile on page 173) and Countess Markievicz, an upper-class Irishwoman married to a Polish aristocrat, had their death sentences commuted to imprisonment.
- In August 1916, Casement – who had first tried to support the rebellion with German weapons and then tried to prevent it from going ahead – was executed for treason.

Reaction to the measures

The harshness of these measures and the callous way in which some of the executions were carried out, together with reports of ill-treatment of prisoners and intimidation of civilians, aroused horror and resentment among all classes in southern Ireland. The prominent Irish writer George Bernard Shaw remarked that the British were 'canonising their prisoners'. Hence, the rebels were given a degree of belated respectability, and Irish nationalists were able to ignore the fact that the rising had been a fiasco. Anti-war and anti-British sentiments in Ireland were hardened, and John Dillon (Redmond's second-in-command) began to take a critical tone towards the government's handling of the situation. While he still condemned the rebels as 'wrong', he also began to talk about their having 'fought a clean fight'. He also completely condemned the executions.

SOURCE C

From a speech by John Dillon in the House of Commons on 11 May 1916, quoted in *Hansard*, HC Deb 11 May 1916, vol 82, cc935–70.

The great bulk of the population were not favourable to the insurrection, and the insurgents themselves, who had confidently calculated on a rising of the people in their support, were absolutely disappointed. They got no popular support whatsoever. What is happening is that thousands of people in Dublin, who ten days ago were bitterly opposed to the whole of the Sinn Fein movement and to the rebellion, are now becoming infuriated against the government on account of these executions, and, as I am informed by letters received this morning, that feeling is spreading throughout the country in a most dangerous degree.

> ? What do you think were Dillon's motives for making the speech quoted in Source C?

As a result of these reactions, as well as of pressure from the US government, Asquith concluded that a new effort must be made to secure an Irish settlement immediately. Lloyd George was put in charge of negotiations. Lloyd George proposed to John Redmond and Sir Edward Carson a Home Rule solution based on the exclusion of the six mainly Protestant counties of Ulster. He managed to get both sides to accept this, but only by being less than clear about the government's intentions. Redmond was led to believe that the exclusion was temporary, while Carson thought that the exclusion of the six counties would be permanent. Lloyd George's attempts to find a solution collapsed anyway, since the key unionists in the coalition government were against any immediate grant of Home Rule. As a result of these discussions, Carson resigned from the government.

For Redmond, the failure of the negotiations was a personal disaster. His apparent willingness to accept the partition of Ireland led to his denunciation by important sections of Irish opinion, and his personal influence, and that of his party, declined ever more rapidly. 'Enthusiasm and trust in Redmond is dead', one Irish MP noted, 'so far as the mass of the people is concerned.' Thus, as the historian F.S.L. Lyons observed in his 1971 book *Ireland since the Famine*, 'the whole constitutional movement, in the last analysis, was the chief casualty of 1916'. It was Sinn Féin – conspicuous by its absence from the negotiations of that year – that now came to occupy the place formerly held by Redmond's Irish Parliamentary Party as the dominant force in Irish nationalism.

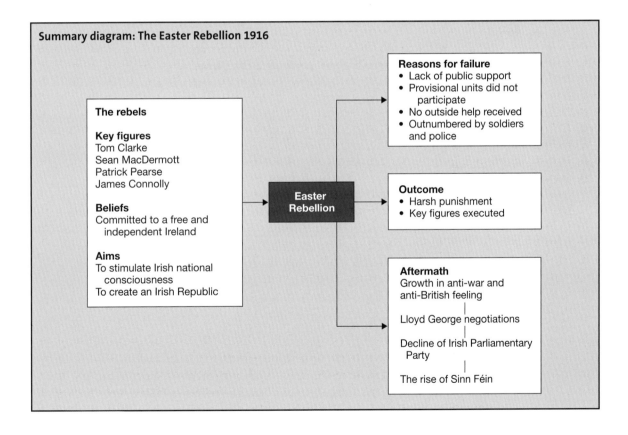

Summary diagram: The Easter Rebellion 1916

The rebels

Key figures
Tom Clarke
Sean MacDermott
Patrick Pearse
James Connolly

Beliefs
Committed to a free and independent Ireland

Aims
To stimulate Irish national consciousness
To create an Irish Republic

Easter Rebellion

Reasons for failure
- Lack of public support
- Provisional units did not participate
- No outside help received
- Outnumbered by soldiers and police

Outcome
- Harsh punishment
- Key figures executed

Aftermath
Growth in anti-war and anti-British feeling
|
Lloyd George negotiations
|
Decline of Irish Parliamentary Party
|
The rise of Sinn Féin

The transformation of Sinn Féin

▶ *How and why did the nature of the Sinn Féin party change?*

Sinn Féin had been founded by Arthur Griffith in 1907 as a militant, but non-violent, Irish nationalist organisation. It had had little influence before the war, and its anti-war stance in 1914 remained a minority view. What changed the situation was the Easter Rebellion of 1916. The cult of 'the men of 1916' as heroes and martyrs, which developed virtually from the moment of their execution, and the growth of the historical myth – cultivated by both their friends and their enemies – that the Easter Rebellion was essentially a Sinn Féin uprising, increased the prestige and influence of Griffith's organisation at the expense of the Irish Parliamentary Party.

Sinn Féin's popularity increased even more as a result of the policies pursued by the British government and the army after May 1916:

- the continuation of martial law and further imprisonments, including that of Griffith, who had always condemned violence
- the creation of fresh martyrs owing to the deaths of a few prisoners on hunger strike
- the spread of revolutionary ideas among the Irishmen brought together in the prisons and internment camps
- the apparent acceptance of the Unionist veto over immediate Home Rule by Asquith and Lloyd George.

By the end of 1916, Sinn Féin had, in effect, remodelled itself. It had become a revolutionary party committed to the establishment of the Irish Republic whose birth had been announced in the Easter Monday Proclamation. The changing trend of opinion in Ireland was seen when, early in 1917, Sinn Féin won two by-elections in usually safe Irish National Party seats. In April, the United States entered the war on the side of the Allies. As a result of pressure from US President Woodrow Wilson for an Irish settlement, Lloyd George (who had replaced Asquith as prime minister in December 1916) released the Irish prisoners held in internment in Great Britain.

All this did was to provide new, more revolutionary, recruits for Sinn Féin. Lloyd George then followed this up by summoning an Irish Convention in July 1917, representing the British government and all parties in Ireland, to try once again to hammer out an Irish settlement. The Convention scheme has been called 'a masterstroke of improvisation', since Lloyd George's real intention was to keep Irishmen talking for as long as possible while he got on with the task of winning the war. In this he was successful, since the Convention staggered on until May 1918. But as far as an Irish settlement was concerned it was a complete failure, since Sinn Féin boycotted the Convention and the Ulster Unionists remained as immovable as ever. This drove another nail into the coffin of the Irish Parliamentary Party, as Redmond had pinned all his last hopes for immediate Home Rule on the Convention. Its failure left him isolated and bereft of ideas. He died in May 1918, during the last days of the conference, a sad and disappointed man.

More significant than the summoning of the Irish Convention in July 1917 was the election that same month of Éamon de Valera as Sinn Féin MP for East Clare. His election was clearly 'a vote for 1916'. Sinn Féin now extended and strengthened its organisation. At its national conference in October 1917, de Valera was elected president in succession to Griffith, and in the following month he became head of the Irish Volunteers, thus combining in his person the leadership of both the political and military wings of the Irish revolutionary movement. By October 1917, there were some 1200 Sinn Féin clubs throughout Ireland, with a total of about 250,000 members. By 1918, Sinn Féin had taken over the position enjoyed by Parnell's Irish Parliamentary Party in the 1880s. What strengthened its position even further was the conscription crisis that emerged in Ireland that same year.

The conscription crisis

As a result of the heavy and continuous demand for manpower that followed the German spring offensive of 1918 on the Western Front, the British government began to contemplate ending existing exemptions and increasing the upper age limit for military service. There was considerable opposition to this, particularly from trade unions and in Ulster unless accompanied by the introduction of conscription in Ireland. The **Conscription Act of 1916** had not been applied in Ireland because it was based on a National Register drawn up by Lord Derby – known as the 'Derby Scheme' – and this had not covered Ireland. Lloyd George, though doubtful about the wisdom of extending conscription to Ireland, realised that the legislation could not get through parliament unless Ireland was included. The necessary legislation was therefore passed through parliament in May 1918. 'All Ireland will rise against you', John Dillon (successor to Redmond as leader of the Irish Parliamentary Party) warned Lloyd George. He was wrong about this, of course, since in Ulster the demand for conscription was strong and had been for some time, whereas outside Ulster opposition was virtually universal.

Dillon and his party displayed their opposition by walking out of the House of Commons and going to Dublin where, in alliance with Sinn Féin, they organised a nationwide campaign against conscription. A one-day strike was also mounted by the Irish trade unions, and the Roman Catholic Church in Ireland denounced conscription as oppressive and inhumane. Lloyd George was convinced that any imposition of conscription in Ireland was only possible if it was accompanied by an agreement on Home Rule. The scale of opposition reinforced his view and consequently conscription in Ireland, although legally available, was never applied. The damage, however, had been done.

 **KEY TERM**

Conscription Act of 1916 Men aged 18–41 were liable to be called up for service unless they were married, widowed with children, or else served in one of a number of reserved occupations considered vital to the war effort.

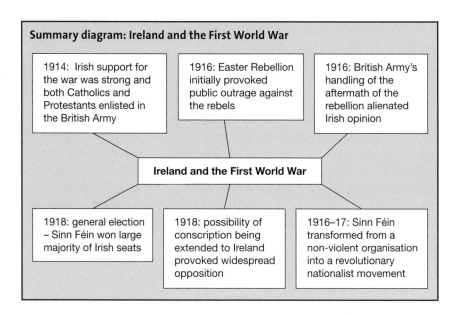

Summary diagram: Ireland and the First World War

1914: Irish support for the war was strong and both Catholics and Protestants enlisted in the British Army

1916: Easter Rebellion initially provoked public outrage against the rebels

1916: British Army's handling of the aftermath of the rebellion alienated Irish opinion

Ireland and the First World War

1918: general election – Sinn Féin won large majority of Irish seats

1918: possibility of conscription being extended to Ireland provoked widespread opposition

1916–17: Sinn Féin transformed from a non-violent organisation into a revolutionary nationalist movement

The 1918 general election

It was Sinn Féin which gained most from this radicalisation of opinion in southern Ireland, and its agitation was directed almost as much against the Irish Parliamentary Party as the British government. As Dillon said, presciently, Sinn Féin's purpose was 'to swallow us up', and indeed the alliance between the two organisations soon collapsed.

An example of the changing trend in Irish opinion is illustrated by the fact that in April 1918 Arthur Griffith (now vice-president of Sinn Féin) was returned for East Cavan by an overwhelming majority. The authorities in Ireland responded to all this by arresting republican leaders – claiming their involvement in a German plot – and clamping down on public meetings and the press. This antagonised public opinion and played into Sinn Féin's hands. The results were seen in the general election held in December 1918, shortly after the signing of the November Armistice which ended the war. In Ireland, the election proved to be a bitter and ugly affair. Its consequences, however, were decisive for the future of the country.

Sinn Féin fought the 1918 election on the basis of the principles enshrined in the Easter Monday Proclamation. This meant support for an independent Irish Republic for all Ireland, and the destruction – by 'any and every means available' – of English power. Any Irish party demanding less than complete independence was to be opposed. The problem of Ulster was ignored: Ulster unionism was, de Valera claimed, 'a thing of the mind only, non-existent in the world of reality'.

Éamon de Valera

1882	Born in New York, then raised in Ireland
1916	Took part in the Easter Rebellion
	Sentenced to life imprisonment
1917	Released from prison under a general amnesty
	Elected MP for East Clare
	Elected president of Sinn Féin
1918	Imprisoned
1919	Escaped from prison
	Elected president of the Dáil
1926	Split from Sinn Féin and formed Fianna Fáil
1932–48	Head of Irish government
1951–4	Head of Irish government
1957–9	Head of Irish government
1959–75	President of Ireland
1975	Died

The (probably) illegitimate child, born in New York, to a Spanish father and Irish mother, de Valera was educated in Ireland and for a time taught mathematics there. He joined the Gaelic League, and later the Irish Volunteers, and fought in the Easter Rising, being the last commander to surrender. Only his American citizenship saved him from execution. After a short period of imprisonment, his reputation as the sole leading figure to survive the rising helped him to become leader of both Sinn Féin and the Irish Volunteers.

In 1918, despite being imprisoned, he was elected an MP, and after breaking out of jail became president of the newly formed Dáil. His political ideal was a Gaelic republic comprising all 32 Irish counties.

For most of the Anglo-Irish War he was in the USA, raising money for the Irish cause. After the truce in July 1921, he held talks with Lloyd George (who commented that negotiating with him was 'like trying to pick up mercury with a fork'), but he controversially absented himself from the crucial talks held in London during October–December 1921. He wanted Michael Collins, whom he disliked and regarded as a rival, to receive the blame likely to attach to an unpopular settlement. It is, however, hard to judge the motives of such an ascetic, wily personality. Certainly, he disapproved of the terms that were reached and led the anti-treaty forces in the Civil War. Then he changed course, splitting with the militant Sinn Féiners in 1926 and forming his own party, Fianna Fáil.

The Irish poet W.B. Yeats once said that he was 'a living argument rather than a living man', but he was undoubtedly the most important Irish politician of the twentieth century.

The result of the 1918 general election was an overwhelming victory for Sinn Féin, and the virtual destruction of the Irish Parliamentary Party:

- Sinn Féin won 73 seats
- the Parliamentary Party just six (compared with 68 in December 1910)
- the Unionists obtained 26
- in the 26 counties of Catholic Ireland, Sinn Féin won 65 per cent of the votes cast.

In terms of the overall popular vote and the wider context of the election, in a much-enlarged electorate that was the result of the **Reform Act of 1918**, the Sinn Féin results were less impressive:

- Overall, 48 per cent of the votes were cast for Sinn Féin.
- Twenty-five of Sinn Féin's successful candidates were returned unopposed.

 KEY TERM

Reform Act of 1918
Granted the franchise to all men over 21 and to all women over 30.

- Thirty-one per cent of electors did not vote.
- The Irish Labour Party did not stand as a separate party.
- There was much electoral malpractice, with some Sinn Féin activists voting more than once. Vinny Byrne, a Sinn Féin activist and later IRA assassin, confessed in the highly acclaimed 1979 BBC documentary *Ireland: A Television History* to having voted over twenty times in his constituency, and added 'I was only one of many'.

The Dáil

Sinn Féin could now claim to represent the will of the Irish majority. The election had given it legitimacy. Its MPs decided, therefore, not to take their seats in the House of Commons and so refuse to recognise the authority of the UK parliament over Ireland. Instead, Sinn Féin summoned all its MPs to Dublin on 21 January 1919, to constitute themselves as the parliament of the Irish Republic (**Dáil Éireann**). Only 27 arrived as many were in prison or in hiding in Ireland or abroad. One of those in prison was the 1916 rebel Countess Markievicz, the first woman to be elected in a UK parliamentary election.

The Dáil issued a Declaration of Independence, demanded an English withdrawal from Ireland, and set up a provisional government under de Valera. In March, the British government, perplexed and bewildered by these recent events, released all the Irish political prisoners, thus strengthening Sinn Féin's hand. The Irish provisional government was soon able to make its authority effective over much of Ireland, where it established its own courts of law and even collected taxes. It was backed up by the power of the Irish Republican Army (IRA), as the Irish Volunteers were now coming to be called, under its brilliant leader, Michael Collins. Collins, who had fought in Dublin during the Easter Rebellion of 1916, was both an outstanding military commander and a practical statesman. He was to organise the intelligence system that proved so vital to the IRA during the Anglo-Irish War of 1919–21, and he also held important domestic posts in the Irish provisional government.

By 1919, the two authorities confronted one another in Ireland, both demanding the allegiance of the Irish people:

- the British government, which rested its mandate on law and established treaty rights
- the Irish provisional government, which claimed to represent the will of the Irish people and embody Irish nationhood.

In January 1919, two policemen in County Tipperary were killed during an IRA attempt to obtain explosives from a local quarry. For Sinn Féin and the IRA this marked the opening shots in what they regarded as a war for Irish independence. By that time, however, the British government was already planning a new constitutional initiative for the whole of Ireland.

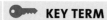

KEY TERM

Dáil Éireann Irish parliament.

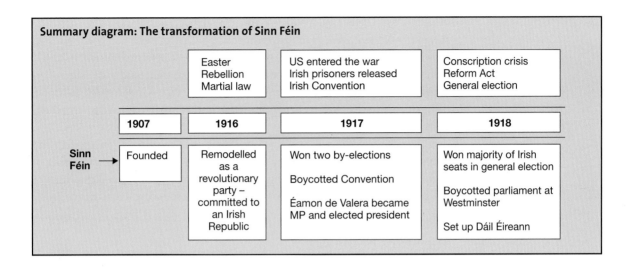

Summary diagram: The transformation of Sinn Féin

	Easter Rebellion Martial law	US entered the war Irish prisoners released Irish Convention	Conscription crisis Reform Act General election
	1916	**1917**	**1918**

	1907	**1916**	**1917**	**1918**
Sinn Féin →	Founded	Remodelled as a revolutionary party – committed to an Irish Republic	Won two by-elections Boycotted Convention Éamon de Valera became MP and elected president	Won majority of Irish seats in general election Boycotted parliament at Westminster Set up Dáil Éireann

5 The Government of Ireland Act 1920

▶ *What were the intentions behind the Act?*

Outside Ireland, the result of the general election of December 1918 was an overwhelming victory for the coalition government of Lloyd George, who was supported by the Conservatives (with nearly 400 MPs) and a section of the Liberals. The other part of the Liberal Party, led by Asquith, together with the Labour Party, were now in opposition. For the government, the Irish question was bound to re-emerge as an important priority, not only because of Sinn Féin's recent victory in the Irish elections, but also because the application of the 1914 Home Rule Act had been postponed only until the end of the war. The Irish question still required a proper answer.

Yet, the profound changes in British party politics since 1914, together with the new emphasis on **national self-determination** enshrined in the declarations of the peacemakers at Paris, were bound to affect the Irish question. Indeed, the coalition government had announced in 1918 that one of its first tasks was to 'explore all practical paths towards a settlement of this grave and difficult question on the basis of self-government'. This consensus over self-government ('we are all Home Rulers now', as one Tory MP observed) meant that the Conservative Party, apart from a few 'diehard' MPs, distanced itself from the Ulster Unionists and was no longer prepared to oppose Home Rule, as long as it could be accomplished with a recognition of Ulster's rights and the retention of Ireland within the British Empire.

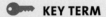 **KEY TERM**

National self-determination The idea that nations should have the right to govern themselves.

Nevertheless, Ulster Unionists were still in a relatively strong position. A number of them were in the government, and Carson (who had been returned for a Belfast constituency in 1918) was still an influential figure outside. In the House of Commons the Conservative Party was dominant; and the Ulster Unionists (who had won 22 out of 37 seats in northern Ireland) formed the only distinct Irish voice at Westminster, since the Sinn Féin MPs refused to take their seats. Moreover, Lloyd George – who remembered his disastrous experience over the Irish negotiations in 1916 – was determined this time to ensure that any proposed Irish settlement received the backing of his Conservative colleagues. Walter Long (a former leader of the Ulster Unionists) was appointed chairman of the government's Irish committee with the task of producing a new Home Rule bill.

The terms of the Act

The main feature of the eventual government plan for Ireland was the application of the principle of Home Rule to both Ulster and southern Ireland. The Government of Ireland Bill of 1920 therefore proposed:

- The establishment of two separate parliaments for northern and southern Ireland, consisting of an elected House of Commons and a Senate (Upper House), together with a government responsible to each parliament.
- Election to the two parliaments was to be by **proportional representation** in order to safeguard the rights of minorities in each region.
- The powers of the parliaments were to be similar to those contained in the 1914 Home Rule Act, which meant that although they were responsible for most internal affairs, the imperial government would still retain considerable control. Thus, the new parliaments were to have no jurisdiction over foreign policy, defence, external trade, customs, police or even the Post Office.
- The supremacy of the UK parliament remained 'unaffected and undiminished over all persons, matters and things in Ireland', in order to justify the British government's intervention in the affairs of Northern Ireland.

As far as the vexed question of the boundaries of Northern Ireland was concerned, the coalition government eventually accepted the Ulster Unionist argument in favour of six counties (see page 168) on the grounds that, owing to their overall Protestant majority, security and stability in the new state would be made easier. Both parts of Ireland were to be represented at Westminster. There was also to be a Council of Ireland, consisting of representatives from both north and south, to deal with common problems; and it was written into the Act that, if both sides consented, one common parliament could be established for the whole country. For Lloyd George, this represented one final appeal to the old Liberal Party ideal of Home Rule for the whole of Ireland.

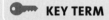

KEY TERM

Proportional representation An electoral system where the number of seats in parliament that a party gains is awarded in direct proportion to the number of votes it gets.

The Ulster Unionists, who had not originally wanted self-government within the UK, eventually came to see the advantages of the new proposals, particularly in the light of the IRA's violent campaign throughout Ireland (described on pages 178–80). 'We see our safety in having a Parliament of our own', wrote Captain Charles Craig (brother of the Ulster Unionist leader); 'we feel that we would then be in a position of absolute security.' The Government of Ireland Bill therefore easily passed through parliament at the end of 1920, and its terms came into operation in May 1921. In the elections for the Northern Ireland parliament that shortly followed, the Unionists won 40 out of the 52 seats, and as a result Sir James Craig became prime minister and began the formidable task of taking over powers from the British authorities and providing peace and stability in the new state.

Failure of the Act

In the south, however, the Act was virtually a dead letter. No elections were contested, and 124 supporters of Sinn Féin (which by that time was still fighting a war against England) were returned unopposed out of 128 candidates. To show their contempt for the Act, the Sinn Féiners then boycotted the new parliament as they had already done with the Westminster parliament after the elections of 1918. Thus, paradoxically, it was the Ulster Unionists who were now the committed Home Rulers. In southern Ireland, on the other hand, the political revolution that had been gathering pace since 1916 had made Home Rule irrelevant as an acceptable option for Irish nationalists. The Government of Ireland Act therefore was essentially constructed to solve the Irish problem as it had stood in 1914, not as it stood in 1920.

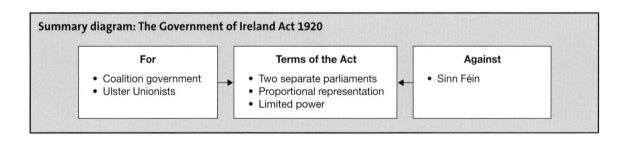

Summary diagram: The Government of Ireland Act 1920

For	**Terms of the Act**	**Against**
• Coalition government • Ulster Unionists	• Two separate parliaments • Proportional representation • Limited power	• Sinn Féin

The Anglo-Irish War 1919–21

▶ *How did the situation in Ireland develop into an armed conflict?*

At the same time as the British government was introducing the Government of Ireland Act, it was also trying to cope with the activities of the IRA throughout much of Ireland. From the beginning of 1919, the IRA, under the leadership of Michael Collins, had launched a campaign of murder and harassment directed mainly against the police and British soldiers, in an effort to destroy English power in Ireland and force England to withdraw. For Sinn Féin and the IRA, their campaign was a legitimate one on behalf of an existing Irish Republic, and they expected to be treated as the soldiers of an Irish national army.

SOURCE D

From the *Volunteer's Journal*, 31 January 1919, quoted in Russell Rees and Anthony C. Hepburn, *Ireland, 1905–1925: Documents and Analysis*, volume 2, Colourpoint, 1998, p. 177.

If they are called on to shed their blood in defence of the new-born Republic they will not shrink from the sacrifice. For the authority of the nation is behind them, embodied in a lawfully constituted authority … Dail Eireann, in its message to the Free Nations of the World, declares a 'state of war' to exist between Ireland and England … [which] can never be ended until the English military invader evacuates our country … The 'state of war' which is thus declared to exist … justifies Irish Volunteers in treating the armed forces of the enemy – whether soldiers or policemen – exactly as a National Army would treat the members of an invading army … Every Volunteer is entitled, morally and legally in the execution of his military duties, to use all legitimate methods of warfare against the soldiers and policemen of the English usurper, and to slay them if it is necessary to do so in order to overcome their resistance.

? What do you think was the most important intended audience for the statement in Source D?

Government policy

The British government found it difficult to know how to respond to these tactics. From its perspective, the IRA were members of a tiny 'murder gang' (in Lloyd George's description), unrepresentative of and alien to the mass of the Irish people. They were not and should not be treated as genuine combatants. But the government had no clear, positive policy to offer, and little understanding of what was really happening on the ground in Ireland. It was subject to the pulls and pressures of the military authorities on the spot and public opinion in Britain.

For a long time, Lloyd George and the Cabinet refused to recognise the existence of a state of war in Ireland, or the alienation of the Catholic masses from British rule and their sympathy with Sinn Féin's demand for independence. Lloyd George, under pressure from his Conservative backbenchers and busy with other problems, therefore reverted to the expedient of repression:

- Sinn Féin and the IRA became outlawed organisations.
- The Dáil was declared illegal.
- Special powers of arrest, imprisonment and arms control were introduced.
- Attempts were made to ban revolutionary publications.

To maintain law and order, the authorities relied at first primarily on the police. But the Royal Irish Constabulary (RIC) was undermanned and much demoralised by the IRA's murder campaign directed mainly against its officers: 176 policemen were killed in 1920, compared with 54 soldiers. The police were therefore strengthened by the recruitment of tough, ex-soldiers, who became known as the **Black and Tans**. Later, the Auxiliaries (see the box on page 180) were formed, consisting of former commissioned officers who were recruited as an elite military force.

The escalation of violence

During 1920, the IRA campaign became more widespread, more calculated and more brutal. It was now directed against civilians who could be regarded as giving comfort to the 'enemy', as well as the police and soldiers, and was accompanied by attacks on public buildings and isolated atrocities. The Black and Tans – and particularly the Auxiliaries – responded in kind, and their unofficial reprisals were, in effect, condoned by the British Army and the government. This attitude did not go uncondemned in Great Britain, especially by the press. Even the staunchly Conservative *Daily Express* proclaimed: 'murder for murder is … a confession of impotence, a return to sheer barbarism'. The Church of England, through its senior bishops, was also vocal in its concern. Criticism also came from the Trades Union Congress and many Labour and Liberal MPs. However, in reality, the politicians had little control over the forces on either side.

In the autumn of 1920, the British government at last accepted that it was engaged in a real war in Ireland, and applied regular troops on a wider scale. Martial law was introduced in the south. Neither side, however, paid much attention to the conventional rules of war. This last phase of the Anglo-Irish conflict became a grim affair of terror and counter-terror, ambush and atrocities, and the intimidation and occasional murder of civilians.

 **KEY TERM**

Black and Tans The name given to the Royal Irish Constabulary Reserve Force, recruited mainly in Britain but also in Ireland to reinforce the Royal Irish Constabulary. They wore uniforms mixing khaki army uniforms with the regular police uniforms to cover the shortage caused by the rapid recruitment.

> ## Auxiliaries
>
> Although often confused with the Black and Tans, the Auxiliaries were an entirely separate body within the RIC officially known as the 'Auxiliary Division'. Unlike the 'Tans', they were composed entirely of ex-officers and relatively highly paid (double the pay of an RIC constable and with extra allowances on top) to denote their intended status as an elite force charged with the task of directly countering the IRA insurgency. Although technically part of the RIC, they operated more or less independently. Many of these men had been promoted from the ranks to become officers during the war and were finding it hard to adjust to civilian life or find work commensurate with their newfound status: many were decorated and three had been awarded the Victoria Cross. By November 1921, the Auxiliary Division reached a peak strength of 1900 men.

Bloody Sunday and its aftermath

One of the worst episodes of the whole war – and illustrative of the nature of the conflict – took place on 'Bloody Sunday', 21 November 1920, in Dublin. Fourteen British undercover agents were killed and six wounded at different places in the city. The assassins were part of a special death squad specially recruited by Michael Collins consisting of twelve men selected for their ability to kill in cold blood. The twelve were ironically dubbed 'The Apostles'. The day of the killings was chosen to coincide with an important Gaelic football game between Dublin and Tipperary because the huge crowds in Dublin for the match would help the assassins move around more easily, avoiding detection. The Auxiliaries retaliated in the afternoon. They infiltrated the sports ground of Croke Park and fired indiscriminately at the players and the crowd, leaving behind twelve dead and 60 wounded.

A week after the events of Bloody Sunday on 28 November, the IRA carried out its most successful action against British forces. A local IRA commander, Tom Barry, a veteran of the First World War, assembled a flying column of 36 IRA men from the West Cork Brigade and ambushed two lorries transporting Auxiliaries near the village of Kilmichael in County Cork. The engagement has become known as the 'Kilmichael Ambush'. Sixteen Auxiliaries were killed at the scene, another who escaped was shot dead later, and one auxiliary survived badly wounded, having been left at the scene by the attackers who had assumed he was dead. Three IRA men were killed. Auxiliary reprisals were swift, terrible and prolonged. Houses, shops and barns in Kilmichael and other local villages were burned. Martial law was declared in the counties of Cork, Limerick, Tipperary and Kerry on 10 December. On 11 December, the centre of the city of Cork was burned by a combined force of Auxiliaries, Black and Tans and regular army soldiers.

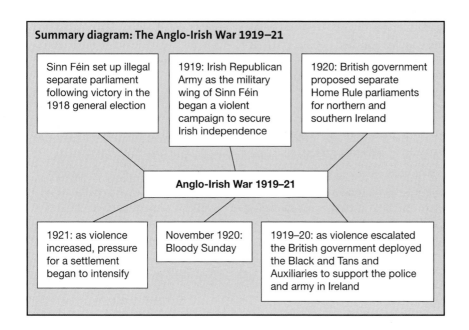

Summary diagram: The Anglo-Irish War 1919–21

Sinn Féin set up illegal separate parliament following victory in the 1918 general election

1919: Irish Republican Army as the military wing of Sinn Féin began a violent campaign to secure Irish independence

1920: British government proposed separate Home Rule parliaments for northern and southern Ireland

Anglo-Irish War 1919–21

1921: as violence increased, pressure for a settlement began to intensify

November 1920: Bloody Sunday

1919–20: as violence escalated the British government deployed the Black and Tans and Auxiliaries to support the police and army in Ireland

7 The Anglo-Irish Treaty 1921

▶ *What were the conditions of the Anglo-Irish Treaty?*

▶ *How should the 1921 Anglo-Irish Treaty be seen in historical perspective?*

By early 1921, however, it was clear that militarily the Anglo-Irish War was winnable by neither side. The IRA (as Collins accepted) was incapable of defeating the British Army, and it was getting short of men and materials as casualties among its members and civilians became heavier. The successful Kilmouth Ambush had killed seventeen Auxiliaries and severely wounded one, a propaganda victory and deeply embarrassing for the supposedly elite Auxiliaries, but in the context of British forces in Ireland numbering over 30,000 it was insignificant. Between January and July 1921, it is estimated that 752 men and women (both IRA and innocent civilians) were killed and 866 wounded. The British government was not prepared to use its full power in an all-out war against Catholic Ireland, which is what real victory would have required. Once these basic facts were recognised there was the possibility of a truce and negotiations between the two sides.

Moreover, by the end of 1920, Lloyd George was profoundly aware of the growing unpopularity of the Anglo-Irish War in Great Britain and anxious to find a way out. There was a deep revulsion against the methods pursued by the Auxiliaries and Black and Tans especially, which was expressed by Church leaders, opposition spokesmen ('a state of affairs prevails which is a disgrace to the human race', said Labour's Arthur Henderson), the trade union movement, and, above all, influential newspapers such as *The Times* and the *Manchester Guardian*. Opinion in the USA had also been shocked, and this was at a time when the British government was trying desperately (and largely failing) to keep the USA involved in world affairs in the face of growing isolationism there.

The prime minister was informed by his military advisers that it would require an army of 100,000 to subjugate Ireland permanently, and it was obvious that public opinion would never stand for such an operation. Hence, as D. George Boyce wrote in his 2004 book, *Ireland in Transition: 1867–1921*, 'it was the revolt of the British conscience, not the defeat of the British army, that obliged Lloyd George to seek terms of peace and settlement with Sinn Féin'. Moreover, the prime minister had at last come to realise that he was faced with opposition not just from a tiny 'murder gang', but from a political movement whose demands for independence were now increasingly supported by the majority of the Irish people outside Ulster.

The truce

In December 1920, Lloyd George put out peace feelers to de Valera in an effort to bring about a truce and negotiations, but these early moves failed. Nevertheless, the fact that a British prime minister was prepared to consider such a step represented a breakthrough in Anglo-Irish relations and (it has been suggested) a psychological victory for Sinn Féin. Lloyd George's determination to persist with his peace efforts was reinforced by reactions to the implementation of the Government of Ireland Act in the spring of 1921. The blunt refusal of Sinn Féin to have anything to do with the Southern Ireland parliament set up under the Act, not only showed its determination to consider nothing less than effective independence, but also raised the question: how were the 26 counties to be governed if Home Rule was ruled out? The alternatives seemed to be either all-out war and military rule, or peace and negotiations, and the first option was in practice impossible. The fact that a separate (six-county) Northern Ireland state was now in existence helped to remove an additional complication to any truce and future negotiations. In that sense, partition effectively cleared the way for a peace settlement.

Peace came quite suddenly. The catalyst has often been taken to have been the words of King George V in a speech given at the opening of the Northern Ireland parliament in Belfast on 22 June 1921: 'I appeal to all Irishmen to pause, to stretch out the hand of forbearance and conciliation, to forgive and forget and to join in making for the land which they love a new era of peace, contentment and good will.'

In reality, these words had no resonance with the Irish republicans. What moved de Valera and Collins more were hard military facts: the loss of men and weapons and the exhaustion produced by the conflict. They could have carried on for only another three weeks, Collins said later. The republican leaders also came to accept that Lloyd George was genuinely seeking a political settlement and was prepared to moderate his original conditions for peace in order to obtain one. The prime minister was, in fact, already thinking in terms of **Dominion Status** as the basis for such a settlement. Both sides therefore agreed to a truce on 11 July 1921.

The treaty

The truce was followed almost immediately by meetings between Lloyd George and de Valera, as well as Sir James Craig, which formed the prelude to a long period of complicated negotiations which lasted almost until the end of the year. The basis of Lloyd George's proposal for a political settlement was the offer of Dominion Status. This was a considerable advance on Home Rule, although it was less than complete independence. Dominion Status for Ireland meant that it would:

- gain full control of domestic affairs
- continue with membership of the British Empire
- remain in allegiance to the Crown.

In addition, the prime minister insisted on naval facilities for Britain in Ireland, and recognition of the state of Northern Ireland, 'which cannot be abrogated [abolished] except by their own consent'.

The British government's original proposals were rejected out of hand by the hard-line republican majority in the Dáil Éireann, for whom the oath of allegiance and membership of the British Empire were too much to stomach. De Valera himself, however, was prepared to accept some sort of connection with Great Britain. What was needed, therefore, was a form of words – and much of the discussion in the long months ahead turned on such verbal niceties – which would reconcile the reality of Irish independence with formal membership of the Empire. De Valera agreed to send a delegation to London on 11 October 1921, to negotiate with the British representatives 'with a view to ascertain how the association of Ireland with the community of nations known as the British empire may best be reconciled with Irish national aspirations'.

The Irish delegation

The five-man Irish delegation which assembled in London in October was led by Arthur Griffith and Michael Collins. De Valera preferred to remain in Dublin as the symbol of 'the republic', unsullied by the processes of bargaining taking place in London. This produced tension between the Irish leaders in Dublin and their colleagues in London, a situation which was worsened by the confusion over the status of the Irish delegates.

 **KEY TERM**

Dominion Status
Granting to Ireland the same constitutional powers as belonged to Canada and other Dominions within the British Empire.

KEY TERM

Plenipotentiaries
Representatives who have full power and authority to make agreements on behalf of their government.

On the one hand, they were described as **plenipotentiaries**, and could therefore sign a binding treaty with the British government on their own authority; on the other hand, de Valera insisted that any draft treaty arrived at be submitted first to the government back home. These misunderstandings among the Irish leaders gave a considerable advantage to the British team, and especially to a man as experienced and skilled in negotiation as Lloyd George. For it was the prime minister who really dominated the London conference. He had three government ministers as his colleagues: Winston Churchill, Austen Chamberlain (leader of the Conservative Party) and Lord Birkenhead. But the last two were there primarily to ensure that Lloyd George received the backing of the Conservative Party for any Irish settlement that he was able to secure.

There were three main questions for discussion by the two groups of delegates:

- British security and defence concerns – these were settled fairly easily when it was agreed that Great Britain should have three naval bases in Ireland.
- The question of Ulster – this did not prove in the end as difficult as might have been expected. None of the Irish leaders in London or Dublin wanted partition but none was really prepared to challenge the existence of the new state of Northern Ireland. Northern Ireland was therefore given the right to opt out of any treaty agreement.

In addition, Lloyd George persuaded the Irish delegates to accept the idea of a Boundary Commission, and led them to believe that its eventual recommendations would be so critical of Ulster's present boundaries that, if carried out, the Northern Ireland state would collapse and have to join up with the rest of Ireland. The prime minister also agreed to bring Northern Ireland into line over this proposal, but this was pure bluff, since there was no way in which Sir James Craig could be coerced into agreeing to cooperate with any such scheme, and in fact later negotiations to alter the boundary between the two states got nowhere.

The powers of the new Irish state, to be called the 'Irish Free State', proved to be the most contentious issue at the conference. The central issue was the problem of Ireland's relationship to the Crown and the Empire. Characteristically, for both sides this was more an argument about symbols than political realities. In the end, however, partly in return for the offer of the Boundary Commission, Lloyd George managed to get the Irish delegates to accept a cosmetic formula over the Crown and Empire issues. The Irish Free State would have Dominion Status rather than the independence Sinn Féin wanted, but the oath of allegiance to the Crown would be watered down, making it less offensive to Irish sensibilities. After much toing and froing between London and Dublin – where there was considerable opposition to the proposed treaty – matters were brought to a head.

SOURCE E

The oath of allegiance for Irish Free State MPs and Senators, quoted in the Constitution of the Irish Free State (Saorstát Éireann) Act, 1922, Articles of Agreement for a Treaty between Great Britain and Ireland, *Irish Statue Book*, Government of Ireland.

I ... do solemnly swear true faith and allegiance to the Constitution of the Irish Free State as by law established, and that I will be faithful to H.M. King George V, his heirs and successors by law in virtue of the common citizenship of Ireland with Great Britain and her adherence to and membership of the group of nations forming the British Commonwealth of nations.

Why was the oath in Source E so offensive to Irish nationalists?

On the afternoon of Monday 5 December, the prime minister laid down a threat. Unless the Sinn Féin representatives accepted the treaty, 'it is war, and war within three days ... We must have your answer by ten pm tonight. You can have until then, but no longer, to decide whether you will give peace or war to your country.' Mesmerised by Lloyd George, fearful of the consequences of rejection and worn out by months of negotiation, Griffith, Collins and their three colleagues reluctantly agreed to sign the Anglo-Irish Treaty at 2.30a.m. on 6 December 1921. Collins insisted, quite rightly, that he was signing his own death warrant. Yet, the irony is that Lloyd George may have been bluffing with his threat to resume the war. Certainly, British public opinion would have been profoundly against a resumption the Anglo-Irish War (which had already tarnished Britain's reputation in the world).

Results of the treaty

In Great Britain the treaty was clearly popular with the public, and, despite the misgivings of many Conservatives, the signatures of their party leaders, Chamberlain and Birkenhead, on the document ensured that it passed comfortably through parliament on 16 December 1921.

In Ireland, on the other hand, the reception was very different: there it brought not unity but discord and conflict. The Irish Cabinet was divided over whether the treaty should be accepted or rejected. Collins believed that there was no possibility of getting better terms from Lloyd George, and no alternative to acceptance but renewed and fiercer warfare. De Valera, who was opposed to the treaty since it included the oath of loyalty to the Crown, resigned as president and was succeeded by Griffith. The Dáil, however, after a series of passionate debates, supported the treaty by the narrow majority of 64 votes to 57 on 7 January 1922. In southern Ireland, as in Britain, public opinion was generally in favour.

The terms of the Anglo-Irish Treaty were carried out almost immediately. A new provisional government was appointed under Michael Collins, and power was formally handed over to it by the British viceroy on 16 January. The British Army then began the process of withdrawing from the Irish Free State's territory, handing over its barracks and facilities to the IRA. In June 1922, a general election was held in the Irish Free State which gave Collins and the pro-treaty group a convincing majority. The anti-treaty faction, however, led by de Valera, refused to accept the verdict, and 'the Troubles' – a civil war in Ireland more brutal and more destructive than the earlier Anglo-Irish War – followed. When the violence spread to Northern Ireland, many Conservatives regretted supporting the scheme, a major factor in Lloyd George's fall in October 1922. In the spring of 1923, however, the rebels made their peace with the Irish Free State government.

The constitution for the Irish Free State

By the end of 1922, the Irish Free State government (now headed by William Cosgrove, following the death of Arthur Griffith in August 1922 from heart failure and the assassination, ten days later, of Collins by the anti-treaty rebels) felt that it was strong enough to promulgate a formal constitution. It was approved by the Irish Dáil in December and accepted by the British government. It was followed immediately by the government of Northern Ireland formally exercising its treaty right to opt out of the jurisdiction of the Irish Free State. By 1923, therefore, partition was accomplished. Two states existed side by side in the territory of Ireland: the Irish Free State and Northern Ireland.

Assessment of the treaty

The Anglo-Irish Treaty of 1921 was in many ways a flawed document, full of ambiguities and unresolved problems:

- The constitutional settlement was the product of no definite plan.
- It rested on no clear-cut principles.
- It did not conform to the original ideals, or the deepest instincts, of any of the participants.

The Ulster Unionists had originally aimed to prevent Home Rule altogether but had reluctantly come round to the idea of a separate status for Ulster within the UK. For the Irish nationalist leaders, the 1921 treaty was a compromise which violated their commitment to a united republican Ireland. The settlement also appeared to undermine the traditional views on Ireland of those Liberals and Conservatives whose thinking had never gone beyond either support for or opposition to Home Rule. For the coalition government too, as the Irish historian J.C. Beckett has observed, 'it was a solution that they adopted rather than created', and they adopted it for one overwhelming reason: they believed that it would finally get rid of the 'Irish question'.

Yet, the 1921 treaty was by any reckoning an outstanding achievement. It brought the Anglo-Irish War to an end. It did more: 'It inaugurated for Ireland', says Beckett (writing in 1965), 'a longer period of general tranquillity than she had known since the first half of the eighteenth century'. In addition, Ireland now obtained a greater degree of independence than had been envisaged by O'Connell, or Parnell or Redmond. The Irish Free State completely controlled its own internal affairs – administration, education, justice, police and army, customs and taxes – and there were no Irish MPs at Westminster. Moreover, the Anglo-Irish Treaty (together with the Government of Ireland Act of 1920) offered the possibility of eventual, peaceful, Irish unity. In return, Great Britain obtained important provisions for its security. The prominent English historian A.J.P. Taylor, in an essay in 1960, felt able to claim that Lloyd George had solved the Irish question 'once and for all', but within a few years the outbreak of serious unrest in Northern Ireland would show that even the greatest of historians can make over-hasty judgements. All that remained of the Act of Union of 1801 was the largely symbolic office of **governor-general** and the purely verbal trappings of the oath of allegiance and membership of the British Empire. As Frank Pakenham (later Lord Longford), author of the standard work on the 1921 treaty, *Peace by Ordeal*, wrote: 'Its deeper consequences transformed the whole system under which Ireland had previously been governed and the whole basis of Ireland's relationship to England. The British supremacy over Ireland first claimed in 1172 was virtually ended.'

KEY TERM

Governor-general The king's representative, which corresponded to the old office of viceroy.

Long-term results of the treaty

The practical implications of this were seen in the following decades. One by one the provisions of the treaty of 1921, which limited the sovereignty of the Irish Free State, were rejected after 1932 by the Irish prime minister, Éamon de Valera, and accepted, more in sorrow than in anger, by Great Britain. In 1937, de Valera produced a new constitution which changed the name of the Irish Free State to Ireland. The oath of allegiance to the Crown was abolished. The new constitution claimed jurisdiction in Northern Ireland, although it was accepted that any Irish legislation would not be enforceable there. In 1949, following the assertion of its neutrality during the Second World War, Ireland cut the last remaining ties with Great Britain and the Commonwealth and became a fully independent republic. Clement Attlee, the Labour prime minister, accepted Ireland's new status, but insisted on passing the Ireland Act that same year. This affirmed the existing constitutional and territorial position of Northern Ireland, and insisted that no change could take place without 'the consent of the people of Northern Ireland' – a commitment that has governed British policy ever since.

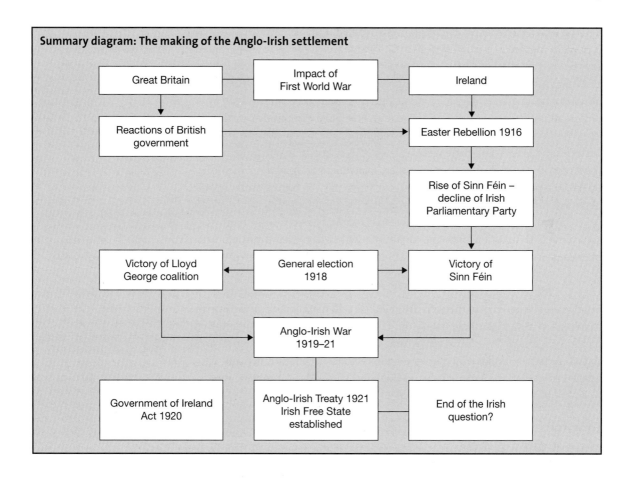

Summary diagram: The making of the Anglo-Irish settlement

Chapter summary

The outbreak of war in 1914 might have brought about a very different outcome for Ireland than conflict and partition. In the first two years of the war up to the rebellion of 1916, Ireland was loyal to the British Crown to a greater extent than at any time since the union. The principle that some form of Home Rule would be granted at the end of the war was established. If there was confusion and disagreement among the elite politicians, British, nationalist and unionist, this had little impact on the broad mass of the Irish people. From all over Ireland, Catholics and Protestants had enlisted to fight the British Empire's war against German aggression. The men and women who planned and carried out the Easter Rising represented a minority. The initially hostile reaction of the Irish public to the rebels confirmed their isolated position. The British government then made the fatal mistake of handing over complete authority to the military in the wake of the rebellion. The policy of martial law, executions and internments rebounded catastrophically. From then on, suspicion and recrimination took over and extremism prospered. The Anglo-Irish Agreement represented the acceptance by Sinn Féin that it had exhausted its capacity to fight the British, and the British government's acceptance that it had gone beyond the legitimate powers of civilisation to impose stability. Neither side was satisfied – neither side deserved to be.

Refresher questions

Use these questions to remind yourself of the key material covered in this chapter.

1 How and why did the nature of Irish nationalism change after 1900?

2 How important were socialist ideas in that process of change?

3 What was the impact of the First World War on Ireland?

4 Why did Irish nationalist support for Britain's war effort begin to evaporate?

5 To what extent did the British government mishandle the 1916 rebellion?

6 Why did the Easter Rebellion fail?

7 Why did Ireland descend into a brutal conflict between 1919 and 1921?

8 How is the growth of Sinn Féin, from rebel organisation to provisional government, best explained?

9 Do you see the Anglo-Irish Treaty's eventual settlement as an example of wise statesmanship or cynical opportunism on the part of a) the British government and b) the Irish nationalists?

10 Why was the treaty accepted by Sinn Féin?

11 What were the immediate consequences of the treaty for Ireland?

12 Should the treaty be seen as a success or a failure?

 Question practice

SOURCE ANALYSIS QUESTION

1 Assess the value of Source 1 below for revealing the impact of socialist ideas on Irish nationalism and the part played by James Connolly in promoting Irish independence from Britain. Explain your answer, using the source, the information given about its origin and your own knowledge about the historical context.

SOURCE 1

James Connolly, writing as 'Vice-President of the Provisional Government of the Irish Socialist Federation' in the federation's journal *The Harp* in 1910. Connolly was the founder of the Irish Socialist Federation, a small Marxist organisation.

The Irish Socialist Federation … is organised against British rule in Ireland … it seeks the Workers' Republic … the work that … lies before the socialists of Ireland … after the inculcation of the principles of socialism … is the proper organisation of the working class of Ireland as a coherent whole in one organisation. That the workers of Ireland be organised not as plumbers, bricklayers, dock labourers, agricultural labourers, etc., but that all these various unions be encouraged to become sub-divisions of one great whole. A militant organisation of the working class of Ireland … would have as dominant and controlling an effect upon the fortunes of the Irish working class as the Land League had upon the fortunes of the Irish farmer. It would create a force which could at any time settle the question of supporting Irish manufacture by refusing to handle all goods whose use or sale in Ireland tended to deprive Irish men and women of a chance to earn their living in their own country. It would do more. The feeling of power, the consciousness of strength which would follow upon this unification of the forces of labour, would develop in our working class an ambition to do and dare greater things, to march forward to the achievement of their emancipation. It shall be our purpose … to work for such a reorganisation of the forces of organised labour in Ireland – into one body of national dimensions and scope, under one executive head, elected by the vote of all the unions, and directing the power of such unions in united efforts in any needed direction.

Some socialists will accuse us of being chauvinistic. But we believe that the toilers of each country should control the industries of their country and they cannot do so if these industries have their location for manufacturing purposes in another country. Therefore, after long and mature deliberation upon the matter in all its aspects we affirm it as our belief that the working class of Ireland should prevent, by united action, the conquest of the Irish market by any capitalist or merchant whose factories or workshops are not manned by members of their organisation.

CHAPTER 9

Conclusion: the Irish Question

The Act of Union of 1800, by incorporating Ireland into the United Kingdom, was in a way the logical outcome of the military conquest of that island in earlier centuries (see Chapters 1 and 2). The Act was undoubtedly conceived in terms of English and Protestant interests, from the point of view of security and defence, property rights and religion. Yet English politicians in the first half of the nineteenth century insisted that Ireland itself gained much from the Union. This was the result of British economic progress and the opportunities opened up for Irish Catholics after the Emancipation Act of 1829 (see Chapter 3), as well as the 'modernisation' of Ireland pursued by successive British governments. Maintenance of the Union therefore became the bedrock of British policy for almost the next 100 years. The effectiveness of this modernisation process was severely undermined, however, by the immense socio-cultural and political shock of the Great Famine (see Chapter 4), which created both a moral reproach to Britain and a moral case for Irish nationalism.

Once it became clear that the Irish majority were unprepared to accept membership of the United Kingdom on these terms, English politicians were faced with the grim reality of the 'Irish question'. This implied a recognition of the fact that Ireland was different from the rest of the United Kingdom and required special treatment; a conclusion most obviously embraced by the Liberal Prime Minister Gladstone (see Chapters 5 and 6). This led to the policy of reform plus coercion which was carried out by successive British governments, since Conservative governments did not reverse Gladstone's reforms and indeed extended the policy of encouraging land purchase by Irish tenants which Gladstone had initiated (see Chapter 7). This programme raised searching questions, however, about the relationship of Ireland to the rest of the United Kingdom:

- Why should time, effort and money be spent on Irish questions which were of no great concern to the majority of the British people?
- How could a pro-Catholic policy of reform be reconciled with the needs of the Protestant minority in Ireland and the intense Protestantism of the British people?
- How could a liberal, and increasingly democratic, state justify the application to Ireland alone of special legislation outside the ordinary code of law?

The conclusion drawn by many Victorian politicians was that the Irish question was, in the words of one of them, 'a troublesome and alien irruption into the British body politic'.

Compared with the earlier Victorian period, therefore, the main aim of British statesmen after 1885 was, in one way or another, to get rid of the Irish question in order to return to 'normal' British politics. The policy of Home Rule may be conceived as a means towards that end. However, by the time that Home Rule did become a practicable policy – after the passage of the 1911 Parliament Act – its Liberal protagonists were faced with the obstinate, unified opposition of the Ulster Unionists until the end of the First World War (see Chapter 7). By the end of the war, as a result of the rise of Sinn Féin, Home Rule was in effect dead as an overall solution to the Irish question (see Chapter 8).

A more advanced alternative to Home Rule for Ireland was 'Dominion Status'. This meant virtually complete independence as far as domestic policy was concerned. It was this solution that eventually was applied by Lloyd George in the Anglo-Irish Treaty of 1921 (see Chapter 8). Unfortunately, it was a solution that rested on the partition of Ireland. It therefore came up against the powerful current of Irish Republican nationalism which had been given a new lease of life as a result of the Easter Rebellion of 1916. In its turn, however, Republican nationalism was faced by the equally intransigent force of Ulster Protestantism based, after 1920, on its own state of Northern Ireland. The consequences of that confrontation – the outcome of nearly four centuries of Anglo-Irish history – remain with us today.

Question practice

ESSAY QUESTIONS

1 To what extent was Daniel O'Connell the most important influence on the development of Irish national consciousness in the period 1774–1870?

2 To what extent was the Act of Union the most significant development for Irish nationalism in the period 1774–1880?

3 To what extent were attempts at armed rebellion the most important factor in developing Irish national consciousness in the period 1774–1923?

4 'The Irish National Party was the most important factor in the campaign for Irish Home Rule in the period 1870–1910.' How valid is this assessment?

5 To what extent was Charles Stewart Parnell the most important individual in the development of Irish nationalism in the period 1800–1900?

6 The reaction of successive British governments to the Irish question throughout the period 1791–1921 was consistently to offer 'too little – too late'. How valid is this statement?

Edexcel A level History

Sources guidance

Edexcel's Paper 3, Option 36.2: Ireland and the Union, *c.*1774–1923 is assessed by an exam comprising three sections:

- Section A is a source analysis assessment. It tests your knowledge of one of the key topics in depth.
- Section B requires you to write one essay from a choice of two, again testing your knowledge of key topics in depth (see page 196 for guidance on this).
- Section C requires you to write one essay from a choice of two. Questions relate to themes in breadth and test your knowledge of change over a period of at least 100 years (see page 200 for guidance on this).

The sections of the exam relate to the sections of the paper in the following way:

Section A and Section B	Test your knowledge of the key topics in depth	• Towards emancipation, 1774–1830 • Industrialisation in Ulster, 1825–55 • The Irish Famine, 1843–51 • The Irish land issue, 1870–82 • Improving working and living conditions: trade union militancy in Ireland, 1907–14
Section C	Tests your knowledge of the themes in breadth	• Irish nationalism: from agitation to civil war • British reaction: from resistance to acceptance

The following advice relates to Paper 3, Section A. Paper 3 is only available at A level, therefore there is no AS level version of this paper.

Paper 3 Section A

Section A of Paper 3 comprises a single compulsory question which refers to one source.

The question

The Section A question will begin with the following stem: 'Assess the value of the source for revealing …'. For example:

> Assess the value of the source for revealing the reasons for the decision of the British government to concede Catholic Emancipation the following year, 1829, and the role played by Daniel O'Connell in this decision. Explain your answer, using the source, the information given about its origin and your own knowledge about the historical context.

The source

The source will be a primary or contemporary source: it will have been written contemporary to *c.*1774–1923, the period that you are studying. The source will be around 350 words long. It will be accompanied by a brief passage which will set out the essential provenance of the source. Here is an example:

SOURCE 1

From a letter written by Mr Vesey Fitzgerald, MP for County Clare, to Mr Robert Peel, the home secretary, from Ennis in County Clare and dated 5 July 1828, quoted in *The Dublin Review*, volume XL, Thomas Richardson & Son, 1856, p. 490.

My Dear Peel,

The election, thank God, is over, and I do feel happy in its being terminated, notwithstanding its results.

I have polled all the gentry and all the fifty-pound freeholders – the gentry to a man.

Of others I have polled a few tenants of [name illegible] only, my own, and not much besides what adhered to me in that way.

All the great interests broke down, and the desertion has been universal. Such a scene as we have had! Such a tremendous prospect as it opens to us!

My aim has been from the beginning to preserve good temper, and to keep down the feelings of my excited friends.

The conduct of the priests has passed all that you could picture to yourself.

The Sheriff declared the numbers to-night. To go on would have been idle. I have kept on for five days, and it was a hopeless contest from the first. Everything was against me. Indeed I do not understand how I have not been beaten by a greater majority.

The Sheriff has made a special Return, and you will say a strange one; but it will force Parliament instantly to take it up. It states that I was proposed, being a Protestant, as a fit person to represent the county in Parliament; that Mr. O'Connell, a Roman Catholic, was also proposed; that he, O'Connell, had declared before the Sheriff that he was a Roman Catholic, and intended to continue a Roman Catholic.

It states that a protest was made by the electors against his return; as well as the certificate that he was called to the Bar as a Roman Catholic.

It states the numbers for each candidate – and thus it leaves the Return.

I shall see you soon, I trust. I shall be able to get away from here, I hope, on Monday. I must have a day's rest, and one day to settle my accounts, and, as far as I can, arrange respecting them.

I care not for anything since I have terminated the contest. For the degradation of the county I feel deeply, and the organization exhibited is so complete and so formidable that no man can contemplate without alarm what is to follow in this wretched country.

Ever yours affectionately, W.V. Fitzgerald

Understanding the question

To answer the question successfully you must understand how the question works. The question is written precisely in order to make sure that you understand the task. Each part of the question has a specific meaning.

> Assess the value of the source[1] for revealing the reasons for the decision of the British government to concede Catholic Emancipation the following year, 1829, and the role played by Daniel O'Connell in this decision[2]. Explain your answer, using the source, the information given about its origin and your own knowledge about the historical context.

1 You must evaluate how useful the source could be to a historian. Evaluating the extent of usefulness involves considering its value and limitations in the light of your own knowledge about the source's historical context. Important information about the context of the source is included in the information given about the source.

2 The question focuses on a specific enquiry that the source might be useful for. This is the reason why the British government decided to grant Catholic emancipation in 1829 and the role of O'Connell.

In essence, you should use the source, the information about the source and your own knowledge of historical context to make a judgement about how far the source is useful to a historian engaged in the specific enquiry.

Source skills

Section A of Paper 3 tests your ability to evaluate source material. Your job is to analyse the source by reading it in the context of the values and assumptions of the society and the period from which it came.

Examiners will mark your work by focusing on the extent to which you are able to do the following:

- Interpret and analyse source material:
  - At a basic level, this means you can understand the source and select, copy, paraphrase and summarise the source to help answer the question.
  - At a higher level, your interpretation of the source includes the ability to explain, analyse and make inferences based on the source.
  - At the highest levels, you will be expected to analyse the source in a sophisticated way. This includes the ability to distinguish between information, opinions and arguments contained in the source.
- Deploy knowledge of historical context in relation to the source:
  - At a basic level, this means the ability to link the source to your knowledge of the context in which the source was written, using this knowledge to expand or support the information contained in the source.
  - At a higher level, you will be able to use your contextual knowledge to make inferences, and to expand, support or challenge the details mentioned in the source.
  - At the highest levels, you will examine the value and limits of the material contained in the source by interpreting the source in the context of the values and assumptions of the society from which it is taken.

- Evaluate the usefulness and weight of the source material:
  - At a basic level, evaluation of the source will be based on making simplistic criteria about reliability and bias.
  - At a higher level, evaluation of the source will be based on the nature and purpose of the source.
  - At the highest levels, evaluation of the source will be based on a valid criterion that is justified in the course of the essay. You will also be able to distinguish between the value of different aspects of the source.

Make sure your source evaluation is sophisticated. Avoid crude statements about bias, and avoid simplistic assumptions such as 'a source written immediate after an event is reliable, whereas a source written years later is unreliable'.

Try to see things through the eyes of the writer:

- How does the writer seek to convey his or her understanding of the situation?
- What assumptions does the writer have?
- Is the writer trying to influence someone or something?
- Is the writer trying to challenge an idea or a potential outcome?

Basic skill: comprehension

The most basic source skill is comprehension: understanding what the source means. There are a variety of techniques that you can use to aid comprehension. For example, you could read the sources included in this book and in past papers. In this context you could:

- Read the sources out loud.
- Look up any words that you don't understand and make a glossary.
- Make flash cards containing brief biographies of the writers of the sources.

You can demonstrate comprehension by copying, paraphrasing and summarising the sources. However, keep this to the minimum as comprehension is a low-level skill and you need to leave room for higher-level skills.

Advanced skill: contextualising the sources

First, to analyse the sources correctly you need to understand them in the context in which they were written. Source 1 (page 192) reflects Vesey Fitzgerald's feelings at the end of a crucial and unsuccessful election campaign. Your job is to understand the values and assumptions behind the source.

- One way of contextualising the source is to consider the nature, origins and purpose of the source. However, this can lead to a formulaic essay.
- An alternative is to consider two levels of context. First, you should establish the general context. In this case, Source 1 was written in the immediate aftermath of the County Clare election. Second, you can look for specific references to contemporary events, people or debates in the sources. For example, when considering the motives of the government for introducing Catholic Emancipation the details in the source can be put in context in the following way:
  - How had the election come about?
  - What was Vesey Fitzgerald's attitude to the basic principle of Catholic Emancipation?
  - What was the position of Peel and what attitude did he have to Catholic Emancipation?
  - What is Fitzgerald referring to when he writes about the 'conduct of the priests' and 'the organization so complete and formidable'?

Use context to make judgements

- Start by establishing the general context of the source:
  - Ask yourself, what was going on at the time when the source was written, or the time of the events described in the source?
  - What are the key debates that the source might be contributing to?
- Next look for key words and phrases that establish the specific context. Does the source refer to specific people, events or documents that might be important?
- Make sure your contextualisation focuses on the question.
- Use the context when evaluating the usefulness and limitations of the source.

For example:

Source 1 is valuable to a historian investigating the British government's reasons for agreeing to introduce Catholic Emancipation in 1829 and the role of O'Connell because it relates to the crucial event that was the immediate catalyst for it changing its previous position. The evidence of the source points to the defeat of the government's candidate Vesey Fitzgerald by the Roman Catholic political leader Daniel O'Connell in the County Clare by-election in the summer of 1828. Fitzgerald was already the MP for County Clare and had been offered and accepted a post in the government by Lord Wellington, the prime minister. At that time, this meant he had changed his status as an ordinary independent MP and was therefore required to seek re-election by his constituents. This suggests that neither Fitzgerald nor the government expected that he would be challenged in this way.

As a Roman Catholic, O'Connell could not take the existing parliamentary oath without abandoning his Roman Catholic faith and so could not actually sit in the House of Commons. In standing he was, therefore, provoking a direct confrontation with the government. The evidence in the source shows that once he took this decision, his Catholic supporters were prepared to elect him. Indeed, the source gives us a valuable insight into the situation because Fitzgerald reveals the limited nature of his support and says that he was actually expecting to be beaten by a bigger margin: the votes stood at O'Connell 2057 and Fitzgerald 982 when Fitzgerald opted to accept defeat. In fact, he agreed to end the voting after five days – not a very long time in the context of the period when polling could go on for two weeks or even longer. Finally, the evidence in the source needs to be seen in the context that Fitzgerald was one of those Tories who actually supported Catholic Emancipation. He was a popular landlord in the county and normally had widespread support from Catholic voters. This was therefore a clear demonstration of Catholic feeling against a man who was normally highly regarded by those who had deserted him.

This passage contextualises relevant details in the source to show why the result of the election indicates a motive for the government's subsequent action. This shows that the passage is of considerable use for this enquiry. However, to score well it would need to be accompanied by a discussion of the limitations of the evidence it contains. For example:

- It only deals with the immediate event that precipitated the crisis.
- It does not reveal that the government faced a majority of opinion in the House of Commons in favour of Catholic emancipation and so could not rely on support there to defend the *status quo*.
- It does not reveal the longstanding nature of the controversy dating back to Pitt's failed attempt to introduce Catholic Emancipation in 1800 or the split this had caused in the Tory Party between those who supported the idea and those, like Peel and Wellington, who resisted it.

Essay guidance (1)

In order to get a high grade in Section B of Paper 3 your essay must contain four essential qualities:

- focused analysis
- relevant detail
- supported judgement
- organisation, coherence and clarity.

This section focuses on the following aspects of exam technique:

- Section B: the nature of the question.
- Planning an answer to the question set.
- Writing a focused introduction.
- Deploying relevant detail.
- Writing analytically.
- Reaching a supported judgement.

Section B: the nature of the question

Section B questions are designed to test the depth of your historical knowledge. Therefore, they can focus on relatively short periods, or single events. Moreover, they can focus on different historical processes or 'concepts'. These include:

- cause
- consequence
- change/continuity
- similarity/difference
- significance.

These different question focuses require slightly different approaches:

Cause	1 'Fear of rebellion in Ireland was the main factor which forced the British government to concede Catholic Emancipation in 1829.' How far do you agree with this statement?
Consequence	2 To what extent did the policies of the British government worsen the effects of the potato famine in Ireland?
Continuity and change	3 To what extent did industrialisation transform Ulster in the period 1825–55?
Similarities and differences	4 'Gladstone's Irish policies in 1868–74 and 1880–2 were both equally inadequate to deal with the problems in Ireland.' How far do you agree with this statement?
Significance	5 To what extent was trade union militancy in Ireland in the years 1907–14 inspired by political rather than social and economic concerns?

Some questions include a 'stated factor'. A common type of stated factor question would ask how far one factor caused something. For example, for question one in the table, '"Fear of rebellion in Ireland was the main factor which forced the British government to concede Catholic Emancipation in 1829." How far do you agree with this statement?', you would be expected to evaluate the importance of 'Fear of rebellion in Ireland' – the 'stated factor' – compared to other factors.

Planning an answer to the question set

It is crucial that you understand the focus of the question. Therefore, read the question carefully before you start planning. Check the following:

- The chronological focus: which years should your essay deal with?
- The topic focus: what aspect of your course does the question deal with?
- The conceptual focus: is this a causes, consequences, change/continuity, similarity/difference or significance question?

For example, for question 5 in the table on page 196 you could point these out as follows:

> To what extent[1] was trade union militancy[2] in Ireland[3] in the years 1907–14[4] inspired by political rather than social and economic concerns?

1 Conceptual focus: significance, specifically to politics and social and economic improvements.
2 Topic focus: trade union militancy.
3 Topic focus: Ireland.
4 Chronological focus: 1907–14.

Your plan should reflect the task that you have been set. Section B asks you to write an analytical, coherent and well-structured essay from your own knowledge, which reaches a supported conclusion in around 40 minutes.

- To ensure that your essay is coherent and well structured, it should comprise a series of paragraphs, each focusing on a different point.
- Your paragraphs should come in a logical order. For example, you could write your paragraphs in order of importance, so you begin with the most important issues and end with the least important.
- In essays where there is a 'stated factor' it is a good idea to start with the stated factor before moving on to the other points.
- To make sure you keep to time, you should aim to write three or four paragraphs plus an introduction and a conclusion.

Writing a focused introduction

The opening paragraph should do four main things:

- answer the question directly
- set out your essential argument
- outline the factors or issues that you will discuss
- define key terms used in the question – where necessary.

Here is an example introduction in answer to question 4 in the table on page 196:

In one sense it is fair to argue that Gladstone's Irish policies were indeed equally inadequate in responding to the problems in Ireland[1]. *This is because in both instances Gladstone's solutions failed to achieve his original stated aim of 'pacifying' Ireland. This can be seen from the fact that the situation in Ireland was so serious by 1880 that he was forced to go further than he had been prepared to do in 1868-74. Furthermore his policies in 1880-2 did not end the demand for at least Home Rule for Ireland, something he had once condemned as an 'absurdity'*[2]. *However, it must be remembered that the situation in 1880 was fundamentally different from that of 1868 and any judgement comparing his policies needs to take this into account*[3].

1 The essay starts with a clear focus on the question.
2 This sentence simultaneously defines 'inadequate' and provides evidence to justify the statement in the first sentence.
3 This sentence sets up the idea of a balanced argument to be explored in the remainder of the essay before a final judgement is offered.

The opening paragraph: advice

- Don't write more than a couple of sentences on general background knowledge. This is unlikely to focus explicitly on the question.
- After defining key terms, refer back to these definitions when justifying your conclusion.
- The introduction should reflect the rest of the essay and make it clear that there is a debate to follow. The tone needs to be provisional, not final – that is reserved for the conclusion. Don't make one argument in your introduction, then make a different argument in the essay.

Deploying relevant detail

Paper 3 tests the depth of your historical knowledge. Therefore, you will need to deploy historical detail. In the main body of your essay your paragraphs should begin with a clear point, be full of relevant detail and end with explanation or evaluation. A detailed answer might include statistics, details of legislation, chronology and technical terms. For example, if you are assessing how adequate Gladstone's 1868–74 policies were in relation to the situation in Ireland you will need specific details about the Church Act (1869), the Land Act (1870) and his proposals for Irish education (1873). You will need to show how these impacted on Ireland, focusing on adequacy and inadequacy, and also explaining what relationship they had to the recent events in Ireland (such as the Fenian Revolt) and the general situation there. You will need to follow the same pattern with 1880–2 and in doing so build in direct comparisons with the earlier period. This will lead you to a summative conclusion.

Writing analytically

The quality of your analysis is one of the key factors that determines the mark you achieve. Writing analytically means clearly showing the relationships between the ideas in your essay. Analysis includes two key skills: explanation and evaluation.

Explanation

Explanation means giving reasons. An explanatory sentence has three parts:

- a claim: a statement that something is true or false
- a reason: a statement that justifies the claim
- a relationship: a word or phrase that shows the relationship between the claim and the reason.

Imagine you are answering question 2 in the table on page 196:

> To what extent did the policies of the British government worsen the effects of the potato famine in Ireland?

Clearly, there are a number of explanations for the catastrophic impact of the potato famine in Ireland. Your paragraph on the policies of the British government should start with a clear point, which would be supported by a series of examples. Finally, you could round off the paragraph with some explanation:

Therefore, the policy of importing Indian Corn could be argued to have made the situation worse[1] because[2] of its poor quality and the risk to health through lack of knowledge about how to cook it[3].

1 Claim.
2 Relationship.
3 Reason.

Make sure of the following:

- The reason you give genuinely justifies the argument you have explained.
- Your explanation is focused on the question.

Reaching a supported judgement

Your essay should reach a supported judgement. The obvious place to do this is in the conclusion of your essay. Even so, the judgement should reflect the findings of your essay. The conclusion should present:

- a clear judgement that answers the question
- an evaluation of the evidence that supports the judgement.
- Finally, the evaluation should reflect valid criteria.

Evaluation and criteria

Evaluation means weighing up to reach a judgement. Therefore, evaluation requires you to:

- summarise both sides of the issue
- reach a conclusion that reflects the proper weight of both sides.

So, for question two in the table on page 196:

> To what extent did the policies of the British government worsen the effects of the potato famine in Ireland?

the conclusion might look like this:

The argument that the British actually intended to worsen the situation cannot be sustained. However, the evidence leads to the inescapable conclusion that, though well intentioned, the policies of the British government did worsen the effects of the famine in Ireland because they were so inadequate to meet the need[1]. It is true that the majority of Irish landlords failed their tenants miserably in the crisis but ultimately they lacked the resources to cope and leaving them to do so was another major failure of the government[2]. It can also be strongly argued that the policies of previous governments were a major factor in making Ireland so vulnerable to the potato blight in the first place because it was these policies that led to the reliance of such a high proportion of the population on the potato for subsistence[3]. In the

last analysis it must be emphasised that the blight was not purely an Irish phenomenon – it affected all of Europe. Only in Ireland were its effects so catastrophic and for this the British government must bear the main responsibility[4].

1. The conclusion starts with a clear judgement that answers the question.
2. This sentence acknowledges an alternative idea (which would have been previously discussed more fully) but shows why it does not weigh heavily enough to affect the verdict.
3. The conclusion reinforces an aspect of British culpability.
4. The essay ends with a final judgement that is supported by the evidence of the essay.

The judgement above is supported in part by evaluating the evidence, and in part by linking it to valid criteria. However, it is important to remember that is only one way of looking at the question. It would be perfectly possible to construct an argument reaching a different conclusion.

Essay guidance (2)

Section C is similar in many ways to Section B. Therefore, you need the same essential skills in order to get a high grade:

- focused analysis
- relevant detail
- supported judgement
- organisation, coherence and clarity.

Nonetheless, there are some differences in terms of the style of the question and the approach to the question in Sections B and C. Therefore, this section focuses on the following aspects of exam technique:

- Section C: the nature of the question.
- Planning your answer.
- Advice for Section C.

Section C: the nature of the question

Section C questions focus on the two themes in breadth:

- Irish nationalism: from agitation to civil war.
- British reaction: from resistance to acceptance.

Questions can address either theme, or both themes. There are two questions in Section C, of which you must answer one. However, you are not guaranteed a question on both themes, therefore you have to prepare for questions on both of the themes.

Section C questions are designed to test the breadth of your historical knowledge, and your ability to analyse change over time. Therefore, questions will focus on long periods, of no less than 100 years.

Section C questions have a variety of forms. Nonetheless, they have one of two approaches. They will focus on either:

- the causes of change: for example, the factors, forces or individuals that led to change

or

- the nature of change: the ways in which things changed.

Significantly, the exam paper may contain two causes of change questions or two nature of change questions: you are not guaranteed one of each. Finally, questions can focus on different aspects of change over time:

- Comparative questions: ask you to assess the extent of change and continuity of an aspect of the period.
- Patterns of change questions: ask you to assess differences in terms of the rate, extent or significance of change at different points in the chronology.
- Turning point questions: ask you to assess which changes were more significant.

Comparative question	'The key factor in promoting British government reforms for Ireland 1790–1914 was the pressure of Irish nationalist agitation.' How far do you agree with this statement?
Patterns of change question	How accurate is it to say that the different campaigns of Irish nationalists consistently failed to achieve the support of the Irish people in the period 1774–1922?
Turning point question	'The key turning point in the development of Irish national consciousness in the period 1798–1918 was the potato famine of 1845–9.' How far do you agree with this statement?

Planning your answer

It is crucial that you understand the focus of the question in order to make an effective plan. Therefore read the question carefully before you start planning. Different questions require a different approach. Here are suggestions about how to tackle some of the common types of question:

Comparative question

'The key factor in promoting British government reforms in Ireland 1790–1914 was the pressure of Irish nationalist agitation.' How far do you agree with this statement?

This is a comparative question which focuses on the causes of change. In this case you should examine the significance of 'the pressure of Irish nationalist agitation', the stated factor, and compare it to other possible causes of change, for example the influence of British politicians such as Gladstone.

Patterns of change question

How accurate is it to say that the different campaigns of Irish nationalists consistently failed to achieve the support of the Irish people in the period 1774–1922?

This is a patterns of change question which focuses on the impact of changes in nationalist activity on the Irish people. Here, you should examine the pattern of the development of Irish nationalism over the period 1774–1922. You should consider how far popular support developed at different times and in different contexts.

Turning point question

'The key turning point in the development of Irish national consciousness in the period 1798–1918 was the potato famine of 1845–9.' How far do you agree with this statement?

This is a turning point question which focuses on the nature of change. Therefore you should examine the significance of the stated turning point for Irish nationalism and compare it to appropriate alternative turning points from the period 1798–1918. When considering how far an event was a turning point you must consider its impact in terms of subsequent similarity as well as difference: that is to say, in what ways Irish nationalism changed as a result and the ways in which it stayed the same.

Advice for Section C

In many ways a Section C essay should display the same skills as a Section B essay (see page 196). However, Section C essays focus on a much longer period than Section B essays and this has an impact on how you approach them.

The most important difference concerns the chronology. To answer a Section C question properly you must address the whole period specified. This means being selective in choosing examples from across the whole range of the period – from the early part of the period, the middle of the period and the end of the period. For example, if you were answering the question:

'The key turning point in the development of Irish national consciousness in the period 1798–1918 was the potato famine of 1845–9.' How far do you agree with this statement?

the question states a possible turning point in roughly the middle of the period. Therefore when you are considering other turning points you should choose one from the earliest part of the period and one as late on as possible. For example:

- early: the Irish Rebellion 1798
- middle: the famine – as specified in the question
- late: the Easter Rising 1916 and the subsequent developments.

However, each question needs to be treated on its merits. The above could not suffice for this particular question as it completely ignores some major factors:

- the Catholic Emancipation campaign in the 1820s
- Daniel O'Connell's impact
- Fenianism
- the Land League
- Parnell.

Obviously, you cannot cover all these elements in depth but with skill and care you can show your awareness of their relative importance. Catholic Emancipation, for example, could be treated quite lightly within the context of a consideration of the overall impact of O'Connell. The same could be done by subsuming Parnell with the Land League. Fenianism could be linked to the eventual Easter Rising of 1916. The key skill is not the depth of your knowledge, so much as your ability to offer judgements throughout an overview of the specified period, and to conclude with a balanced judgement based on your discussion as to the relative importance of the famine in the wider context of the period as a whole.

OCR A level History

The OCR Unit Y316 Britain and Ireland 1791–1921 focuses on the relationship between mainland Britain and Ireland during the period from 1791 to 1921. Students should consider how far, and for what reasons, this relationship changed. The strands identified below are not to be studied in isolation to each other. They are not self-contained and students need to examine the interrelationship of religious, political, social, economic and cultural factors.

Students are not expected to demonstrate a detailed understanding of the specification content, except for the named in-depth studies, but are expected to know the main developments and turning points relevant to the theme.

There are two elements to the component:

- The thematic essay, which will require you to consider developments over approximately 100 years. You will answer two essays from a choice of three.
- The in-depth interpretation element, where you will comprehend, analyse and evaluate the ways in which the past has been interpreted by historians.

The total duration of the exam is 2 hours and 30 minutes.

The two thematic essays should be allocated around 45 minutes each for completion; together they provide 50 marks out of a total of 80. The in-depth interpretation question accounts for the remaining 30 marks and requires around one hour.

Thematic essay guidance

Essay skills

There are a number of skills that you need to develop if you are to reach the higher levels in the marking bands:

- understand the wording of the question
- plan a thematic answer to the question set
- write a focused opening paragraph
- avoid irrelevance and description
- write analytically and thematically
- make comparisons within the themes, showing similarity and difference across the whole period
- write a conclusion which reaches a supported judgement based on the argument in the main body of the essay.

The skills are made very clear by both mark schemes, which emphasise that the answer must:

- focus on the demands of the question
- be supported by accurate and relevant factual knowledge
- be analytical and well structured
- reach a supported and developed judgement about the issue in the question
- demonstrate evidence of well-developed synthesis across the whole period.

These skills are the same as those you have developed for essay writing in Units 1 and 2. However, in this unit there is a significant emphasis on *synthesis* across the whole period.

Understanding the wording of the question

To stay focused on the question set, it is important to read the question carefully and focus on the key words and phrases. Unless you directly address the demands of the question you will not score highly. Remember that in questions where there is a named factor you must write a good analytical paragraph about the given factor, even if you argue that it was not the most important.

Types of questions you might find in the exam	The themes you might consider in answering them
1 How important was the impact of economic factors on the development of Irish nationalism in the period from 1798 to 1921?	You should weigh up the impact of economic factors, both positive and negative, against other factors in the development of Irish nationalism: • Role of nationalist leaders • External influences • Significant events • British attitudes and policies.
2 The creation of the Irish Land League was the most important turning point in the course of Irish nationalism.' How far do you agree with this view of the period from 1798 to 1921?	You might consider the relative importance of the creation of the Land League by comparing it with other turning points • Attempted rebellions, such as Wolfe Tone (1798), Emmet's Rebellion (1803), Fenian outrages (1867) and so on • The decisions/actions of political leaders • Other significant events that are arguably turning points, such as Catholic emancipation or the Great Famine
3 Assess the view that revolutionary nationalism did more to damage opposition to the Union than to advance it in the period from 1798 to 1921.	You should consider a range of factors, including the positive and negative impact of revolutionary nationalism, that might include: • Economic change • British concessions • Role of individuals.
4 'The most important factor in the decline of the Protestant Ascendancy in Ireland was the reforms of successive British governments'. How far do you agree with this view of the period from 1798 to 1921?	You should consider whether the decline of the Protestant Ascendancy was most affected by British government reforms or by: • Specific issues such as Home Rule or Catholic Emancipation • The role of constitutional nationalists such as O'Connell or Parnell • The impact of economic developments • Revolutionary nationalism.

Planning an answer

The marker will look for an organised answer where arguments move logically towards your conclusion: it is difficult to do this if you have not planned out the sequence of your points. It is vital that you start the answer with a clear idea of what your conclusion is going to be. Note this down at the outset and keep it in mind as you work through your answer. Avoid making assertions that are unsupported: the marker wants judgements from you but these must be supported by evidence.

Many plans simply list dates and events – this should be avoided as it encourages a descriptive or narrative, rather than an analytical answer. The plan should be an outline of your argument; this means you need to think carefully about the issues you intend to discuss and their relative importance before you start writing your answer. It should, therefore, be a list of the themes or issues you are going to discuss and a comment on their relative importance in relation to the question.

You should spend at least five minutes and no more than ten minutes on planning out of around 45 minutes for completing each essay. Remember you will write more quickly if you have a clear idea of what you are going to argue and how you are going to support your arguments. This is the primary purpose of the plan.

How to answer turning-point questions

The mark scheme used by examiners is exactly the same for turning-point questions as it is for other thematic essays. This suggests that the approach should be exactly the same as it is for other themes essays and that the structure should be thematic and not chronological. It is much easier to compare the significance or importance of different turning points if a thematic approach, rather than a chronological one, is adopted.

Key themes in the relationship between Great Britain and Ireland

Opposition to the Union

Revolutionary nationalism including Wolfe Tone and the United Irishmen, Young Ireland, the Fenians, the Land League, Sinn Féin, the Easter Rising 1916, the Anglo-Irish War 1919–21; constitutional nationalism including O'Connell, Parnell and Redmond, Catholic Emancipation and the Home Rule movement; cultural nationalism 1798–1921 including the Enlightenment, Young Ireland and the Gaelic Revival; the role of the Roman Catholic Church in opposition.

Support for the Union

Protestant Ascendancy and its decline from the 1870s; Unionism and the rise of Ulster Unionism 1886–1921 and its strategies; the policies and approaches of the Conservative, Whig and Liberal parties and their leaders; the role of the Anglican and Presbyterian Churches in support for the Union.

The Union and reform

The creation of the Act of Union; reform within the Union from 1829 including Catholic Emancipation 1829, reforms in administration, education, land and local government; Home Rule and Partition.

The Irish economy and the link to Irish Nationalism

Agrarian underdevelopment and population pressures, land and economic issues in their own right and in relation to nationalism, the impact of the Famine 1845–9; industrialisation and Ulster; North/South and regional differences.

Example turning-point question

Look at question 2 in the table on page 205:

> 'The creation of the Irish Land League was the most important turning point in the course of Irish nationalism.' How far do you agree with this view of the period from 1798 to 1922?

There other events that might be considered to be the most important turning point in the course of Irish nationalism and could be evaluated against the creation of the Land League including:

* the Wolfe Tone Rebellion 1798
* the Act of Union
* Catholic Emancipation 1829
* the Great Famine 1845–9
* the Fenian Rising 1867
* the Second Land Act 1881
* the failure of Home Rule in either 1886 or 1893
* the Easter Rising 1916.

This is not an exhaustive or exclusive list.

A potential essay could analyse, evaluate and compare such events (in order to show synthesis), but it would make for a very cumbersome structure and would be difficult to undertake in 45 minutes. It would be far easier to adopt a thematic approach which would allow you to compare the events. The following themes could be considered:

* political
* economic
* social
* cultural.

You would then select examples from the period and compare their relative importance and significance in terms of being a turning point for each theme.

Ultimately, you would reach a judgement on which event was politically, economically, socially and culturally the most important, before going on to reach an overall judgement as to which event was the most important turning point. This means that the skills you have considered in the previous chapters are just as applicable to turning-point questions as to other essays. Consider the following responses to the question above.

Response A

The creation of the Irish Land League was not the most important turning point in the course of Irish nationalism in this period. Although it was significant in that it helped to bring about the Second Land Act of 1881, this was a measure intended by the British government to appease Irish national grievances and curb Irish nationalism rather than encourage. However, the League was also important in that it gave a wider political platform to Parnell as its president as well as leader of the Irish National Party and helped stimulate the campaign for Home Rule. Even so, the main importance of the League was in forcing Gladstone's government to confront the land agitation that was in full swing by 1880. Although Gladstone responded with a new Coercion Act initially to clamp down on the League, this was quickly followed by the Second Land Act that granted the long-demanded three 'Fs', giving Irish tenants much more security over their tenancies and a fair rent system. The Land Act also opened the way through the 'Bright clause' for tenants to buy out their landlords using government mortgages. However, the League was only a temporary influence and Parnell came to see it as a political liability by late 1882. He then moved to wind it up and introduced a new more broadly based 'Irish National League' to replace it. The Land League was basically a short-term nationalist response to the terrible social and economic conditions in Ireland that developed in the late 1870s rather than a key turning point for Irish nationalism.

Analysis of Response A

Strengths:

- The paragraph shows good knowledge of the Irish Land League and its impact.
- The knowledge is used to support an argument about the significance of the League.
- In putting forward the argument the paragraph offers a balanced discussion about the significance of the League.

Weakness:

- There is no synthesis or comparison of the Act with other measures to establish whether it was the most significant turning point.

Response B

In terms of the land issue, the most important turning point was the Second Land Act of 1882. **This was more important than the creation of the Land League as that simply started a violent campaign to try to force the British government to act. The Land Act of 1881 on the other hand replaced to largely ineffective 1870 Land Act with a measure that changed the situation entirely.** As a result of the Second Land Act, Irish tenants obtained important security over the tenancies through fairer rents and guaranteed compensation for improvements they made to their holdings if the tenancy ended. They also obtained the right to government mortgages to buy the land they farmed if the landlord wished to sell. This amounted to a revolution in landholding in Ireland over the next two decades. **In comparison to the impact of the Land Act, the actions of the Land League made the image of Irish nationalism to British politicians even less acceptable than it already was.** Even Parnell, who had agreed to become president of the League soon realised that it was an embarrassment rather than an asset. In contrast, the 1881 Land Act was not only significant in social and economic change.

Its success in improving the situation on the land still failed to end the political agitation for Home Rule which convinced Gladstone that Home Rule must be considered if Ireland was to be pacified. This was of huge significance in the course of Irish nationalism because it committed the Liberal Party to a permanent policy of introducing Home Rule. Finally, the situation in Ireland by 1880 when Gladstone came to power was so critical that some further land reform was inevitable. The violence of the Land League arguably delayed the Second Land Act as much as encouraging it.

Analysis of Response B

Strengths:

- A clear comparative argument is offered: the Second Land Act was more important than the creation of the Land League.
- There is a direct comparison between the Land League and the 1881 Land Act, which is seen in the boldface text.
- The argument is explained and justified.
- The impact of the 1881 Land Act examined in some detail and contrasted with that of the League.
- The significance of the changes brought about by the Dawes Act is then compared with the changes at the end of the period.
- The different themes of the topic are addressed by reference to political, social and economic implications.

Activity

Write thematic paragraphs that compare the importance of the creation of the Irish Land League with other events in terms of culture, economic progress, social change and political change.

Interpretations guidance

For each of the in-depth interpretation elements, three topics are listed in the specification and a question will be set on one of the topics. The three topics for Britain and Ireland 1791–1921 are as follows:

- Irish rebellions and British responses 1791–1803.
- O'Connell and British governments 1823–41.
- The crisis over Home Rule 1908–14.

Although this is an A level paper it is not a historiography paper. The aim of this element of the unit is to develop an awareness that the past has been interpreted in different ways. The question will require you to assess the strengths and limitations of the two interpretations of an issue related to one of the specified in-depth topics. The interpretations will always be from historians and will not be primary sources.

You should be able to place the interpretation within the context of the wider historical debate on the key topic. However, you will not be required to know the names of individual historians associated with the debate or to have studied the specific books of any historians.

There are a number of skills you will need to develop if you are to reach the higher levels in the mark bands:

- Remain focused on the question throughout the answer.
- Assess and evaluate the two interpretations in the wider context of the historical debate about the issue.
- Apply your knowledge of the topic to the interpretations in order to evaluate their strengths and weaknesses.
- Ensure that you consider both interpretations.
- Reach a supported judgement as to which interpretation you think is more convincing.

Approaching the question

You should aim to spend around one hour on this question. You will need to read both passages carefully. You will also need to refer to them as you write in order to ensure that you are evaluating them accurately and as fully as possible.

It might be helpful to think of a three- or four-paragraph structure:

- In the first paragraph, explain the interpretations in the two passages and place them in the wider debate.
- In the second/third paragraph, apply your own knowledge to the passages to evaluate the validity of their views about the issue in the question. In doing this, own knowledge should be used to analyse the strengths and weaknesses of the view in the interpretation. Depending on what you find in the passages, and the wider knowledge you need to deploy, you may decide to write separate paragraphs for the passages or for different aspects of your knowledge.
- In the final paragraph, reach a supported and balanced judgement as to which view you think is more convincing.

You do not need to evaluate the provenance of the interpretation and therefore comments on the author and their background will not gain marks.

Questions set will be similar to the one below:

Evaluate the interpretations in both of the passages and explain which you think is the more convincing explanation of the impact of the Act of Union of 1800 in Ireland.

PASSAGE I

Adapted from 'The Act of Union' by Jonathan Bardon in the Act of Union Virtual Library website, Queen's University, Belfast, 2005 (available at: www.actofunion.ac.uk/actofunion.htm).

'The mass of the people do not care one farthing about the Union', Cornwallis remarked and there was much truth in this statement. The bad harvest of 1799 was of much greater concern. Cornwallis came very close to promising emancipation forthwith and, for that reason, most educated Catholics were in favour of the Union. The Union came into force on 1 January 1801 and was in being only for a few weeks when it received a body blow: George III flatly refused to consider Catholic emancipation and declared: 'I shall reckon any man my personal enemy who proposes any such measure'. Pitt, who was convinced that emancipation was essential to ensure the success of the Union, resigned on 3 February 1801. Protestant parliamentarians who had vehemently opposed the Union Bill were soon won over. One reason,

undoubtedly, was that the prospect of immediate Catholic emancipation quickly faded. In another respect the sky did not fall in: a separate Irish administration was retained in Dublin Castle and this meant that coveted jobs, mainly in the civil department, could still be obtained and monopolised by the Ascendancy. Fear of growing Catholic self-confidence persuaded the great majority of Protestants of all classes – including descendants of Presbyterians who had fought in 1798 – to become passionate supporters of the United Kingdom. A sprinkling of Protestants could be found in the nationalist camp, such as Robert Emmet, but they were members of the intelligentsia and the vast majority of humbler Protestants became unwavering unionists.

PASSAGE 2

Adapted from E. Llewellyn Woodward, *The Age of Reform*, Oxford University Press, 1962, p. 328.

To the English the outbreak of the [1798] rebellion was another example of Irish treachery; to the Irish, the suppression of the rebels was another example of English ruthlessness. Thus the act of union appeared to one side as a measure of political necessity against rebels, and to the other side a demonstration of force unsupported by right. The terms of the union were never laid down before the Irish people, and the two houses of the Irish parliament voted their own abolition only after a shameful distribution and acceptance of money and titles. Catholics had some reason for believing that the union would not be altogether to their disadvantage. The Irish Catholics thought that, if they accepted the act of union, the parliament of the United Kingdom would put them on terms of equality with Protestants. Pitt wanted Catholic emancipation, but the king would not consent to it.

The Irish Catholics could not accept the subordination of their interests. From their standpoint, they had been betrayed. If the Catholics had received emancipation as a gift immediately after the union it is still doubtful whether Irish opinion would have been conciliated. Irish grievances were not merely religious and political; they were also the result of Irish economic conditions. The source of the trouble was deep-seated, affecting property as well as politics and religion. After the union successive British governments must bear an even greater responsibility for the continuance and aggravation of Irish economic distress. British ministers, with the support of parliament and public opinion, would not allow the Irish to carry out their own agrarian revolution, and would not make it for them.

In answering the question, the opening paragraph could consider the views of the two interpretations and place them in the context of the debate:

Historians usually approach the issue of the impact of the Act of Union in Ireland by considering the merits of two distinct perspectives. One perspective holds that the Act of Union was potentially a long-term solution for the 'Irish question' which failed due to the alienation caused to Catholics by the refusal to grant Catholic Emancipation as part of the settlement. The second perspective sees the Union as essentially a measure to ensure British control of Ireland with the promise of emancipation simply thrown in as a sweetener. From this perspective the Act of Union was irrelevant to the fundamental problems of Ireland[1]. Passage 1 emphasises the failure to grant emancipation as the key issue in defining Catholic and Protestant reactions to the Union. In particular, Passage 1 points to the way in which Protestant opposition, originally a significant issue, largely crumbled away once it was realised that emancipation was off the agenda. The passage focuses on the original enthusiasm of educated Catholics for union based on the expectation of emancipation while asserting that in the wider context the Union attracted little attention due to economic conditions. Passage 2 on the other hand, while acknowledging the sense of betrayal felt by Catholics over the failure to grant emancipation, focuses mainly on the view that the Union did not impact on the basic problems of Ireland and goes so far as to suggest that even if emancipation had been granted this would still have been the case. The interpretations therefore diverge considerably, with Passage 2, for example, not even mentioning the issue of initial Protestant opposition[2].

1 The opening places the Act of Union in the wider context of the debate about its impact.
2 The next part explains Passages 1 and 2 in relation to the issue raised in the question and supports this by summarising part of the interpretations.

The answer for the question should then go on to evaluate the passages in the light of your own knowledge:

The immediate context for the passing of the Act of Union was in response to the rebellion of 1798, which had threatened the security of the British hold on Ireland at a time of war against revolutionary France. Passage 1 completely ignores this event in favour of arguing that the more immediate context was the impact of a poor harvest which distracted attention from the Union debate. Passage 2, however, places the rebellion at the heart of the issue. While these interpretations do not directly address the issue of the subsequent impact of the Union, they represent important and differing interpretations of the impact that the proposal for the Union had in Ireland and the context in which the whole debate was carried on. To this extent, Passage 2 is more convincing since poor harvests were hardly an unusual event in Ireland, whereas the rebellion had been accompanied by a French invasion and resulted in many civilian and combatant deaths, variously estimated from 10,000 to 50,000[1].

On the other hand, the issue of Catholic Emancipation was unquestionably central to the way the Union was perceived and its refusal had a massive effect on the impact of the Union subsequently. This is rightly given full prominence in Passage 1, which shows how educated Catholics reacted to the prospect of the Union. Even more importantly though, it shows how the prospect of Union affected Protestants, creating a significant opposition and the subsequent impact of the refusal to grant emancipation which brought almost all Protestants onside. In contrast, Passage 2 ignores the Protestant viewpoint entirely, indeed the only reference to the Protestants comes purely as a point of reference to explain the Catholic standpoint[2].

1 The opening paragraph focuses on the immediate historical context in which the Union was proposed and how the two passages interpret its impact. The paragraph compares the two and evaluates their strengths and weaknesses, reaching an interim verdict broadly in favour of Passage 2.

2 The next paragraph continues the evaluation of the two passages, this time looking at the subsequent impact of the Union with reference to the refusal to grant Catholic Emancipation as originally intended. Again an interim verdict is offered, this time in favour of Passage 1.

In this instance, each paragraph has resulted in a different interim verdict in terms of which passage is more convincing. However, each question has to be treated on its merits and it is not necessary that this pattern be followed unless that is your genuine decision. So long as your discussion shows that you are approaching the evaluation in a balanced way, you will be meeting the requirements of the marking scheme.

In the conclusion it might be argued:

Both passages have convincing elements to the interpretations they offer. Both show the centrality of Catholic Emancipation to the way the Union eventually affected Ireland and both seek to place the Union in an immediate context as a proposal[1].

Overall, Passage 2 seems to be the more convincing of the two. This is because it is the more complete picture. The big difference between the passages is that Passage 1 concentrates heavily on the Protestant opposition with little comment on the Catholic reaction – especially once emancipation was rejected. Passage 2 is almost exactly the reverse in approach. However, Passage 2 develops a more complete interpretation. The impact of the proposal for the Union on Ireland cannot really be divorced from the impact of the Wolfe Tone Rebellion and this is ignored by Passage 1. Furthermore, Passage 2 sets the impact of the

Union subsequently into a wider context than just the king's blocking of Catholic Emancipation. Passage 2 shows that there was a wider context to Irish grievances and questions whether the Union could have been accepted even had Catholic Emancipation not been refused[2].

1 The first two sentences underline the fact that a balanced evaluation has taken place and recognise that both passages have value in different ways.

2 The rest of the conclusion is devoted to the overall verdict in favour of one passage, which is explained and supported.

Timeline

1541	Henry VIII declared himself King of Ireland by a Royal Proclamation enacted in the following year
1610	'Plantation of Ulster'
1641	Ulster Rebellion
1690	Battle of the Boyne
1750s	The Patriots formed
1760	The Catholic Committee formed
1779–80	Free trade for Ireland
1782	Constitutional reform in Ireland
	Irish parliament achieved legislative independence
1791	Society of United Irishmen founded
1795	Orange Order in Ulster
1798	Irish Rebellion
1800	The Act of Union passed
1823	Formation of the Catholic Association
1828	O'Connell elected MP for County Clare
1829	Roman Catholic Emancipation Act
1833	Coercion Act
1835	Lichfield House Compact
1840	Repeal Association founded by O'Connell
1843	Repeal meeting at Clontarf banned
1845	Beginning of potato blight
1845–9	The Great 'Potato Famine' resulted in around a million deaths; perhaps as many as 2 million people emigrated from Ireland
1846	Repeal of the Corn Laws
	Peel replaced as prime minister by Lord Russell
	Young Ireland leaders left the Catholic Association
1847	Death of O'Connell
	Soup kitchens provided relief

1848	Poor Law used as means of relief
	Young Ireland rebellion failed
1849	Better conditions returned
	Encumbered Estates Act
1850	Irish Tenant League founded
1858	Irish Republican Brotherhood (Fenians) founded
1867	Fenian outrages in Ireland and England
1868	Liberal victory at general election
1869	Irish Church Act
1870	Gladstone's first Irish Land Act
1872	Ballot Act introduced secret voting
1873	Defeat of Irish Universities Bill
	Home Rule League founded by Isaac Butt
1874	Conservative victory at general election
1877	'Obstructionism' in the House of Commons
1879	Foundation of Irish National Land League
1880	Liberal victory at general election
	Parnell elected leader of the Irish Parliamentary Party
1881	Coercion Act
	Gladstone's second Irish Land Act
	Parnell arrested, Land League outlawed
1882	Kilmainham Treaty between Parnell and Gladstone
	Phoenix Park murders
	Formation of the National League
1884	Third Parliamentary Reform Act passed
1885	Parnell supported Conservatives: Gladstone resigned
	Conservatives in power under Lord Salisbury
	General election: Irish Party won 86 seats and held the balance of power
	Herbert Gladstone flew the 'Hawarden kite'

1886	Loyalist Anti-Repeal Union set up
	Parnell supported Liberals: Gladstone formed his third ministry
	Gladstone's First Home Rule Bill – rejected by Commons
1889	Captain O'Shea sued for divorce, citing Parnell as co-respondent
1890	Gladstone opposed Parnell as Irish leader
	Irish Party split over leadership
1891	Death of Parnell
1892	General election: Gladstone formed fourth ministry, with Irish support
1893	Second Irish Home Rule Bill passed by Commons but rejected by Lords
1900	Reunion of Irish Parliamentary Party under John Redmond
1903	Wyndham's Land Act
1905	Ulster Unionist Council formed
1906	Liberal landslide victory at general election
1907	Liberals' Irish Councils Bill dropped
1910	General elections wiped out Liberal majority
1911	Parliament Act
1912	Third Home Rule Bill introduced
	Solemn League and Covenant signed
1912–14	A third attempt at Home Rule provoked a crisis as Ulster resisted the move
1913	Ulster Volunteer Force (UVF) set up
	Irish Volunteers formed
1914	Curragh 'Mutiny'
	Larne gunrunning incident
	Home Rule Bill passed
	Home Rule Amending Bill rejected by Lords
	Buckingham Palace Conference
	Howth gunrunning incident
	Britain entered First World War
	Home Rule Bill became law

1915	Formation of Asquith's coalition
1916	Beginning of Easter Rebellion
	Rebels surrendered
	Execution of rebel leaders
	Formation of Lloyd George coalition
1917	Meeting of Irish Convention
	De Valera elected leader of Sinn Féin
1918	Conscription proposed for Ireland
	Landslide victories for Sinn Féin in Ireland and Lloyd George coalition in Britain
1919	Beginning of Anglo-Irish War
	Dáil Éireann met; de Valera elected president of Irish Provisional government
	Dáil declared illegal
1920	Black and Tans recruited
	'Bloody Sunday' in Dublin
	Martial law proclaimed in southern Ireland
1921	Opening of Northern Ireland parliament by George V
	Truce in Anglo-Irish War
	Anglo-Irish Treaty signed
1921–2	End of the Act of Union: Northern Ireland remained part of the UK; the rest of Ireland became a New 'Dominion' of the British Empire – the 'Irish Free State'
1922	Anglo-Irish Treaty accepted narrowly by the Dáil
1923	End of civil war

Glossary of terms

£10 household suffrage   The vote to the male head of every household possessing £10 a year or more.

40-shilling freeholders   Those who possessed a 'freehold' (a property held for life or in unconditional inheritance) worth at least 40s. a year in rental value, which entitled them to vote.

Absolute veto   The ability to stop any law going through.

Agrarian   Rural (usually but not always) and agricultural.

Anglican Church of Ireland   Established as the State Church in Ireland by Henry VIII.

Anti-Corn Law League   Organisation formed in 1839 to work for the repeal of the English Corn Laws. The Corn Laws, which regulated the grain trade and restricted imports of grain, were repealed in 1846, although in reality this was not solely due to the campaign of the League.

Anti-papal   Opposition to the Pope and/or Roman Catholicism more generally.

Benburb   A battle won by Owen Roe O'Neill, commanding forces of the Irish Confederacy, which supported Charles I in the Civil War. He defeated forces from Scotland that invaded Ulster with the intention of purging Roman Catholicism and imposing Presbyterianism on Ireland in 1646.

Black and Tans   The name given to the Royal Irish Constabulary Reserve Force, recruited mainly in Britain but also in Ireland to reinforce the Royal Irish Constabulary. They wore uniforms mixing khaki army uniforms with the regular police uniforms to cover the shortage caused by the rapid recruitment.

Blight   General term for any sudden and severe plant disease.

Boycott   The word came into the language after Captain Boycott, a land agent in County Mayo, was isolated – without servants, mail delivery or service in shops – as a result of the Land League's policies because he refused to charge lower rents and evicted tenants.

Brinkmanship   The policy of seeking advantage by creating the impression that one is willing and able to push a dangerous situation to the limit rather than to concede.

Cash crop   A crop grown for sale rather than for feeding the producer's livestock or family.

Chartist movement   The Chartists took their name from the 'People's Charter', drafted in 1838. The Charter made six demands: votes for all men; equal electoral districts; abolition of property qualifications for MPs; payment for MPs; annual general elections; and secret voting. It was presented in petitions to the House of Commons in 1839, 1842 and 1848 – and rejected each time. After 1848 the movement quickly declined.

Clontarf   A battle won by Brian Boru, High King of Ireland in 1014, against a joint force of Vikings and Irish rebels.

Coalition government   Government composed of different groups or political parties.

Coffin ships   Ships that carried Irish immigrants escaping the effects of the famine. These ships, crowded and disease ridden, with poor access to food and water, resulted in the deaths of many people as they crossed the Atlantic.

Conscription Act of 1916   Men aged 18–41 were liable to be called up for service unless they were married, widowed with children, or else served in one of a number of reserved occupations considered vital to the war effort.

Constitutional Nationalists   Nationalists who rejected the use of physical force as a means of achieving Home Rule. Instead, they supported means within the rule of law.

Cottier   An Irish tenant holding land.

Dáil Éireann   Irish parliament.

Demagogue   A popular orator who appeals to the passions and prejudices of his audience.

Devolution   A transfer of powers from central government to local government.

Disendow   To take away the endowments (funds and property) of an Established Church.

Disestablish   To deprive a Church of established status and official government support.

Dispensary   A place where medical care and medicines are available.

Doctrinaire   Committed to carry principles to their extremes without compromise; in this case the cause for an independent Ireland.

Dominion Status   Granting to Ireland the same constitutional powers as belonged to Canada and other Dominions within the British Empire.

Established Church   A Church that is constitutionally and legally recognised as the official Church of the nation.

Executive   The top-level part of a government which makes the key decisions on policy; in the UK this is the Cabinet, which comprises the prime minister and other leading government ministers.

Extra-parliamentary   Political methods that go outside politics. Direct action and civil disobedience are examples of extra-parliamentary tactics.

Fenian movement   Revolutionary society organised in 1858 in the USA and called the 'Fenian Brotherhood', aiming to achieve Irish independence from England by force. Its counterpart in Ireland was officially known as the Irish Republican Brotherhood (IRB) but the term Fenian became the umbrella term. The IRB was a forerunner of the Irish Republican Army, which emerged after the 1916 Easter Rising.

Governor-general   The king's representative, which corresponded to the old office of viceroy.

Guillotine   A parliamentary procedure whereby debate on specific clauses of a bill could be terminated.

Hanoverian dynasty   The English royal house that reigned from 1714 to 1901 (from George I to Victoria).

Home Rule plus 'exclusion'   The policy of excluding Ulster from a self-governing Ireland.

Interdenominational   With the participation of various religious denominations.

Internment   The practice of detaining persons considered dangerous during a war or a crisis.

Invocation of saints   The belief that saints can be prayed to in order that they may intercede with God on behalf of the person praying. The Anglican Church does not agree with the Roman Catholic view of this and some other Protestant Churches completely reject this idea.

Irish Board of Works   Established in 1831 to carry out public works schemes such as road building.

Irish Dissenters   Protestants who disagreed with the teachings of the Church of Ireland.

Irish National Invincibles   A terrorist splinter group of the Irish Republican Brotherhood usually known simply as 'the Invincibles'.

Irish republican nationalism   The desire for the establishment of an Irish Republic.

Irish Volunteers   A militia force established to try and ensure the passing of the Home Rule Act.

Jacobite rebellions   A series of military campaigns attempting to restore the Stuart kings to the throne. A Jacobite was a supporter of James II of England or of the Stuart pretenders after 1688.

JP   Justice of the peace; a local magistrate.

Labour movement   The organisation of the working classes so that they can achieve better conditions.

Labour Rate Act   Passed in 1846, this Act stated that Irish hunger relief and work creation schemes were to be funded from Irish local taxation.

Laissez-faire   An approach where the government avoids intervening in economic and social matters, allowing market forces to operate freely.

Laity   The main body of Church members who do not belong to the clergy.

Land tenure   The manner in which land was owned by an individual, who was said to 'hold' the land.

Legislature   The body which has the power to pass laws. In a democracy this is an elected parliament.

Leinster   One of the counties of Ireland in 1170 (see Figure 1.1).

Linen cloth   A cool and very durable textile made from the fibres of the flax plant. Its manufacture is documented as far back as written records exist. When the tomb of the Egyptian Pharaoh Ramses II – who died in 1213BC – was discovered in the 1880s, the linen wrappings were found to be perfectly preserved.

Loyalist   Supporter of the British government.

Male household suffrage   The principle that all men who owned or legally occupied as tenants any property should be entitled to vote regardless of the value of the property. The 1867 Act caused a debate over whether women householders should also be included – an idea that was rejected in parliament.

Martial law   Rule by military authorities, imposed on a civilian population especially in time of war or when civil authority has broken down.

Migratory workers   People who move from one area to another in search of work.

Militant   Engaged in violence as part of a struggle for the achievement of a political goal.

Militia   An army that is made up of civilian volunteers, as opposed to a professional army of regular, full-time soldiers.

Mixed farming   The use of a single farm for multiple purposes, such as the growing of crops and the raising of livestock.

Moratorium   A period of delay.

National rising   A revolt or revolution carried out with the support of a large part of the population of a country.

National self-determination   The idea that nations should have the right to govern themselves.

Nationalist   A person who seeks to promote the interests of a particular nation.

New Model Army   The parliamentary army as remodelled by Cromwell in 1645.

New World   The American continent and associated Caribbean islands reached by Columbus in 1492.

Non-denominational   Not aligned to any one denomination of the Christian Church.

Non-sectarian   Not limited to or associated with a particular religious denomination.

Nonconformist   Member of those Protestant Christian Churches who did not 'conform' to the teachings of the Anglican Church of England. Examples would be Presbyterians, Methodists and Baptists.

Obstruction   Causing a delay in the running of the business of parliament, usually by continuing talking at great length and organising a series of speakers to immediately replace each other and keep the delay going. Since the House of Commons operated on the premise that members were 'gentlemen' and would behave appropriately, there was no official procedure to deal with this abuse of the system.

'Old Country'   The country of origin of an immigrant; in this case Ireland.

Orange card   Churchill was referring to the power and influence of the Orange Order in Ulster.

Partisan   Biased in support of a particular party; in this case the Conservatives.

Partition   Division of a country into separate nations or separately governed regions.

Pastoral farming   Rearing of livestock rather than growing crops.

Patronage system   The award and distribution of favours.

Penal laws   The body of discriminatory and oppressive legislation directed against Roman Catholics and Protestant nonconformists.

People's Budget   The main terms of the budget that the Lords objected to were that the standard rate of income tax was to be raised on annual incomes of up to £3000 and there would be a new 'super tax' on incomes over £3000 a year.

Plenipotentiaries   Representatives who have full power and authority to make agreements on behalf of their government.

Political apathy   A lack of interest in or concern with politics.

Poor Law Unions   After 1838, workhouses in Ireland were administered locally by groups or unions of electoral divisions.

President of the Board of Trade   The title of a position in the government that was sometimes given Cabinet status and sometimes not. It is now a secondary title of the Secretary of State for Trade and Industry.

Price mechanism   The process of supply and demand by which markets set prices. When supply outstripped demand prices would naturally fall and, in reverse, prices would increase with limited supplies.

Proportional representation   An electoral system where the number of seats in parliament that a party gains is awarded in direct proportion to the number of votes it gets.

Reactionary   Resistant to any form of progressive change.

Reform Act of 1918   Granted the franchise to all men over 21 and to all women over 30.

Revisionist   A historian who has significantly 'revised' or challenged the previously accepted view of a particular historical question.

Roman Catholic Emancipation   Prior to this 1829 Act, the Parliamentary Oath of Allegiance required MPs or peers to make statements disavowing fundamental Roman Catholic beliefs in order to sit in the Commons or the Lords.

'Scorched earth' policy   Burning any land, crops or trees so as to leave nothing salvageable to the enemy.

Scottish Union   Scotland had been united with England in 1707.

Sectarian   Part of an extreme religious movement.

See   A bishop's official seat or area of authority.

Separatism   Principle of separating Ireland from Great Britain.

Sequestration clauses   Parts of the Irish Church Act that authorised the seizure of Church property.

Sinn Féin   Gaelic term meaning 'we, ourselves'. Sinn Féin was founded in 1905. Officially non-violent, it was quickly infiltrated by members of the Irish Republican Brotherhood.

Socialist Workers' Republic   Political system where government is based on the principle of a socialist state controlled by the working classes.

Spiritual lords   High-ranking churchmen such as bishops.

Subsistence-level wages   The minimum amount needed to provide for the necessities of life in order to survive.

Temporal lords   Peers of the Realm with the right to sit in the House of Lords. In descending order of seniority, these are dukes, marquises, earls, viscounts and barons.

Test and Corporations Acts   Acts of 1661 and 1673 excluding Roman Catholics, Protestant Dissenters, and followers of Judaism and other faiths from public office.

Three Fs   A series of demands issued by Irish nationalists in their campaign for land reform. The 'Fs' were fair rents, free sale and fixity of tenure.

Tillage   The cultivation of land for raising crops.

Tithe   All landholders, irrespective of their religion, had to pay an annual tithe (or religious tax) to the Church of Ireland of ten per cent of the value of the agricultural produce of their land.

Tithe war   Violent resistance to paying the tithe that lasted from 1831 to 1838.

Tory   A member of the Conservative Party.

Transport   To send abroad to a penal colony.

Transubstantiation   The belief that during the Roman Catholic Mass the bread and wine of the sacrament are literally transformed into the body and blood of Christ – rather than the Anglican belief that this is a symbolic transformation.

Ulster   A province of Ireland; the larger part of this is today's Northern Ireland and still within the United Kingdom.

Ulster Presbyterians   The largest Protestant group in Ireland; of Scots–Irish descent.

Underemployment   The condition of having too large a part of the labour force unemployed due to the demand for labour being less than the supply of labour available for work.

Unionists   Those people who wanted the political union between Great Britain and Ireland – as set up by the 1800 Act of Union – to continue.

Whigs   A political party that had always been more sympathetic to reform and tolerance in Ireland but which had been largely excluded from government before 1830.

William of Orange   A Dutch Protestant Prince married to James II's Protestant daughter, Mary.

Yeomanry   Volunteer regiments.

Young Ireland   Radical Irish nationalist movement founded by Irish intellectuals in 1841. It promoted the study of Irish history, the Irish language, Irish national ideas and independence. Its belief in violent agitation led it to break away from O'Connell in 1846.

Index